Game of My Life
DODGERS

MARK LANGILL

Martha —
Hope you enjoy
these stories of Dodger
Baseball!
Mark

SportsPublishingLLC.com

2·22·22

ISBN 10: 1-58261-799-6
ISBN 13: 978-1-58261-799-2

All interior photos courtesy of the Los Angeles Dodgers.

Publishers: Peter L. Bannon and Joseph J. Bannon Sr.
Senior managing editor: Susan M. Moyer
Acquisitions editor: Mike Pearson
Developmental editor: Laura E. Podeschi
Art director: K. Jeffrey Higgerson
Dust jacket design: Joseph Brumleve
Interior design: Kathryn R. Holleman
Photo editor: Erin Linden-Levy

Sports Publishing L.L.C.
804 North Neil Street
Champaign, IL 61820
Phone: 1-877-424-2665
Fax: 217-363-2073
SportsPublishingLLC.com

Printed in the United States of America

CIP data available upon request.

FOR MARK AND MICHAEL RAYALA,

WITH LOVE AND GRATITUDE TO THE WORLD'S
GREATEST NEPHEWS.

HISTORIANS ARE NEUTRAL; PROUD UNCLES ARE NOT.

CONTENTS

INTRODUCTION vii

CHAPTER 1 **CARL ERSKINE** 1

CHAPTER 2 **BUZZIE BAVASI** 13

CHAPTER 3 **VIN SCULLY** 25

CHAPTER 4 **WILLIE DAVIS** 35

CHAPTER 5 **MAURY WILLS** 45

CHAPTER 6 **WES PARKER** 55

CHAPTER 7 **LOU JOHNSON** 65

CHAPTER 8 **STEVE YEAGER** 75

CHAPTER 9 **JIMMY WYNN** 87

CHAPTER 10 **FRANK JOBE** 97

CHAPTER 11 **STEVE GARVEY** 107

CHAPTER 12 **MIKE BRITO** 119

CHAPTER 13 **JERRY REUSS** 131

CHAPTER 14 **STEVE SAX** 143

CHAPTER 15 **JAIME JARRIN** 155

CHAPTER 16 **NANCY BEA HEFLEY** 169

CHAPTER 17 **JIM GOTT** 177

CHAPTER 18 **TOMMY LASORDA** 191

CHAPTER 19 **DON DRYSDALE** 201

INTRODUCTION

Flip through the pages of any baseball record book and the facts, the final tally of either a team or a player from a particular year, are indisputable. There is no romance or opinion to these accounting ledgers, only precise entries such as "Ruth 714," "DiMaggio 56," "Wills 104," and "Spahn 363" to formally code the folklore.

A fire-and-brimstone lawyer might still crow about the 1962 San Francisco Giants, who stole the pennant from the Dodgers with a ninth-inning comeback in the third and deciding playoff game in Los Angeles. But certain things will never change. For example, Willie McCovey's screaming line drive always ends up snared in the glove of Yankees second baseman Bobby Richardson to end Game 7 of the World Series. And so lives the range of emotion from such moments, especially if the lawyer, as an impetuous youth, broke his television screen after missing a championship by just a few feet.

Every new baseball game brings a blank palette, no matter what the level of competition. It also has a chance to remain forever etched in someone's heart. One's favorite game or most vivid recollection doesn't require a set of guidelines or regulations: getting your first hit in Little League; learning to keep score with a parent in the grandstands; screaming at the top of your lungs as a hometown player circles the bases; watching your son or daughter catch a baseball and hand it to a younger child.

Since moving to the West Coast in 1958, the Dodgers have played before more than 135 million fans at the Los Angeles Coliseum and Dodger Stadium. The franchise brought a storied history dating back to its Brooklyn roots in the 1880s and continued its popularity and success with five championships, Hall of Fame performers, and unforgettable personalities. And although he is considered a Brooklyn Dodger for his baseball career, the life of Jackie Robinson falls under the category of "Great American," as he forever impacted the social consciousness of the United States while breaking the sport's color barrier in 1947.

This *Game of My Life* volume offers the stage for former players, executives, and broadcasters to fill in the gaps with their memories. Their experiences range from a World Series showdown in late October in front of 55,000 screaming fans to one's first day in the major leagues, when the clock starts ticking for an indefinite period.

As the players share their stories, the rich fabric of the Dodger organization expands like the patches on a memory quilt. And some of the men who wore the 10 retired uniform numbers in history are bound to come up in conversation, whether Pee Wee Reese (1), Tommy Lasorda (2), Duke Snider (4), Jim Gilliam (19), Don Sutton (20), Walter Alston (24), Sandy Koufax (32), Roy Campanella (39), Robinson (42), or Don Drysdale (53).

At age 80, Carl Erskine recalls with great detail throwing the first pitch on the West Coast on Opening Day 1958 at the Los Angeles Coliseum. At 92, former executive Buzzie Bavasi still can't figure out how his Dodgers won the 1959 World Series. Bobby Castillo knows his life forever changed with one fateful pitch in a semi-pro game in East Los Angeles, also opening doors for Mike Brito and Fernando Valenzuela.

A note of disclosure must be made regarding Jimmy Wynn, the outfielder whose spectacular 1974 season helped the Dodgers win a pennant. Wynn's most memorable game is also shared by the author, who as a nine-year-old watched his favorite player slug a September grand slam against the dreaded National League West rival Cincinnati Reds. Every kid should feel such joy. The photo caption under Wynn's swing in the next morning's newspaper said it all—"That Grand Moment."

One unique chapter in this book is dedicated to the memory of Don Drysdale, who spent his entire playing career with the Dodgers from 1956-1969. Drysdale was a Dodger broadcaster in June 1993 when he sat down for a lengthy interview to reflect on his Hall of Fame career. The occasion was the 25th anniversary of Drysdale's streak of six consecutive shutouts and 58⅔ scoreless innings in 1968.

But Drysdale passed away just a few weeks later at age 56, suffering a heart attack at the team hotel in Montreal. The cassette tape remained unplayed for years until this project came along. With the permission of his gracious widow, Ann Meyers Drysdale, the recollections from "Big D" can be enjoyed again in his own words, punctuated with the trademark three-beat chuckle of Drysdale, one of the most enduring personalities to those around him. Ann also reflects on Drysdale's life and raising their three children: sons D.J. and Darren and a daughter, Drew.

The lion's share of statistical research for this book is from Project Retrosheet (retrosheet.org), the amazing website led by David W. Smith, baseball historian extraordinaire whose "day job" is associate professor of biological sciences. Imagine the research available from someone who, when asked by *Sports Illustrated* to find every box score of every major-league game in history, replied, "Counting all the grains of sand is overwhelming, but not infinite. There is an end point." Fortunately, Smith also has a sense of humor and a four-decade gratitude to Lou Johnson for providing the only offense in Sandy Koufax's 1965 perfect game.

Other Society of Baseball Research (sabr.org) members who contributed include David Vincent, Lyle Spatz, Tom Owens, and Bill Carlye.

Dick Beverage of the Pacific Coast League Historical Society keeps alive the memories of baseball in Los Angeles before the Dodgers arrived, staging annual reunions in both the Los Angeles and Oakland areas. He also serves as executive director of The Association of Professional Ballplayers of America (apbpa.org), a benevolent organization that, since 1924, has provided financial assistance for those former professional baseball players, coaches, umpires, scouts, and clubhouse men who are in need. While some players have no problem feeling nostalgic about their baseball careers, others are trying to deal in the present tense. The care administered by Beverage and those with similar perspectives is truly heroic.

Others contributing to research and historic materials for this volume include Bob Hunter Jr., Richard Lederer, Greg Pine, Tracy Fukagawa, Robert Schweppe, Dr. Alan Blum, David Schwartz, Astrid Omdal, Bob Wall, Phil Panacci, Ron Lewis, Luz Cortinas, Rob Menschel, Tot Holmes, Morgan Muir, Ted Sobel, Bob Keisser, Sal LaRoca, Thelma Erickson, Chad Clark, Ben Platt, Bette Burke, Joe Hendrickson, Mikako Niwa, and Pete Bonfils.

And special thanks to family members, ballpark colleagues, and the fleet of morning pre-dawn stationary bicyclers at the South Pasadena YMCA who have provided a sane balance to the seemingly never-ending pursuit of obscure trivia and other random information since a first trip to Dodger Stadium at age seven. In the 35 years leading to a book entitled *Game of My Life*, I've had the time of my life.

Chapter 1

CARL ERSKINE

NAME:	Carl Daniel Erskine
BORN:	December 13, 1926
BIRTHPLACE:	Anderson, Indiana
YEARS WITH THE DODGERS:	1948-1959
POSITION:	Pitcher
UNIFORM NUMBER:	17
CAREER HIGHLIGHTS:	Compiled 122-78 record in 12 seasons with Brooklyn and Los Angeles; set single-game World Series record with 14 strikeouts against the New York Yankees in 1953 World Series; only Dodger right-hander in 20th century with two career no-hitters (1952, 1956).
THE GAME:	April 18, 1958; Los Angeles Dodgers vs. San Francisco Giants at Los Angeles Coliseum

WELCOME TO THE WEST COAST

You only get one chance to make a positive first impression.

At least that's how Carl Erskine felt when given the starting assignment for the Dodgers' first game at the Coliseum in Los Angeles on April 18, 1958. More than 75,000 Southern California residents were expected to

1

jam the converted football stadium to watch the transplanted Brooklyn ballclub face the Giants, their New York rivals dating back to the 1880s. Erskine knew these weren't necessarily Dodger fans, but rather curiosity seekers who wanted to be part of history.

"When I got the assignment, oddly enough, of all the other things I could hope for, I wasn't thinking of anything past the first pitch," Erskine said. "I kept thinking to myself, 'The first pitch in Los Angeles has to be a strike.'"

The Dodgers' cross-country journey occurred after the team exhausted a 10-year campaign to build a new ballpark in Brooklyn to replace Ebbets Field, a cozy but aging facility in the middle of a Flatbush neighborhood with a 32,000-seat capacity and parking for 700 cars. It began in 1946 when Walter O'Malley, then a Dodger vice president, wrote a letter to New York architect Emil Praeger asking for ideas to enlarge or replace the stadium.

About the same time, team president Branch Rickey was assembling a team later dubbed "The Boys of Summer" by author Roger Kahn. The powerful lineup included catcher Roy Campanella, shortstop Pee Wee Reese, first baseman Gil Hodges, outfielders Duke Snider and Carl Furillo, and pitchers Don Newcombe, Preacher Roe, Johnny Podres, and Clem Labine. Jackie Robinson broke baseball's color barrier in 1947, and the Dodgers won six National League pennants during the athlete's 10-year career through 1956.

"It was a thrill for a skinny, 165-pound kid from a small town to be a part of that Dodger system and to be mentored by Branch Rickey, who was a brilliant man," Erskine said. "He has a lot of critics. But when he dealt with his players one on one, he helped us understand the game. He had a lot of insight into the game itself, but also into the character of the players he dealt with and the players he kept and the players he traded. When he assembled his team and Campanella, Hodges, Robinson, Reese, Cox, Furillo, and Snider, this team had character. It had Hall of Fame talent and competitiveness beyond any team I had ever played on. We expected to win every game we played. It wasn't a case of putting in a season. This was a contending team that was not only a great offensive team. This team could play defense. I mean, they made the double play, they threw to the right bases. This was a real bunch of pros."

Erskine was called up to the Dodgers at age 21 in 1948, but he didn't stay in Brooklyn full time until 1951, O'Malley's first season in charge after succeeding Rickey as team president. From 1951-1956, Erskine went 92-

From left to right: Roy Campanella, Duke Snider, and Carl Erskine are ready for photos during the Brooklyn Dodgers' 1956 Goodwill Tour of Japan.

58, including a career-high 20 victories in 1953. He is also the only Brooklyn Dodger to pitch two no-hitters (1952, 1956).

The Dodgers won the World Series in 1955 and repeated as National League champions in 1956. But even as the Dodgers celebrated their pennant-clinching victory over Pittsburgh at Ebbets Field, O'Malley raised the subject of a new ballpark when interviewed by television announcer Happy Felton in the jubilant Brooklyn clubhouse. Clearly, the success on the field was not going to interfere with the business side of baseball.

"There were rumors about the Dodgers leaving Brooklyn back in 1956, somewhere in that range," Erskine said. "You have to realize the players were kind of out of the loop. I was the player representative and O'Malley was always pretty good at calling me into the office and telling me some things. One of the things he did as early as 1955 was to call me into his office at 215 Montague Street. That was a famous address for the Brooklyn Dodgers. He showed me a domed stadium model that had been made by a young architect. And that was the first time I ever heard or knew there was even a concept of a stadium that was completely enclosed and roofed. He said, 'This may be the future.' And that was amazing. Because there are accounts of Walter O'Malley all over the place of his futuristic thinking, and this is one of those examples. That was maybe a hint of something to come, but he still wanted to keep the team in Brooklyn."

Following the 1956 postseason goodwill exhibition tour of Japan, the Dodgers returned to the country and stirred more controversy, trading Robinson to the New York Giants for pitcher Dick Littlefield and $35,000. Robinson chose to retire, announcing the news in an exclusive magazine interview. Getting scooped didn't sit well with the local newspaper reporters, so instead of honoring arguably the most significant athlete in American sports history, petty grievances surfaced against Robinson. General manager Buzzie Bavasi suggested Robinson might play for the Giants if the price was right, but Robinson stood by his decision and became a vice president with the Chock Full o' Nuts company in New York.

With Robinson leaving the stage, the rest of the team was in jeopardy. Real estate developer Marvin Kratter had purchased Ebbets Field in 1953 with plans to eventually raze the ballpark and build a $22-million apartment complex. The Dodgers retained a five-year lease on the property. On January 15, 1957, the Dodgers received an additional three-year lease in case Los Angeles couldn't secure the land needed to build a stadium. Meanwhile, the Dodgers played a series of "home" games (15 overall) at Jersey City's Roosevelt City in 1956 and 1957.

On May 28, 1957, the National League gave permission for the Dodgers and Giants to move to Los Angeles and San Francisco if the clubs sought to make the shift together by October 1.

So the innocence of Brooklyn Dodger fans inevitably began to disappear, along with hopes of keeping the Ebbets Field lifestyle intact. "It was a special time to play the game," reliever Clem Labine said. "So many things have changed in today's game. We played for the love of the game." But less than two years after the city's first championship, it was suddenly time to say goodbye.

"There was disappointment on the streets in Brooklyn when we'd run into people," Erskine explained. "They'd say, 'This is terrible,' and 'What's O'Malley doing this for?' But the players were not called in on progressive meetings, whether they were about moving or the status of the negotiations with the city. We didn't get any of that, except through the newspapers and hearsay. So it was just out there.

"Also, you have to realize that players, at least in those days, pretty much were detached from the operations side of the game. We were all working on one-year contracts and we were all fighting to keep our jobs. The Dodgers had a big system, and a lot of players in the minor leagues were terrific, especially the pitching staff, which had a lot of turnover. We were just battling to stay in the big leagues. We were like the population out there in Brooklyn. We knew what was happening by what was being announced and what was in the paper."

The 1957 Dodgers finished in third place at 84-70, 11 games behind the Milwaukee Braves. Erskine went 5-3 with a 3.55 ERA in just 15 appearances, seven of which were starts. Only 6,702 fans attended the final home game on September 24 when left-hander Danny McDevitt blanked the Pittsburgh Pirates 2-0.

On October 7, the Los Angeles City Council voted 10-4 to pass a motion to officially ask the Dodgers to relocate and enter into a contract with them. The next day, the Dodgers announced they were moving. When the players returned to training camp four months later, the only immediate difference was the team's initials, which changed from "B" to "L.A." on the Dodgers' caps.

"Prior to the 1958 season, we reported to Vero Beach, Florida, and the Dodgertown camp, which had been set up as a training site in 1948," Erskine said. "In the back of our heads, we're thinking, 'OK, we're going to Los Angeles.' But everything seemed the same in spring training. We played the same amount of games against the same teams, put in our time, and got ready. The realization hit all of us when we broke camp. Before, we played our way north from Florida to New York, maybe with the Braves. We'd play in Mobile, Jacksonville, come up to Atlanta, Nashville. We traveled on a train in those days.

"Instead of that routine, we packed our gear in the clubhouse and we went to the small airport in Vero Beach, boarded the Dodger plane, and flew west. Now that's when the team had this sudden and definite feeling, 'There is no more playing our way north, there is no more Brooklyn. We're heading to this unknown place.' The pioneers must've felt that way, thinking, 'What's on the other side of the mountain?' We didn't know. We were in limbo as to what was coming next."

THE GAME OF MY LIFE

By Carl Erskine

We didn't go to Los Angeles to start the 1958 season, we went to San Francisco. And we didn't go to a major-league stadium, we went to a minor-league ballpark to open the season—Seals Stadium, the home of the old Pacific Coast League team. It was new, strange, and it did not seem like the big leagues. It was just as new to the West Coast as it was to the players. Here are these teams that the fans probably read about, but there was no identity with the fan base. They didn't know the players yet. OK, here come the Giants and Dodgers. But as far as the players were concerned, we were playing the same team that we played in New York. There wasn't a whole lot of difference. It was the surrounding atmosphere that seemed so different. It was like playing an exhibition game at Seals Stadium. This was a minor-league ballpark and the grandstands weren't as big. The game went on, but it was like, "This is not quite real yet." So I think the players went through this adjusting time of "Hey, this is the big leagues. And we are playing a major-league Opening Day in San Francisco."

We didn't play well in the series. We lost the first game 8-0 and ended up dropping two of three games. It was not an auspicious beginning for us, but the rivalry among the players didn't change much. We were facing the same players and no matter where we played, it was still the Giants and their black and orange colors versus the Dodgers' blue and white. We were still the same competitive players. Now all the hype of the rivalry was done through the front office, through the public relations department, and through the ticket sales.

And of course, there's a good story about Duke Snider and a fan who called him "horse face" all the time at the Polo Grounds. It drove Duke crazy, and when we were moving to the West Coast, I'm sure he was thrilled to finally shake this guy. When we stepped off the bus in San Francisco, a voice said, "Hello horse face, I'll bet you thought you got rid of me." Here's this same person with a hat, overcoat, and a bunch of rolled-up greasy newspapers under his arm. That was one indication that the rivalry did indeed move west, because this same irritating fan who was bothering Duke in New York was now going to be at Seals Stadium.

It was a little bit of a surprise that Walter Alston chose me to start the opener in Los Angeles on April 18, because I did not have a very good spring and I was at the tail end of my career. It was a question mark of whether I should've even played in 1958 and 1959, because I had arm trouble. My 10 years in Brooklyn were my best years. Given all that, the only logical explanation for Alston selecting me to pitch the opener was that it was such a big day in Los Angeles with the parade and the hype—the first game ever played in Los Angeles, the Dodgers moving in. And all of that buildup was much bigger than I sensed it was in San Francisco. I never asked Alston, "How did you happen to pick me?" I had been in five different World Series and we played in lots of hot pennant races in our days in Brooklyn, so I had been through a lot of settings where there was a lot of pressure. And with the Coliseum expecting between 75,000 and 80,000 people and all the bands playing and the hype, maybe Alston thought, "I need somebody to pitch who isn't going to be affected as much as a younger pitcher might be." That's the only reason I can think of—I had pitched well for Walt, so he knew he could get a good game out of me now and then.

But Alston also surprised me. He called me in to his office before the game and told me that San Francisco had a new rookie infielder who had a terrific spring in Arizona and a great series against us at Seals Stadium. His name was Jimmy Davenport. So Alston says, "Hey, I know you don't normally want to do this. I'm not going to ask you to do this, I'm going to order you to do it. I want you to get a strike on Davenport, and then I want you to flatten him. Let's welcome him to the National League." He must've told me that the day before, because that was part of the reason I wanted that first pitch to be a strike.

So the game starts. "Play ball!" Johnny Roseboro was the catcher. Roy Campanella had been my catcher in Brooklyn for 10 years. John was new and a rookie and he was trying to keep the job after Campy's automobile accident ended his playing career. The first pitch was a fastball. Strike one. Boy, that was a relief to me, because I got that first pitch in there. Now the second pitch, John gave me the knockdown sign, which is kind of the flip of the thumb. I threw a good knockdown pitch; it was just at the bill of his batting helmet. Davenport went down like a sack of rocks, his cap went one way and the bat went the other way and he hit the ground. He got up, and you learn over time that the most important pitch after a knockdown is the next pitch. You'd better make a good pitch. So my next pitch I think was a fastball and Jimmy lined a single off the new fence in center field. So I look over the to dugout and Alston shrugged his shoulders, like "What are you going to do?" We did all we knew to do and it didn't work. But then we went on to play a ragged ballgame and we won at the end, 6-5.

One incident that happened Opening Day also involved Roseboro. After the first pitch and the knockdown of Davenport, on the next couple of pitches, John fired the ball back to me and almost hit me in the face. He was so pumped up. Campy always returned the ball very soft and easy. I called time and met John halfway from home plate. I said, "John, the catcher's not supposed to throw the ball harder than the pitcher." His eyes were as big as silver dollars. That settled him down.

As far as the game itself, you're concentrating here on the next pitch, the next hitter, the number of outs, who's on base, and the score. That keeps your mind down there on the field. You're not aware too much of what's going on in the stands. The diamond looks about the same and you've got the umpires and foul lines. About the second or third inning, I happen to glance toward our dugout, and there were about six guys craning their necks and looking into the crowd. There was a whole group of movie stars—Danny Kaye, Bing Crosby, Ray Bolger, Lana Turner, Jeff Chandler. There were a lot of movie stars there because it was a historic day in Los Angeles. It wasn't a baseball crowd yet. It was a curiosity crowd. They came and they wanted to be part of the big event. It was a social event more than a rousing, hyped-up fan base like we used to have in Brooklyn. But they didn't know any of us. We were all just names that maybe they had heard about. On the field and in the game, we weren't too concerned with what was going on outside. It was a strange feeling to play in that new configured ballpark. But it didn't affect the game itself a whole lot.

There was one play in the first inning when Daryl Spencer hit a bunt and the ball popped into the air. Here comes this fly ball to me, and I'm still standing on the dirt part of the mound where I finished my delivery. I looked up to catch this fly, but as it came down, the sun was coming down right along the top edge of the Coliseum and it blinded me. I had to duck my head. Then the ball hit the ground in front of me. On one hop, I picked it up and turned it into a double play. Everybody thought that was a smart play. I never told anyone that I actually lost the ball in the sun. The runner on first couldn't run because it looked like I was going to catch it.

When we moved to Los Angeles, some of us had never been to the West Coast before. It was a strange place for us. We didn't know the streets, we'd get lost going to the ballpark. I got there the night before and I didn't have anyone to put on the pass list because my family was still in Indiana. I thought, "Gee wiz, I wish I had somebody I could invite to the game. I don't know anyone." Then I remembered Matt Brinduse, a guy I knew in Anderson, Indiana. He went to our church and later moved to Los Angeles some years ago. He worked delivering laundry in Long Beach. So I looked in the phone book and sure enough, there's Matt Brinduse. So I invited him to the game.

Well, Matt was a real outgoing guy, a real fun-loving guy. After that, I had a lot to do to get ready for the ballgame, so I forgot about Matt. We had this wild finish in the ninth inning and Davenport made a mistake on the bases, failing to touch third base while scoring the apparent tying run. We trapped him on the basepaths and ended up winning the game.

So now the game was over and we'd won the first game in Los Angeles. I got the victory and Clem Labine got the save after reliving me in the eighth inning. We went inside the clubhouse and I wasn't privy to what happened next, I was later told of it. There was a press conference after the game, and usually the players never went to those things. It was for the manager to handle. Walter Alston was talking after the game to a lot of people he didn't know, because the writers and TV guys were new. After a couple of questions, a voice in the back said, "Mr. Alston, Erskine pitched great today."

Walt said, "Oh yeah, Carl did a good job."

Couple questions later, the same voice in the back said, "Mr. Alston, Erskine has been one of your great pitchers."

Alston said, "Yeah, Carl has been a good pitcher for us."

After a few more questions, the same voice said, "Mr. Alston, wouldn't you say Erskine is the ace of your pitching staff?"

Walt looked at Lee Scott, our traveling secretary, and said, "Who in the hell is that?"

It was Matt Brinduse, my pass for the day, from Long Beach. That gave me a big chuckle, because knowing Matt, I could picture him talking his way past the security and into the press conference.

THE RESULTS

In the first home game in Los Angeles history, the Dodgers defeated the San Francisco Giants 6-5 in front of 78,672 at the Coliseum. Carl Erskine scattered four runs on 10 hits in eight-plus innings, and Clem Labine recorded the save. Third baseman Dick Gray hit the only home run for the Dodgers, a solo shot off Johnny Antonelli in the seventh inning, to give Los Angeles a 6-3 lead. Left fielder Hank Sauer hit two home runs for the Giants off Erskine in the fourth and eighth innings.

And general manager Buzzie Bavasi still remembers public relations whiz Arthur "Red" Patterson trying to keep the Hollywood crowd happy. "Red was supposed to stop by one of Walter O'Malley's private boxes and check on three guests: actress Lauren Bacall, singer Jo Stafford, and her husband, Paul Weston. He stopped by every few innings with some food," Bavasi laughed. " I can still see Red trying to offer a soda to Lauren Bacall."

THE LONG GOODBYE

Plagued by arm problems, Erskine started only 11 more games. In 40 overall appearances after Opening Day 1958, he compiled a 3-7 record and 5.70 ERA. Most struggling players draw their outright release, but the respect garnered by Erskine during his career made it difficult for him to retire. Teammates and team officials kept stalling the inevitable.

"I was ready to retire much earlier than when I actually did," he said. "I was not as productive and I was putting a lot of pressure on myself. I had a lot of tension. I had always been a starting pitcher and was at a place where I couldn't really produce anymore. But Don Drysdale and Duke Snider and two or three other guys would say to me, 'You can't quit, Carl. You're throwing good, I hit against you in batting practice.' Then I would stay on a little longer and have a bad outing. I was in this dilemma in 1959 about when to quit. I told Buzzie Bavasi this and he said, 'Well, don't do it yet.' So even he kept me hanging around for a few more starts.

"And then finally, in Pittsburgh, it was over. Ironically, my first inning in the big leagues was at Forbes Field in Pittsburgh. I relieved Hugh Casey and I got the win. Twelve seasons later, I started the game at Forbes Field and it was one of those 'extended' starts that I really didn't want, because the others kept encouraging me to continue. Well, I started the ballgame by striking out Bill Virdon, and that was the last out I ever got in the big leagues. The Pirates combed me for four runs. The problem was my earned run average was always 3.75, in that range, and the two seasons in Los Angeles, it boosted my ERA higher than I wanted at the end of my career."

So many times, the end of an athlete's career means a lonely trip back home, the connection with teammates suddenly severed by the business of the sport. There is also the awkward feeling of "civilian" status, which often reminds the active players of their own vulnerability in a uniform.

A tribute to his character, Erskine stayed with the Dodgers and made the transition. He could have returned to Indiana a happy man, but chose to delay his homecoming after Bavasi asked if he would stay as a coach.

"You might say the only two contributions I made to Los Angeles were the Opening Day start in 1958 and retiring on June 15 in 1959," Erskine said. "Roger Craig replaced me and he won 11 games that last half of the season. In fact, the players voted me a half-share of the World Series, probably because I quit. After that, I threw a lot of batting practice for the team. I helped Maury Wills learn to hit, because he just had been switched from a right-handed hitter to a switch-hitter by Bobby Bragan at Spokane. When they brought Wills to Los Angeles in the middle of the 1959 season, he could not hit left-handed. He couldn't get around on a good fastball. I was still throwing well if I was not interrupted. If I had to quit between innings, I couldn't stay loose. So I could throw an hour or an hour and a half of batting practice. He finally got around on the ball and we went up to San Francisco for a two-game series. They had a prize, the MVP of the series won a trip to Hawaii or something like that. Wills won that prize, and that's when his career took off.

"The other piece of trivia was that I also helped Wally Moon by pitching hours of batting practice. Wally was a left-handed hitter and he learned to hit those 'Moon Shots,' which were home runs hit over the towering left-field fence just 315 feet from home plate at the Coliseum. Those were behind-the-scene events, but I do feel I made a contribution to the 1959 team, even though I didn't win any games for us."

After his playing career, Erskine became a successful businessman. He sold life insurance from 1960-1975 and later became president of Star Financial Bank in Indianapolis from 1982-1993. He also coached 12 seasons at nearby Anderson University.

In 2005, he wrote a book, *What I Learned From Jackie Robinson*, which includes a memorable chapter comparing the challenges of Robinson and the fourth child of Carl and Betty Erskine, who was born in 1960 with Down Syndrome. Doctors suggested little Jimmy could enjoy life somewhere away from home, but the Erskines wanted him to be a part of the family. When Erskine later attended a meeting in town to discuss a possible group home for youngsters like Jimmy, neighbors opposed it, describing these children as "lunatics and insane people." They were also concerned property values would drop.

Jimmy Erskine stayed with his family and later got a job at the local Applebee's restaurant. He participated in Special Olympics during his youth and also accompanies the Erskine family to the Dodger Adult Camp in Vero Beach. The highlight at camp occurs after the campers-instructors game at Holman Stadium, when Jimmy, dressed in a Dodger uniform, runs around the bases and slides into home plate, just as he saw Tommy Lasorda do a decade earlier.

"Jackie and Jimmy, because of tradition, superstition, ignorance, fear, and arrogance, felt the bitterness of rejection," Erskine wrote. "Society considered them second-class citizens or worse. The whole Robinson experience, which I had lived through as a player, now seemed to arise in our lives. Jimmy was facing many of the same barriers. Only now I was coping with this experience as a father.

"Some of those who uttered these terrible words were people I knew quite well. I felt a good dose of pain and rejection Jackie told me he used to feel. I'd never known how fearful people could be about someone who was different. I used to ask myself, 'Why are all these harsh things being said about my son?' Jimmy didn't do anything to deserve this."

Erskine and Robinson remained friends until Jackie's death in 1972. Carl and Betty traveled to Washington, D.C. in 2005 as Robinson was posthumously honored with the Presidential Medal of Freedom. And early in 2007, Erskine received a letter from the Commissioner's Office, inviting him to Dodger Stadium in Los Angeles for the 60th anniversary celebration of Robinson's major-league debut on April 15. There aren't very many teammates left to tell the story, and Erskine is always ready and willing.

When most ballplayers look back on their careers, usually the statistics and memorable game performances are the main topics of conversation. Erskine realizes his personal "sports career," even his first pitch in Los Angeles, can't compare with one of the most significant times in American history. His character and perspective made him well equipped for the ride.

"It's hard to say how life works out for you," Erskine said. "I almost signed with the Braves. I was in the Navy and stationed in Boston, throwing batting practice as an 18-year-old for the Braves. They desperately tried to sign me. I preferred the Dodgers because they scouted me in high school and treated me first-class. I called the Dodgers and said, 'I don't want to play for the Braves, I want to play for the Dodgers.' Branch Rickey told me to sit tight, because I couldn't sign a contract since I was under 21. So they sent for my parents at the 1946 All-Star Game in Boston, which was at Fenway Park. The night before the All-Star Game, my parents and I were at the Kenmore Hotel in Boston in Mr. Rickey's suite. And he signed me to a Dodger contract. That, right there, set the stage for me to have one of the most fantastic experiences any player in baseball could have, and that was to play for a team that Mr. Rickey was putting together, which included Jackie Robinson, of course."

Chapter 2

BUZZIE BAVASI

NAME:	Emil Joseph Bavasi
BORN:	December 12, 1914
BIRTHPLACE:	New York City, NY
YEARS WITH THE DODGERS:	28
POSITION:	Executive vice president/general manager from 1950-1968; worked in Brooklyn minor-league system from 1939-1943, 1946-1949 (served in U.S. Army as an infantry machine gunner from 1943-1946, earning the Bronze Star).
CAREER HIGHLIGHTS:	Graduated from DePauw (Indiana) University in 1938; his Dodger teams won eight National League pennants and four World Series titles; named 1949 Minor-League Executive of the Year at Triple-A Montreal; named 1959 Major-League Executive of the Year by *The Sporting News*; founding president and part-owner of San Diego Padres; general manager of California Angels from 1978-1984.
THE GAME:	October 8, 1959; World Series Game 6; Los Angeles Dodgers vs. Chicago White Sox at Comiskey Park.

BUZZIE BASEBALL

Perhaps more than any other person from the 20th century, Buzzie Bavasi is the foremost authority on Dodger history. His baseball career spanned six decades and enough generations to roll with a variety of high-profile executives: Larry MacPhail, Branch Rickey, Walter O'Malley, Ray Kroc, and Gene Autry.

And, at age 92, Bavasi still provides any audience with an unbeatable one-two punch, his wonderful sense of humor sprinkled into countless stories. His razor-sharp memory paints a vivid picture as he recalls how a baseball novice turned into a street-smart executive. Those who marvel at the vigor in his voice when storytelling only need to know his mother nicknamed her son "Buzzie" because of the way be "buzzed" around the house.

His family's friendship with Ford Frick, National League president and later commissioner of baseball, helped Bavasi get his foot in the door with both the Dodgers and Larry MacPhail, Brooklyn's team president.

"I was the college roommate of Fred Frick, Ford's son, and we both went to DePauw University, which is Ford's alma mater," Bavasi said. "And when my dad died in 1933, Ford sort of became my other father. When I graduated from college, my mother gave me a great present—a new car and a year to do anything I wanted. Well, the best thing I wanted to do was to go to Florida and watch the ball games.

"And I was sitting in Clearwater Stadium watching the Dodgers play in spring training when Ford came by and said, 'What are you doing here?' I told him and he said, 'No longer. Be in my office tomorrow morning.' So I went back to New York the next day and went to his office. He took me to Brooklyn to meet Larry MacPhail."

During his Hall of Fame career as an executive with the Reds, Dodgers, and Yankees, MacPhail contributed many innovations to the sport, such as nighttime baseball, regular game televising, and the flying of teams from game to game. The temperamental MacPhail was a colorful character who often clashed with his Dodger manager, the equally fiery Leo Durocher. Brooklyn languished in the standings until MacPhail's arrival in 1938, and the Dodgers returned to the postseason for the first time in 21 years in 1941.

The Dodgers' fortunes, along with Bavasi's life, were about to change when he walked into MacPhail's office with Frick in 1939.

"So you want to get into baseball?" MacPhail asked.

Buzzie Bavasi was the Dodgers' executive vice president and general manager from 1950-1968.

"I certainly do," Bavasi replied.

"What do you know about the game?"

"Nothing. I played in college, but that's about it."

"Good. Surprised you don't know anything about the game, but it will do you some good, because we have too many people around here who know everything."

Bavasi's career began as an office boy in Brooklyn, although he waited nearly 13 weeks before receiving his first paycheck from MacPhail. In

1940, Bavasi became business manager for Class D Americus of the Georgia-Florida League. He switched to Class D Valdosta in 1941-1942 and Class B Durham in 1943 until he was drafted into the Army during World War II. MacPhail resigned from the Dodgers in 1942 to join the Army.

Rickey was president of the Dodgers in 1945 when he contacted Bavasi following the war. Resting at home in Georgia after returning from his assignment in Italy, Bavasi didn't realize the biggest challenge of his career would come so early in the minor leagues.

During this time, Rickey decided to break baseball's color barrier by signing Jackie Robinson, a former UCLA multisport star currently playing for the Kansas City Monarchs of the Negro Leagues. Robinson and pitcher Johnny Wright would spend the 1946 season at the Dodgers' top farm club in Montreal.

Rickey asked Bavasi to find a suitable location for a club in the newly reformed New England League. Bavasi thought Rickey might sign other African-American players, so he looked for a community with a racially progressive newspaper and a significant French-Canadian population, believing such a place would be more accepting. He chose Nashua, New Hampshire.

Bavasi negotiated a lease for the city-owned Holman Stadium and spoke with *Nashua Telegraph* editor Fred Dobens about the city's racial climate. By March 1, the Dodgers had signed catcher Roy Campanella and pitcher Don Newcombe, but the transactions were not announced for a month in order to give Bavasi time to integrate the team into the community. Bavasi arranged for local war veterans to try out for the team and made French-Canadian ballplayers a priority. He named the newspaper editor, Dobens, president of the club. The Dodgers also promoted the local ties of Brooklyn coach Clyde Sukeforth, who scouted Robinson, Newcombe, and Campanella. Sukeforth briefly played minor-league ball in Nashua in 1926.

Bavasi wanted former Dodger outfielder Stanley "Frenchy" Bordagaray to manage the club, but Bordagaray was assigned to Class C Trois Riviers, Quebec. Walter Alston, the future longtime manager of the Brooklyn and Los Angeles Dodgers who Bavasi chose in 1953 to succeed Charlie Dressen, became Bavasi's next preference. The former St. Louis Cardinals farmhand started as a player-manager at first base in 1946, but an injury that season kept Alston in the dugout.

The Nashua Dodgers placed second that year but won the league championship in the playoffs. Campanella was named league MVP, and Newcombe went 14-4.

His associations with Alston, Newcombe, and Campanella at Nashua played a pivotal role in Bavasi's career. He clearly displayed that he could handle the pressure in tough situations, especially after defending Newcombe and Campanella following a game against the Lynn Red Sox in 1946.

Throughout the matchup, Lynn manager Pip Kennedy and his players subjected Newcombe and Campanella to racial taunting. Bavasi waited until after the game when team officials arrived to collect their share of the gate receipts, then challenged Kennedy to a fight as the rival team stood in the background. Bavasi made sure he was close to the burly Alston—just in case.

"If it weren't for Buzzie Bavasi, I'd have nothing in baseball," said Newcombe, who, with the Dodgers, became the only man in history to win the Rookie of the Year, Most Valuable Player, and Cy Young Awards. "These guys from the opposing team were calling us names and we promised Branch Rickey that we would keep our heads. We couldn't do anything, Roy and I, but Buzzie did."

In 1947, Robinson led the Dodgers to the National League pennant, earning Rookie of the Year honors. Rickey added another star each season—Campanella in 1948, Newcombe in 1949. O'Malley took over the Dodgers following the 1950 season, naming Bavasi as the team's executive vice president and general manager. The Dodgers lost the pennant in Bavasi's first season on Bobby Thomson's ninth-inning home run in Game 3 of the National League playoffs against the Giants.

"We never won a World Series in Brooklyn for over 60 years until 1955," Bavasi said. "But that 1955 team wasn't our best club. I thought the 1952 Dodgers was the best team we ever had, with either a Hall of Famer or an All-Star at every position. But we lost in seven games to the New York Yankees, so that team isn't remembered as much as the 1955 team, because they did something we had tried to do for years—beat those 'Damn Yankees.' And anyone who watched that final game in 1955 will say it was their most memorable when we were in Brooklyn."

Despite the success on the field, O'Malley yearned for a ballpark larger than Ebbets Field, built in 1913 and unable to be expanded because of its neighborhood location. Ebbets Field was sold to a developer in 1953 and the Dodgers retained a three-year lease, though the writing was on the wall for a franchise move. In 1956, the Dodgers also played one game against each National League opponent at Roosevelt Stadium in Jersey City.

As the landscape was changing, so was the roster. Bavasi made a controversial trade after the 1956 season, sending Robinson to the New York Giants for pitcher Dick Littlefield and $35,000 cash. Robinson had already decided to retire, but he couldn't tell Bavasi because he had signed a contract with *Look Magazine* in 1955 for a three-part biography and a future promise of the exclusive retirement announcement, whenever that was to be. Robinson hinted to Bavasi in a telephone conversation prior to the winter meetings not to trade third baseman Randy Jackson, because he wasn't sure whether he wanted to play in 1957.

The Giants reportedly offered Robinson a $60,000 contract in the hope it would help the team's sagging attendance. Any thoughts of a comeback ended when Bavasi suggested in the press that Robinson's magazine story was merely a scheme to get more money from the Giants. Had Robinson accepted the contract and sparked the franchise, it's debatable whether the Giants would've gone along with O'Malley's plan to move two teams to California.

But the Dodgers and Giants did relocate to the West Coast in 1958. The Giants ventured to Seals Stadium of the Pacific Coast League while the Dodgers played in the cavernous Los Angeles Memorial Coliseum, which staged track meets and football games. The year began with tragedy when Campanella was paralyzed in a car accident while driving home from work on a snowy night in Long Island in January. Newcombe opened the season 0-6 and was traded on June 15 to Cincinnati for four players, including pitcher Art Fowler and first baseman Steve Bilko. The 1958 Dodgers limped to the finish line with a 71-83 record, 21 games behind the Milwaukee Brewers.

Was this any way to prepare for a championship in 1959?

THE GAME OF MY LIFE

By Buzzie Bavasi

During our first year in Los Angeles in 1958, I think most of the players were unhappy, because at that time, only two had been west of the Mississippi. They didn't acclimate themselves that well. We finished in seventh place, although if Roger Craig had fielded a bunt correctly, we would've won the final game and finished in fifth place.

We won the title our second year in Los Angeles. To me, we had as good a ballclub in 1958 as we did in 1959, but the attitude wasn't there. The players were disappointed. They weren't happy. The Hodges family never came to California, not once. I think that had a big effect on the attitude of the players. In 1959, they realized they had backing from the fans in California and decided this was where they wanted to play.

We spent our first four seasons at the Coliseum, and the dimensions of the ballpark were not fair to Duke Snider, our great hitter who had 43 home runs during his last year in Brooklyn. Duke hit only 15 home runs in 1958. The Coliseum was 480 feet to right field. Duke was a great outfielder, but asking him to hit home runs at the Coliseum was terrible.

After the 1958 season, I decided we needed to get a left-handed hitter. I had always liked Wally Moon, who I had seen years ago in 1951 at Rochester. He looked like the kind of player who could be a Dodger. He hustled all the time. When I had a chance to get him, we got pitcher Phil Paine and Wally from the Cardinals for Gino Cimoli. Wally turned out to be a knowledgeable hitter. He wasn't a great player like Duke Snider, but he learned how to hit the ball to left field, which Duke never did. Duke didn't want to because he was so powerful. But without Wally, there's no doubt in my mind that we wouldn't have won anything in 1959.

We brought up Maury Wills during the summer of 1959. Don Zimmer was our shortstop in 1958. Don broke the big toe on his right foot and he really couldn't get around that well. One day I noticed his shoe was torn. He had made a hole in the front of his shoe so he could play. There was no way it was going to work out, but Don wasn't about to admit it. Meanwhile, we had Bobby Bragan, who was the manager at Spokane at the time. He made a switch-hitter out of Maury, and that made the big difference. Maury came up and you know what he did— the record speaks for itself. But I have to give credit to Bobby Bragan, because he's the one who saw that Maury could be a great switch-hitter.

The 1959 season was also the time Sandy Koufax became more of a pitcher. We decided in the middle of the season to put Sandy in the rotation. Don Drysdale became a great pitcher. But the biggest thing that happened was Wally Moon learning how to hit the ball to left field.

Playing at the Coliseum changed the strategy of a lot of managers. You couldn't play for the home run, so Earl Weaver definitely could not have managed at the Coliseum. Earl was a great manager, but he always depended on the home run and he always had at least three guys who could hit a lot of home runs and three pitchers who could win 20 games or more. But at the Coliseum, you had to manufacture runs.

Walter Alston was great at manufacturing runs, especially with our team in 1959. The hit-and-run, bunt and squeeze—we didn't go for the home run. To me, it made it an interesting game, more interesting than waiting for a home run. The fans liked it.

The 1959 regular season ended in a tie and we faced the Milwaukee Braves in a playoff for the National League pennant. That was one of the most interesting times of my life. I say that because I wasn't sure if we could win. Of all the Dodger clubs I had, the 1959 club was one of the weakest, because we had a second baseman playing the outfield, a first baseman playing left field, and Norm Larker and others playing all over the place. We had no set positions.

The job that Walter Alston did in 1959 was the best job he ever did for the Dodgers. Let me tell you a little story. Walter O'Malley was a good baseball man. He knew nothing about the game itself, but he was a great businessman. After 1958, he wanted to fire Walter Alston. I told him, "Well, if Walter goes, I go." He said, "Well, we're out here with all these people and we should have a big name." He wanted Leo Durocher back as manager. There was no way I was going to take Leo back, so I said, "Let's talk to (coach) Charlie Dressen and (team captain) Pee Wee Reese." So he said, "Fine." He figured they'd say, "Let's get rid of him." But they told Walter right in the hotel room, "You fire Alston and we quit, too." So that settled it.

In the 1959 playoffs, the Dodgers were motivated by pride. They weren't motivated by money. The team and the office staff were motivated by pride, everybody in management, too. I think that's what won it for us—the attitude of players. Milwaukee had a great club and great management, but I think our players wanted it more than Milwaukee did.

I give credit to John Corriden for the 1959 World Series, believe it or not. John was a scout around 80 years old, living in Indianapolis. And I believe in old scouts. I called him during the season and said, "John, we need a relief pitcher. Find one for me." He scouted the minor leagues and finally called, saying, "I found one for you."

"Who?"

"Larry Sherry."

"C'mon, John. He's been with us for two years and he can't pitch."

"What are you paying me for Buzzie? You want information and I'm giving it to you. If you don't bring him up to the Dodgers, then I quit, so help me."

So we brought Larry up to the Dodgers and the rest is history. Carl Erskine retired and Larry, along with Roger Craig, took his place. We finished the regular season tied with the Braves for first place.

During the first playoff game against Milwaukee, Larry was brought out of the bullpen in the second inning while John Corriden was home in Indianapolis, seated in front of his television set. As Larry was coming into the game, he asked his wife, "Could you bring me a lollipop?" That was John's phrase for a beer. She said, "Sure." When she came back to give John the beer, he was dead in his chair. He never saw Larry pitch that first playoff game. Larry wound up pitching 7⅔ innings in relief of Danny McDevitt that afternoon.

I think Larry did a helluva job, but I think he was doing an even better job because of John Corriden. What can I say about Sherry's performance against the White Sox? All I can do is praise him. Everyone knows Larry Sherry won the World Series for us.

THE RESULTS

After both teams posted 86-68 records to end the regular season, the Dodgers defeated the Braves in the best-of-three National League playoff. Sherry pitched the final 7⅔ innings of a 3-2 victory in the first game at Milwaukee's County Stadium. Sherry didn't pitch in the second game in Los Angeles, won by the Dodgers 6-5 in 12 innings, as right-hander Stan Williams pitched three hitless innings of relief and earned the decision when Milwaukee shortstop Felix Mantilla's two-out throwing error allowed Gil Hodges to score from second base in the bottom of the 12th.

When the Dodgers faced the Chicago White Sox in 1959, it was the first time they had squared off in a World Series against a team other than the New York Yankees since 1920. Between 1941 and 1956, the Dodgers and Yankees met seven times with Brooklyn winning only once, in 1955.

The Dodgers lost the first game of the 1959 World Series 11-0 at Comiskey Park. But Los Angeles took control of the Series with three consecutive victories. The turning point occurred in Game 2 with the Dodgers trailing Bob Shaw 2-1 in the sixth inning. With two out, manager Walter Alston batted Chuck Essegian for his pitcher, Johnny

Podres. Essegian, a former Stanford halfback who played only 24 games in 1959 as a reserve outfielder, hit a home run. Jim Gilliam followed with a walk and Charlie Neal's two-run homer chased Shaw to give the Dodgers a 4-2 cushion. Sherry scattered a run on three hits in the final three innings to preserve Podres' victory.

In Game 3, Dodger starter Don Drysdale allowed 11 hits and four walks in seven-plus innings, but Chicago managed only one run. Sherry pitched the final two innings of a 3-1 victory. Game 4 was tied 4-4 until Gil Hodges hit a leadoff home run in the eighth against Gerry Staley. Sherry held the 5-4 margin with two scoreless innings.

Sherry took the day off in Game 5 as Sandy Koufax and Stan Williams pitched brilliantly in a 1-0 defeat. The only run of the game was scored in the fourth when Sherm Lollar grounded into a double play with runners on first and third.

Back in Chicago, the Dodgers closed out the Series with a 9-3 victory in Game 6. Staked to an 8-0 lead by the fourth inning, the White Sox crept back into the game. Ted Kluszewski hit a three-run home run, and when Podres walked the next batter, Alston went to the bullpen. Sherry allowed a single and walk to load the bases, but he escaped further damage when Luis Aparicio popped to shortstop to end the inning. Sherry restored order with 5⅔ scoreless innings and was named the Series MVP with a 2-0 record, two saves, and a 0.71 ERA in 12⅔ innings. The Dodgers also became the first team to win a championship after finishing in seventh place the previous season.

ONCE A DODGER,
ALWAYS A DODGER

If the 1959 championship caught Dodger fans by surprise in Los Angeles, great expectations became the attitude in the early 1960s when the Dodgers made three World Series appearances in a four-year span from 1963-1966. The first year at Dodger Stadium in 1962 ended with heartbreak as the Giants won the National League playoff with a ninth-inning rally in Game 3 similar to 1951, when the teams battled in New York. In retrospect, it was the biggest disappointment of Bavasi's career, because he knew O'Malley wanted a World Series for the stadium's debut.

The Dodgers rallied and swept the Yankees in the 1963 World Series. Sandy Koufax and Don Drysdale packed a 1-2 punch on the pitcher's mound while Maury Wills terrorized the basepaths and Tommy Davis notched his second consecutive batting title.

"The 1959 World Series was just the beginning of many postseason success stories in Los Angeles, especially in the early 1960s when we reached the World Series in 1963, 1965, and 1966," Bavasi said. "I didn't believe it, but the Chamber of Commerce told me that every time we got to the World Series, it meant an additional $150 million for the city of Los Angeles. They said, 'You don't know how much people pay for hotels, cabs, food, and entertainment. If the Series went seven games, it meant $150 million.' So at least we were doing something for the city. Of course, Walter O'Malley wasn't doing too bad, either."

Prior to the 1966 season, Koufax and Drysdale staged their famous holdout. The Hall of Fame duo combined for 49 victories, 47 complete games, and 644 innings in 1965. In an era before free agency, Koufax and Drysdale didn't have agents; rather, they met together with Bavasi for better leverage. According to Bavasi, each pitcher sought a three-year contract for $500,000. In 1965, Koufax had made $85,000 and Drysdale $80,000. The pitchers missed most of spring training while Bavasi and O'Malley, wielding all the power, enjoyed the publicity of "the great holdout."

"Walter played along with it brilliantly," Bavasi later wrote in his 1986 autobiography. "He knew how to agitate the situation by calling the boys at a propitious time—when they were out. He'd leave messages for them to call him, and they would religiously return their calls. Then, Walter would tell the reporters that the boys were getting anxious to come back, that they were calling every day."

Actor Chuck Connors, a former Brooklyn Dodger farmhand, brokered a meeting among Bavasi, Koufax, and Drysdale. Koufax received $125,000 and Drysdale $110,000, although Bavasi graciously offered $117,500 each if they still insisted on receiving the same salary.

The Dodgers won the pennant again in 1966, but there wasn't a Round II in negotiations. Following a 27-win season, Koufax retired at age 30 due to arthritis in the left elbow.

"I've often wondered how much Koufax and Drysdale would command if they were playing today and came in together and asked for $2 million each," Bavasi said. "What would you do? Make them partners in the club?"

The Dodgers went south in the standings, finishing eighth in 1967, and Bavasi left the Dodgers in June 1968 to join the expansion San Diego

Padres, set to join the National League in 1969. San Diego owner C. Arnholt Smith, a banker by trade, encountered personal financial trouble, and the early Padres teams were horrible, even after McDonald's restaurant chain owner, Ray Kroc, took over in 1974.

Bavasi joined the Angels in 1977. While he enjoyed the resources of Gene Autry, the dawn of free agency and arbitration hearings began to take the fun of the game away from Bavasi. His relationship with Hall of Fame pitcher Nolan Ryan became strained when Bavasi decided Ryan wasn't worth $1 million a year following a 16-14 campaign in 1979. Bavasi uttered his most infamous one-liner at the time, explaining that the Angels could replace Ryan "with a couple of 8-7 pitchers."

Eleven years later when Ryan pitched his sixth career no-hitter, Bavasi sent Ryan a telegram: "Nolan—Some time ago I made it public that I made a mistake. You don't have to rub it in."

During Bavasi's tenure, the Angels made their first two playoff appearances in team history as American League Western Division champions in 1979 and 1982. Bavasi left the Angels in 1984, but he remained active in his retirement, especially with the advent of cable television and e-mail.

"He outgrew the sport and the sport outgrew him," wrote Hall of Fame outfielder Reggie Jackson in the introduction to Bavasi's book, *Off the Record*. "He wanted the game to stay old school, though I don't think he refused to change with it. He just didn't want to change his way of life. He dealt with us as if he were our uncle—our Uncle Buzzie. Buzzie wanted people to come to him with their problems and seek his help or advice. ... Buzzie was taught under the tutelage of a very knowledgeable baseball man, Branch Rickey. You can't do better than that. To me, Buzzie is the kind of guy who was born at the age of 60 and will always be 60. He is always your dad, always your father. He has the jowls, the receding hairline, a heavyset way about him. I knew Buzzie when I was 19 years old. When I was 19, he looked 60. When I was 40, he still looked 60."

And the man who haggled with ballplayers over $500 bonuses in the early 1950s later watched his son Bill Bavasi, general manager of the Seattle Mariners, lavish a combined $114 million in contracts to a pair of free agents, third baseman Adrian Beltre and outfielder Richie Sexson, after the 2004 season. Buzzie's reaction? "I told my wife we must've brought the wrong baby home from the hospital."

Chapter 3

VIN SCULLY

NAME:	Vincent Edward Scully
BORN:	November 29, 1927
BIRTHPLACE:	New York City, NY
YEARS WITH THE DODGERS:	1950-Present
POSITION:	Broadcaster
UNIFORM NUMBER:	17 (at Fordham University)
CAREER HIGHLIGHTS:	Named top sportscaster of the 20th century in July 2000 by more than 500 national members of the American Sportscasters Association; inducted into the National Baseball Hall of Fame in 1982; voted "Most Memorable Personality" in Los Angeles Dodger history by fan balloting in 1976; called play-by-play events for the National Football League and PGA Tour events for CBS-TV (1975-1982), Major League Baseball for NBC-TV (1983-1989), and the World Series for CBS Radio (1990-1997).
THE GAME:	May 13, 1952; St. Louis Cardinals vs. Brooklyn Dodgers at Ebbets Field

THE VOICE OF BASEBALL

Without historical perspective, there is a natural tendency to dub the head of one's generation as the "greatest of all time."

Although he developed into a Hall of Fame baseball announcer, Vin Scully didn't invent the conversational play-by-play style that millions of Dodger fans adopted as part of their daily routine. The seeds of Scully's encyclopedic baseball knowledge were planted long before the major leagues expanded west of the Mississippi.

As an impressionable New York youngster, Scully worshiped New York Giants home run hitter Mel Ott. He marveled at the sounds emanating from the furniture-sized radio in his family's living room, sometimes crawling under the table with his crackers and milk.

The roar of the crowd first drew Scully's imagination to the radio, and that sound would always complement—not compete with—his future broadcasts. After falling in love with baseball, Scully penned a grammar-school essay proclaiming that one day he would like to become a sports announcer.

The relative infancy of broadcasting sporting events coincided with Scully's childhood dreams, a contrast to other famous names who planned other careers before discovering radio, such as Graham McNamee (singer) and Mel Allen (lawyer).

"When I was in high school and college and an outfielder of sorts, I would stand out there and actually do the play-by-play of a game I was playing," Scully recalls.

During Scully's youth, the most distinctive radio voice belonged to Walter Lanier "Red" Barber, whose Southern accent and homespun tales gave a distinctive flavor to Brooklyn Dodger broadcasts. Barber's ability to entertain an audience for hours on a daily basis attracted Scully to the theater of radio.

When he first enrolled at Fordham University in 1945, Scully thought he might become a writer. As a freshman, Scully penned a column for the school newspaper formerly written by noted journalists John Kiernan and Arthur Daley. But after a stint in the Navy, Scully landed a job at the campus FM radio station, thus returning to his original goal.

Scully received a degree in communication arts at Fordham in 1949. He sent out 150 letters to prospective employers. Only one radio station responded with a legitimate offer, WTOP in Washington, D.C., where Scully worked as a summer replacement. Scully returned to New York

Hall of Fame broadcaster Vin Scully was originally hired by the Brooklyn Dodgers in 1950.

that fall and met Barber, who was also the CBS radio sports director. Scully left his name with Barber and expected nothing further to happen.

But Barber called a few days later with an assignment for CBS. Scully arrived at Boston's Fenway Park expecting to cover the Boston University-Maryland football game from the comfort of the press box.

"When I got to the park, I found that there was no radio booth for me," Scully said. "It was a bitterly cold day. The big CBS game that afternoon was Notre Dame-North Carolina, but that one fell apart. My game turned out to be the craziest thing you ever saw.

"And there I was, on the roof of the stadium with 50 yards of cable and a microphone. If somebody ran 20 yards, I ran 20 yards with him—and believe me, I was glad to do it to keep warm."

As the studio host of the college football roundup show, Barber was impressed with Scully's updates throughout the afternoon. But the real impression occurred several days later when Barber discovered Scully's predicament—battling the cold without an overcoat while trying to make sense of the game from the press box roof. Scully never mentioned these conditions to his listeners, nor did he complain to Barber after the assignment.

A few weeks later, Barber nominated Scully to Dodger president Branch Rickey as a candidate to replace No. 3 announcer Ernie Harwell, who left the Dodgers after the 1949 season to join the New York Giants. By February, Scully was reporting to the team's spring headquarters in Vero Beach, Florida, to cover the reigning National League champions with Jackie Robinson, Roy Campanella, Pee Wee Reese, and Duke Snider, among others.

Behind the scenes, Scully watched Barber's preparation for every game. Wanting the youngster to succeed, Barber offered sincere and fatherly advice. He once admonished Scully for having a beer with his pregame lunch in the press room, explaining other media members might get the wrong impression in the event of an on-air mistake. Scully, whose boyhood jobs included washing silverware at a hotel, delivering milk, and slotting mail, never forgot his roots or his lessons from Barber.

"Red was my teacher ... and my father. I don't know, I might have been the son he never had," Scully remembered in 1982 upon his election to the Baseball Hall of Fame. "It wasn't so much that he taught me how to broadcast. It was an attitude. Get to the park early. Do your homework. Be prepared. Be accurate. He was a stickler for that. He cared. He was very much a taskmaster, or I might have developed bad habits."

THE GAME OF MY LIFE

By Vin Scully

In the early 1940s, probably the best athlete at Fordham Prep in New York was a fellow named Larry Miggins, who was one year ahead of me in school. He could play many sports, but his strong suit was baseball. One day, we were sitting in the back row of the school auditorium, daydreaming about what we wanted to do when we were older.

Larry said he wanted to be a professional baseball player. I said that I'd love to become an announcer. I took it a step further and said to Larry, "How about if it came to pass that you became a major-league player and I became a major-league broadcaster, and I wind up broadcasting a game in which you play?" And we shook our heads after considering the odds and said, "Well, that has to be one in a trillion."

We continued our love of sports at Fordham University. Eventually, I graduated, as did Larry. He went into the Merchant Marine Academy. I went into the Navy. Time elapsed and I lost track of Larry for a while. And then I got the job broadcasting the Dodgers. One day I was reading *The Sporting News* about the ascendancy in the Cardinals' organization of a player named Larry Miggins. I thought, "Wow, he's on his way. And I'm here with the Dodgers. The odds might begin to dwindle a little bit."

In May of 1952, the Cardinals came to New York and they were going to play the Giants, and then they were going to play the Dodgers. Several of us from school got together and we had dinner. Included in the group was Larry Miggins. At dinner, I told him I was looking forward to seeing him at Ebbets Field, and Larry wasn't even sure if he was going to play against the Dodgers in that series. But sure enough, it came to pass on that day that Larry was in the starting lineup for the St. Louis Cardinals. The Dodgers had a crafty left-hander pitching that day named Preacher Roe.

Now in those days, just to really hype up the odds, I only did two innings. I did the third inning and the seventh inning. Red Barber and Connie Desmond were the principle announcers. The odds suddenly came down one to one because in my one inning while I was on the air, who was coming to bat but Larry Miggins. I was overwhelmed over the thought that I'm describing this tall, right-handed hitter who is stepping in against Preacher Roe.

And then miracle upon miracles—and I don't know how in retrospect I didn't break down and begin to cry—because Larry hit a home run against Preacher Roe. And I described the home run. So if you want to talk about truth being stranger than fiction, that's it—from the back row of the auditorium on the campus of Fordham University and as high school kids at Fordham Prep to a home run in Ebbets Field about eight years later. I'm describing the home run we thought was impossible. And that's the story of Scully and Miggins, or Miggins and Scully. A one-in-a-trillion event.

If there is a residue of Larry Miggins, Vin Scully, and the home run in 1952 at Ebbets Field, it's the fact that although both of us felt the ultimate dream was impossible, the answer to the story is that dreams are not impossible. Oh sure, the chances are they might not come true. But at the same time, in the face of all those odds, you should not only dream, you should dream big and let it go. And no matter how many people may discourage you, you must keep trying. Because you never know, it might just come about.

THE RESULTS

The Brooklyn Dodgers defeated the St. Louis Cardinals 14-8 on May 13, 1952 at Ebbets Field. The Dodger offense recorded 14 hits against six St. Louis pitchers, including home runs by Gil Hodges and relief pitcher Ben Wade. Dodger starter Preacher Roe allowed four runs on seven hits in three-plus innings, including the home run by Miggins and a pair by Stan Musial. Wade (1-1) earned the victory in relief and added a double in the eighth inning. Miggins' home run was his only hit in five at-bats. Prior to the game, Dodger catcher Roy Campanella received his 1951 National League MVP award from National League president Warren Giles.

THE PRIDE OF THE DODGERS

Larry Miggins' major-league career lasted only 43 games—one game in 1948 and the other 42 games with the Cardinals in 1952. His only other home run was hit against the Boston Braves' Warren Spahn. Miggins quit baseball in July 1954 and soon embarked on a 25-year career with the United States Probation and Parole Department.

Scully became the lead voice of the Dodgers when Barber left the team following the 1953 season.

"I'm so proud of Vincent," Miggins says today from his home in Houston. "He became the best announcer there ever was."

When the Dodgers moved to Los Angeles in 1958, Scully's voice and stories made visitors carry their portable transistor radios to the cavernous 90,000-seat Coliseum. Just as Brooklyn's "Boys of Summer" ballclub gave Scully great moments to describe early in his career, so did the Los Angeles crew, which won championships in 1959, 1963, 1965, 1981, and 1988.

"Vin Scully taught people about baseball in Los Angeles," said former Dodger general manager Buzzie Bavasi. "Even those who didn't know about the sport liked to hear him on the radio. He was the most important person in making the Dodgers as popular as they are today."

Scully made the transition to television with ease, never competing with the crowd during critical moments and always deferring to the picture if self-explanatory. Using a phrase from Barber, Scully "knew when to shut up." This simple approach also explained why for decades, whether on radio or television, Scully kept Barber's tradition of having only one broadcaster at a time behind the microphone.

Another key to Scully's success was the contribution of Jerry Doggett, who joined the Dodgers during Labor Day weekend in 1956 after 15 years with the Texas League as a broadcaster and publicity director. Doggett was 11 years older than Scully and accepted his role as the Dodgers' No. 2 announcer without jealousy. Scully and Doggett forged a genuine friendship, and their 32-year tenure is the longest in baseball history. Doggett retired in 1987 and passed away at age 80 in 1997.

"Vin is very humble and low-key," Doggett said in 1982. "He doesn't like a public image. He's embarrassed to be recognized in a public place. I'm sure he's aware of his impact, but he likes to suppress it. He hasn't changed much. He is thoughtful, considerate, friendly. He will stop and talk to everybody. He is outgoing and very gracious. He gets attention and gets noticed everywhere, and he handles it very well. It would drive some people crazy."

Dodger Stadium opened in 1962 as baseball's first privately financed stadium since Yankee Stadium, which was built by a brewery in 1923 and dubbed "The House That Ruth Built," thanks to the popular home-run-hitting Babe Ruth.

Goldy Norton, a former Southern California public relations executive, reveals a story about the construction of Dodger Stadium that carries a similar theme regarding Scully's magnitude. A significant source of income was a deal with Union Oil to become the initial radio/TV sponsor for Dodger Stadium, signage and the service station in the stadium parking lot.

"They wouldn't make the deal unless the Dodgers locked up Vin with a long-term contract," Norton said. Because the industry's union prohibited contracts longer than seven years, Scully's reported decade-long pact included three option years.

In the middle of the Hollywood scene in the 1960s, Scully appealed to both baseball fans and movie stars who liked to visit the ballpark, such as comedian Danny Kaye, who penned "The Dodger Song" in 1961 with lyrics to an imaginary Dodgers-Giants showdown.

"Vin is to broadcasting what Sandy Koufax was to pitching," Dodger manager Walter Alston once said.

But the Dodgers couldn't keep Scully's talent from attracting other suitors. After hosting other local programming in Los Angeles in the late 1960s and early '70s, Scully joined CBS television in 1975 to broadcast football, golf, and other non-baseball events.

Scully was voted "Most Memorable Personality" in L.A. Dodger history in 1976 in fan balloting conducted by the ballclub. But there were also fears in 1976 that Scully's Dodger days were numbered because of his network television commitments.

The crisis was averted when Scully agreed to stay with the Dodgers on a part-time basis. The headline in one newspaper the next morning read: "YOU CAN RELAX: SCULLY SIGNS DODGER PACT". The team added local sportscaster Ross Porter in 1977 as the No. 3 man in the booth to share Doggett's workload when Scully was out of town on assignment.

If learning to share Scully with the rest of the world was tough on Dodger fans, it became impossible for them to imagine his inevitable departure from the scene. Unlike a Hall of Fame player whose talents carried an expiration date, Scully kept rolling along through the generations without losing his distinctive style.

While honesty and credibility are his cornerstones, the rich voice, silky smooth delivery, and human-interest stories catch the attention of even the most novice followers. And when running out of platitudes, some simply describe Scully as "the fabric of the Dodgers"—the common thread during recent ownership changes.

Scully actually donned a Dodger uniform in Brooklyn and Los Angeles, one occasion for each Hall of Fame manager: Alston (1954-1976) and Tommy Lasorda (1976-1996). Alston convinced Scully to wear a Dodger uniform during a "B" spring training game in the early 1950s.

Three decades later, Lasorda cajoled Scully to wear a Dodger uniform and anonymously sit in the dugout at Chicago's Wrigley Field. Cubs manager Don Zimmer, a member of the 1955 world champion Brooklyn Dodgers, knew about Lasorda's special visitor during the game.

"Zimmer kept sending over baseballs to our dugout," Lasorda said. "One of the baseballs had a message saying, 'Hey Scully—If a fight breaks out, I'm coming after you!'"

When asked about his broadcasting philosophy over the years, Scully offered a different recipe or analogy, depending on the type of interview at the time:

- "It's not long work, but it demands complete concentration. Baseball's unlike other sports because the action is not continuous. And you really have to know the game, I think. You can broadcast a football game without being an expert because things are happening all the time. But in baseball, it's tough to fool anyone."
- "An announcer's virtue is not blowing his top unless for extreme provocation—and that doesn't occur very often."
- "Let the crowd noise carry the excitement. The announcer's first job is to inform."
- "People think I'm not excited. I am excited. I have to cram it down all the time. But that's my idea of the way to do the job."

Scully accepted the network job, in part as a personal challenge. Assigned to telecast a full schedule of football games, Scully enrolled in a memory school to help him remember the names and numbers of more than 1,000 players. When covering other assignments such as a Jimmy Connors-Rod Laver tennis match, Scully immersed himself in the subject, reading books, interviewing other stars of the sport, and playing sets with an instructor who knew the styles of both Connors and Laver.

While Scully worked alone during his Dodger broadcasts, network assignments usually meant sharing the booth with a color man. Hall of

Fame manager Sparky Anderson once had a chance to work with Scully on CBS Radio during a World Series, a most memorable experience.

"Vin is the best there ever was," said Anderson, a former Brooklyn Dodger minor-league infielder. "There was a gift given to him—no one could ever argue that point. You couldn't possibly work at becoming that good. You have to start with a gift, and he did."

Chapter 4

WILLIE DAVIS

NAME:	William Henry Davis
BORN:	April 15, 1940
BIRTHPLACE:	Mineral Springs, Arkansas
YEARS WITH THE DODGERS:	1960-1973
POSITION:	Center Field
UNIFORM NUMBER:	26, 3
CAREER HIGHLIGHTS:	All-time Los Angeles franchise leader in hits (2,091), extra-base hits (585), at-bats (7,495), runs (1,004), triples (110) and total bases (3,094); set team record in 1969 with 31-game hitting streak; member of two world championship teams (1963, 1965); won three Gold Glove Awards (1971-1973).
THE GAME:	September 8, 1960; Los Angeles Dodgers vs. Cincinnati Reds at Crosley Field

FAST TRACK TO THE MAJOR LEAGUES

The life of Willie Davis forever changed one afternoon in 1958 when the world-class high school sprinter from Southern California caught the attention of Kenny Myers, a career baseball man whose stocky frame and trademark cigar seemed out of place at a track and field meet.

"In two years, I'm going to make you the center fielder of the Los Angles Dodgers," Myers predicted.

Such a wild prediction might cause laughter or skepticism in some youngsters. But although pro baseball wasn't on his radar screen at the time, the Roosevelt High School star didn't flinch.

"I wasn't doubting him," Davis recalls. "But things go through your mind when someone tells you something like that. The relationship that Kenny and I had was golden; it was so solid. And after a while, I said, 'You're right, Kenny. Let's go for it.'"

Major League Baseball had not yet established the amateur draft, so teams were free to sign any player in the United States upon his high school graduation. The Dodgers signed Davis to a $13,000 bonus on June 20, 1958. The contract included an additional $7,000 when he reached the major leagues.

Instead of joining a Dodger minor-league team, the 18-year-old Davis was assigned to the Dodgers' "Rookie Program," which originated in Brooklyn in 1940 to allow New York-area youth to play on an all-star team with proper instruction and supervision. It was also a chance to keep an eye out for talent, and an estimated 50 percent of the players who participated were signed into baseball either by the Dodgers or another organization.

The Dodgers kept this rookie-team concept when they moved to the West Coast following the 1957 season. The timing couldn't have been better for Davis, who learned the intricacies of baseball in Southern California. Davis played alongside amateurs, and his official Dodger contract wasn't publicized, although several teammates knew that he had already signed.

Myers was one of the coaches for the 18-member Dodger rookie team, along with Pacific Coast League veteran coach Jackie Warner and future Los Angeles Dodger coaches Harold "Lefty" Phillips and Dwight "Red" Adams. The 21-game Dodger rookie schedule included such opponents as the Camp Pendleton Marines, Culver City Merchants, San Luis Obispo Blues, Sawtelle Pirates, and Maywood All-Stars.

The rookie team played its home games at Wrigley Field, the former Pacific Coast League home of the Los Angeles Angels, located at 42nd and Avalon. The Dodgers were originally going to relocate to the 22,000-seat ballpark for the 1958 season, but a last-minute deal allowed them to

Rookie Willie Davis receives tips from scout Kenny Myers, who originally discovered Davis as a high-school track standout.

play at the cavernous Los Angeles Coliseum. The smaller ballpark became a perfect low-key setting for the Dodger rookies.

"At the time, Southern California was a hotbed of talent and, with the Dodgers being the new team in Los Angeles, every kid in town was trying to get on that rookie team," said Wally Wasinack, a left-handed pitcher from Garden Grove High School. "We went through five or six tryouts, and they had 400 to 500 kids trying out. Willie at the time was very talented, but he needed a lot of work. We knew he was a track star, but no one had heard of him as a baseball prospect. He could hit the ball well if it was a fastball, but he wasn't a natural left-handed hitter and also had trouble with curveballs. When our rookie season started, he would strike out frequently. Gradually, you saw the improvement. By the end of the season, he was our best hitter.

"Willie gave me the impression he was a little more mature than the other players on the rookie team. Maybe it was the environment that he lived in that gave him a little more street smarts. He wasn't that talkative, but if you engaged him in a conversation, he was friendly and happy-go-lucky. He never struck me as being real serious, but he was serious when he was playing ball or spending time with Kenny."

After a couple weeks at Green Bay of the Wisconsin League, the Dodgers reassigned Davis to warmer weather once more. He spent most of the 1959 campaign at Class-C Reno of the California League. The transition to playing with professionals was smooth, and he led the league with a .365 batting average, 187 hits, 40 doubles, and 16 triples while adding 15 home runs, 90 RBIs, and 33 stolen bases.

Meanwhile, the Dodgers took their West Coast fans on a roller-coaster ride from 1958-1960 while playing at the Coliseum, its football field transformed into a makeshift baseball field as the future Dodger Stadium was under construction. The Dodgers finished in seventh place in 1958 with a 71-83 record. The familiar names from Brooklyn, such as infielder Pee Wee Reese and pitcher Carl Erskine, gradually gave way to a crop of youngsters.

The 1959 Dodgers became surprise contenders during the summer when minor-league journeyman Maury Wills replaced an injured Don Zimmer at shortstop and relievers Larry Sherry and Roger Craig joined the bullpen. After defeating the Milwaukee Braves in a playoff for the National League pennant, the Dodgers outlasted the Chicago White Sox in a six-game Fall Classic, which general manager Buzzie Bavasi later classified as the most surprising championship in his 29-year association with the franchise.

But the magic disappeared in 1960 as the Dodgers were beset with disappointment and controversy. Veteran first baseman Gil Hodges batted only .198 in 101 games. Outfielder Carl Furillo was released on May 17, but sued the ballclub for the balance of his 1960 salary, claiming he was injured at the time. Furillo was later awarded $21,000, but the episode was a disappointing ending for the former National League batting champion nicknamed "Skoonj" during his days in Brooklyn.

Promising left-hander Sandy Koufax, who tied a major-league record with 18 strikeouts in a game in 1959, opened the 1960 campaign with a 1-8 record. He lasted only 1⅓ innings in a 4-3 loss at home against Cincinnati on June 10. The only hit allowed was a second-inning grand

ng on a major-league uniform for the first time was a unique
ace, because I never imagined as a kid that I would be playing pro
. I was an athlete and a sprinter. I ran track in high school, but I
d in all the sports. I'm pretty sure I could've been a pro in any
chose, whether baseball or basketball. I knew right off the bat that
going to mess around with football because I didn't want to wreck
body. And circumstances didn't lay well for me to get into football
I had a little paper route. I was making money, five or six dollars
nd I wasn't going to give that up to practice football.

In't watch much baseball on television as a kid and I didn't really
y role models. I did my own thing. I figured out that if you learn
damentals in anything, and they are the correct fundamentals, if
actice them, you can't miss. You're going to be successful.

en I first attended a Dodger training camp, the young players were
mentally sound. The Dodgers not only stressed the fundamentals,
d the guys to teach you correctly. And you loved it because it was
ly atmosphere. ... Maury Wills, Wally Moon, Frank Howard,
y Davis, Joe Pignatano, Jim Gilliam, and John Roseboro—many
might not know them for their careers, but man, those guys were
ic off the field.

my first game, manager Walter Alston put me in the second slot
batting order. Smith also started that afternoon, batting sixth and
g third base. The Reds' starting pitcher that day was right-hander
ook, who later pitched for the New York Mets.

ury Wills was our leadoff hitter, and he singled to start the game.
very first at-bat, I hit a single that bounced in front of the Reds'
ielder, Gus Bell. Maury raced to third base and I had a chance to
things out at first base. I looked back into the dugout and saw how
everyone was. They were smiling and they were probably thinking,
wow, he's got some speed. This is going to be great." And so the
continued. It was a wonderful feeling being out there.

batted around during a four-run first inning against the Reds.
faced only five batters before being replaced by Joe Nuxhall, a left-
r. In the second inning, Maury and I opened with singles, and the
ers scored three runs for a 7-0 lead. The good start was fortunate
se we didn't score again that afternoon. Reds' left-hander Claude
n replaced Nuxhall in the fourth and shut us out for the next five
gs. I didn't know it at the time, but Claude would later become one
longtime teammates. After two hits in my first two at-bats, I flied

slam by Cincinnati backup catcher Dutch Dot
the Dodgers to a season-high six games under .

While Los Angeles looked anything b
champions, the Dodger farm system was ready
The Dodgers' 12 minor-league affiliates were
league teams (Milwaukee and Philadelphia were
and four Dodger affiliates won league titles in
Coast League), Atlanta (Southern Associati
League), and Panama City (Alabama-Florida Le

In 1960, Davis sparked Spokane to the PCL
games over Tacoma. In 147 games with the Indi
runs, 43 doubles, and 75 RBIs. His other cate
average, 126 runs, 216 hits, and 30 stolen bases—
obvious the former sprinter was ready for the nex

THE GAME OF MY

By Willie Davis

Although I was tearing up the Pacific Coast L
didn't focus on whether the Dodgers were going to
minor leagues. The news finally came during the fi
when our Spokane team was on a road trip. Pre
manager and he received a phone call from the Dod
Charley Smith and I were supposed to meet the
Cincinnati. Right away, I was excited because thin
Spokane. But the major league is a different leve
anything. I was more or less excited to just get ther

Charley and I arrived at old Crosley Field. Wov
rather old place to play ball. But it was going to be m
in the majors, and I was going to enjoy it.

Some players get a chance to join a pennant race
case in 1960. The Dodgers were in fourth place; the
I walked into the clubhouse and there was uniform
in my locker. I didn't ask for the number, which I wor
training camp in Florida. At the time, the uniform n
to me. It's funny, though, because the next year I got
for the past 45 years have been known as "The 3 Do

Put
experie
baseba
was go
sport
I wasn
up my
becaus
a day,

I d
have a
the fu
you p

Wl
funda
they
a fan
Tomr
peopl
fanta:

Fo
in the
playii
Jay H

M
In m
right
chec
happ
"Oh
gam

Hoo
hanc
Doc
beca
Ost
inni
of n

out to center in the third and sixth innings against Osteen and grounded out to shortstop in the ninth against reliever Bill Henry.

Meanwhile, Sandy Koufax was pitching a great game. I was told Sandy had his problems earlier that season, but you wouldn't know it that day in Cincinnati.

THE RESULTS

Koufax went the distance and struck out 10 batters in a 7-4 victory. Davis went 2-for-5 with two runs scored. Maury Wills went 3-for-5 and Norm Larker and Tommy Davis added two hits apiece. In his major-league debut, third baseman Charley Smith went 0-for-3 with two RBIs. The Reds scored in the sixth on Vada Pinson's home run and added three in the eighth, two on Cliff Cook's home run.

CENTER OF ATTENTION

One of Dodger broadcaster Vin Scully's favorite stories involves Davis on defense during a close game in his rookie season in 1960. With two out in the top of the ninth inning, an opposing batter lofted a towering fly ball toward Davis in center field at the Coliseum. Davis glided under the ball and seemingly snared the ball at belt-high level with ease.

On the postgame show, Scully asked how a rookie could remain so calm in a critical situation. Today, Scully remembers the answer by borrowing Davis' rich baritone voice and smooth delivery:

"It's not my life … it's not my wife … so why-yyyyyy worry?"

Davis was perfectly content to flourish away from the spotlight in the early 1960s as Wills, Koufax, Don Drysdale, and others helped Los Angeles become a perennial pennant contender. Davis' first full season with the Dodgers coincided with the opening of Dodger Stadium in 1962. Davis loved the new ballpark and overall he batted .285 in 157 games with 10 triples, 21 home runs, and 85 RBIs.

The Dodgers lost a three-game playoff against San Francisco at the end of the 1962 season, but rebounded in 1963 with a World Series sweep of the New York Yankees. After a disappointing 1964 season in which Koufax was injured, the Dodgers won the championship in 1965 and returned to the World Series again in 1966.

"It was a diamond-like experience," Davis said. "If anybody went through those experiences with these guys, they would enjoy it. There was something about that time period and these guys where something suddenly clicked. Alston was a no-nonsense guy. And guys sensed that from him, because if you got off track, he'd come to you and say, 'If you don't want to play baseball, you can take off your uniform and get out of here.' To have the guts to say that to star ballplayers, boy, you have to have the support from somebody. He had the support from the front office, and he used it. But we all liked each other, so the results were fine."

Koufax retired following the 1966 season and other roster moves gradually made Davis the elder statesman on the ballclub in terms of service time. Davis remained a cornerstone in the Dodger lineup, but Los Angeles didn't win a pennant for seven years—the longest drought since the Brooklyn days from 1921-1940.

The honeymoon finally ended after the 1973 season when the Dodgers wanted to make adjustments and Davis, at age 33, was ready for a change of scenery. He was traded to the Montreal Expos in exchange for relief pitcher Mike Marshall, who won the 1974 Cy Young Award while helping Los Angeles win the pennant. Davis spent his last five seasons with the Expos, Texas Rangers, St. Louis Cardinals, San Diego Padres, and California Angels.

Always the optimist, Davis found the positives even during his non-Dodger years. Gene Mauch, known as a stern taskmaster when managing the second-division Expos, greeted Davis in 1974 by saying, "OK, you're on my team now, so we're friends."

Davis replied, "Well then, let's rock 'n roll."

As a member of the Rangers, Davis met legendary golfer Ben Hogan at a Texas sports banquet. Davis was thrilled to receive golf "secrets" from the usually reticent Hogan.

"Those kind of memories, even today, they are so valuable," Davis said. "Because when you pass on what you learn, it's a grand feeling. You can't even imagine until you do it. I'd advise anyone who is in sports to learn the fundamentals of their sport. Get to where you know them, and don't be selfish with them, in case anyone asks you about them. That's the way to go about it, so it spreads. And if that feeling spreads, you're going to have a successful route."

Today, Davis still lives in the Los Angeles area and is a member of the Dodger Speakers Bureau. In 2006, he was elected to the Roosevelt High School Hall of Fame, completing a circle that began nearly 50 years earlier.

"I had so many great moments, it's hard to separate them," said Davis, "But just being a part of the Dodger organization and learning the fundamentals, that was so much fun, too. You sensed that if you got these things done that you were going to be around. This is my feeling. I always had that feeling in the beginning. You know, Buzzie Bavasi, the Dodgers' general manager, was kind of like my father, adopting me because I was from the Los Angeles area. He knew in advance how fast I was, but I don't think he knew how good of a hitter or a player I would be until he saw me during spring training. Right from the get-go, I was one of the favorites there. I was a California boy and you know I was groovin' and feeling so good about the whole situation. Walter Alston was giving me encouragement all the time and I always appreciated that."

Chapter 5

MAURY WILLS

NAME:	Maurice Morning Wills
BORN:	October 2, 1932
BIRTHPLACE:	Washington, D.C.
YEARS WITH THE DODGERS:	1959-1966, 1969-1972
POSITION:	Shortstop
UNIFORM NUMBER:	30
CAREER HIGHLIGHTS:	Stole 586 career bases in the major leagues from 1959-1972 and 281 bases in the minor leagues from 1951-1959; earned National League Most Valuable Player honors in 1962; still holds the top two single-season stolen base marks in Dodger history: 104 in 1962 and 94 in 1965; member of three World Series championship teams in 1959, 1963, and 1965; won the Gold Glove Award at shortstop in 1961 and 1962.
THE GAME:	October 3, 1962; San Francisco Giants vs. Los Angeles Dodgers at Dodger Stadium

THE MENTOR

Perhaps the most famous stolen base in major-league history occurred during the 2004 American League Championship Series between the New York Yankees and Boston Red Sox, although some might nominate Brooklyn Dodger icon Jackie Robinson's home-plate steal in the 1955 World Series, replayed on television more often because of catcher Yogi Berra's animated reaction to umpire Bill Summers' "safe" call.

But former Dodger outfielder Dave Roberts changed the fortunes of the Red Sox franchise after Boston lost the first three games of a best-of-seven format to their bitter rivals. The Red Sox trailed 4-3 entering the bottom of the ninth inning of Game 4 at Fenway Park. Yankees' ace closer Mariano Rivera looked to polish off the four-game sweep and leave Boston still aching for its first World Series title since 1918.

When Kevin Millar drew a leadoff walk, Roberts was inserted as a pinch runner, obviously aiming to steal second base against Rivera and catcher Jorge Posada to get into scoring position. After a few pickoff attempts, Roberts took off on Rivera's first pitch to Bill Mueller. Roberts slid safely head-first into second base on a close play and scored on Mueller's single to center field. The Red Sox prevailed 6-4 in 12 innings. Boston won its next seven games, sweeping aside the Yankees and then breezing past the St. Louis Cardinals in the World Series. Roberts didn't even have an at-bat during Boston's three playoff series, leaving the Red Sox via free agency that winter. But in team history, his contribution is simply known as "The Steal."

"When I was with the Dodgers, Maury Wills once told me that there will come a point in my career when everyone in the ballpark will know that I have to steal a base, and I will steal that base," Roberts said. "When I got out there, I knew that was what Maury Wills was talking about."

All the while, Wills watched this drama unfold on his television in Southern California. The man who revolutionized the game himself in the early 1960s and stole a then-record 104 bases in 1962 had come full circle, bursting with pride over a pupil reminiscent of his Triple-A manager, Bobby Bragan, more than 40 years earlier. It was Bragan who taught the speedy Wills to become a switch-hitter at Spokane during the second half of the 1958 season, his eighth year in pro ball.

Bragan thought of the idea only because Wills jumped into his last batting-cage session and swung left-handed to save time.

Speedster Maury Wills stretches his legs during spring training in Vero Beach, Florida.

"Sometimes you just notice things," Bragan wrote in his 1992 autobiography. "He looked natural doing it." Bragan worked with Wills on batting left-handed an hour before regular batting practice for the next four weeks. Wills started to experiment in games after a long homestand, figuring there would be less pressure on the road.

The Dodgers sold Wills' contract during spring training in 1959 on a "trial" basis, but the Tigers were unimpressed and returned him. Wills returned to Spokane and was promoted to the Dodgers at age 26 during the summer of 1959, only because starting shortstop Don Zimmer was nursing a broken toe.

As a minor-league instructor, Wills tutored Roberts in 2002 when Roberts, at age 29, was a non-roster player trying to keep his career alive after eight seasons of primarily bouncing around the minor leagues. One of the biggest challenges in baseball is trying to impress the team brass while doing "the little things" required of a catalyst during otherwise relaxed spring conditions.

"When I was watching the playoffs, it took me back to when I first met Dave at Dodger Stadium for the pre-spring training workouts," Will said. "We used to work out every Monday, Wednesday, and Friday from the first of the year until it was time to leave for Florida. Only the first day was mandatory for certain major leaguers. After the first day, only the minor leaguers showed up. There were a few major leaguers now and then, but Dave lives in Carlsbad, which is about 70 miles away from Los Angeles. Dave would show up every Monday, Wednesday, and Friday, the only major leaguer. And he wanted a chance and he worked hard and listened."

Originally sixth on the 2002 outfield depth chart—even behind non-roster invitee Dante Bichette, whose sudden retirement that spring helped Roberts' chances—the long shot made the team, eventually wearing uniform No. 30 in honor of Wills.

"In spring training, I remember being on a distant field with Dave Roberts, Marquis Grissom, Tom Goodwin, and McKay Christensen," Wills said. "The four of them were on a half-diamond every morning. Marquis Grissom was making $4.5 million, so you knew he was going to play somewhere. Tommy Goodwin was making $2 million and had been around a long time and was a proven major leaguer, so you knew he was going to be in there. And Christensen was brought into camp by the general manager, so you knew he had a good shot at making the ballclub. So that left Dave at the bottom of the totem pole. He was the least likely one to make the ballclub. I remember they were all good working with me, but halfway through the spring, the rest of them seemed to peel off. Dave Roberts was still there working with me. And he started getting really involved, and that hard work paid off. He made the ballclub, made a good salary, and alternated in center field with Marquis Grissom. And then going on to Boston to steal that historic base to help beat the Yankees, the Red Sox went on to become world champions.

"Today, he just signed an $18-million contract. But I don't take any credit for that. Now I see what Bobby Bragan means. He was the one who found me in the minor leagues when I was going nowhere. He made me a switch-hitter and I give credit to him. I give credit to Bobby Bragan for everything Maury Wills was able to accomplish. But I couldn't understand why he wouldn't take any credit. He'd say, 'It was all Maury, it was all Maury.' Now I can understand why he said that. It wasn't me—it was Dave Roberts helping himself. I credit Dave for being such a good student and wanting it enough. That's a work ethic that's hard to find in the game of baseball today. If we had more, you'd see more players like Dave Roberts."

THE GAME OF MY LIFE

By Maury Wills

Before I mention my most memorable game, I want to preface it by talking about three other games. There was a game in the prime of my career and I remember playing a Sunday doubleheader against the Cincinnati Reds. I had something like six hits in the two games, four in the nightcap, and I hit a home run to win the game. I think it was a three-run home run. Nobody could believe it. Then there was a game at the Los Angeles Coliseum in 1961 when, after 1,100-something at-bats, I hit a home run over that short screen in left field. They made a big deal of it because I didn't have any home runs. I also didn't have a home-run trot, which meant I almost tripped over second base. When I got to the dugout, I thought everyone was going to be there to greet me and congratulate me. Instead, they were all sprawled on the floor of the dugout as if they had fainted.

But the game I'll remember is the final game of the 1962 season. We were tied with the Giants and played three extra games, a best two-of-three playoff. The Giants won the first one, we won the second game at Dodger Stadium, and now we're playing the final rubber game. I had three hits and stole three bases. The stolen bases were numbers 102, 103, and 104. And on the 104th steal, I went home after the throw to third base sailed into left field. That gave us a 3-2 lead, and at that point, we had spent our World Series money. Then the Giants rallied with four runs in the ninth inning and beat us 6-4.

Looking back at the stolen bases, I wasn't thinking about the record until late June or early July when the writers were talking about it one night in St. Louis. The previous record was 96 steals by Ty Cobb with the Detroit Tigers in 1915. It turns out that was going to be the Dodger attack during the 1962 season—I would get on, get into scoring position with a stolen base, Jim Gilliam would get me over to third with one out, and I'd score on a sacrifice fly or ground ball. One run was usually enough for Sandy Koufax or Don Drysdale. They would shut out the other team 1-0. So that wasn't by design, it just happened. When we saw the pattern, we just stuck to basics. One time I was on base with nobody out and the situation called for a sacrifice bunt. Walter Alston, our manager, let me steal second and then Gilliam bunted me to third. The 1962 season was very memorable, but it did hurt at the end when we lost to the Giants, so I don't bring it up very often.

I started switch-hitting in 1958, my last year in the minors. In 1959, I'm in the big leagues. In my first full year in the big leagues in 1960, I hit .295 and was in the top 10 among hitters in the league. That gave me the confidence that I needed. I got 2,134 hits in my career after coming up late.

Another game I remember occurred in 1969 when I was caught up in the expansion draft. The Montreal Expos selected me from the Pittsburgh Pirates, where I had been exiled after leaving the Dodgers during their 1966 tour of Japan without permission. I found out that you just don't do that. I was sent to the Pirates and played in Pittsburgh for two years and then was drafted by the Expos. It was so cold in Montreal. I actually quit the game for three days. They finally sent me back to the Dodgers, along with Manny Mota, in a trade.

When I came back to the Dodgers in July, a very memorable public address announcer, John Ramsey, appealed to about 45,000 people in the stands. He said, "Ladies and gentlemen, why don't we stand and welcome back Maury Wills?" About 45,000 people stood and applauded for about four minutes. The umpire tried to get the game started again, but Hank Aaron of the Braves wouldn't step into the batter's box because the cheering wouldn't stop. He was acknowledging the crowd, too. That same day, Walter O'Malley came by the Dodger clubhouse and put a sign over my locker, "Welcome Home Maury." And I was told that was the only time he ever came to the Dodger clubhouse.

That stays with me even today. The fact that 45,000 people stood for four minutes, I don't think it was because I stole 104 bases, or because I was captain of the team, or because we won four in a row against the Yankees in the 1963 World Series. I always felt it was because they liked me as a person. That stood out in my mind. I've always been a fan-friendly person, which is a good lesson in life.

I can't believe it's been 35 years since I retired from baseball. Wow. It's still my life. I do other things in life for my income, but I've always been involved in baseball and still want to be until it's time I "go to the other side," so to speak. I feel good, I feel young, and I feel vibrant. And I'm still beating those guys in the first step when I'm teaching them base stealing. I'm still putting them through the tests in bunting, so I feel good about that. I like encouraging those young players because God blessed me with meeting Bobby Bragan and he turned me around, so one person can make a difference. We think of that as a cliché, but it's a truism. I'm a witness to it. Bobby Bragan made the difference.

I wanted to quit 100 times. I just couldn't go through with it because I loved the game so much.

THE RESULTS

The Dodgers lost the third and final game of the 1962 National League playoff on October 3, 1962—exactly 11 years after Brooklyn lost the pennant to the New York Giants 5-4 on Bobby Thomson's three-run home run in the ninth inning at the Polo Grounds. In both the 1951 and 1962 games, the Dodgers took a 4-2 lead into the ninth inning. Wills stole three bases and went 4-for-5, including singles in his first four at-bats against Giants starter Juan Marichal. The Giants scored four runs in the ninth inning to prevail 6-4. The winning pitcher was Don Larsen, then a journeyman reliever who pitched the only perfect game in World Series history as a member of the Yankees against the Dodgers in 1956.

THE OTHER INSPIRATION

While Bobby Bragan turned around Wills' career, it was Jackie Robinson who caught the attention of Wills as a youngster. Wills was 14 years old when Robinson broke baseball's color barrier with the Dodgers in 1947. Living in the projects of Washington, D.C., Wills asked neighbors in his all-black neighborhood about Jackie Robinson.

"They told me about Jackie," Wills said. "Then I asked, 'Where's Brooklyn?' and 'Where's New York?' I remember right then and there I was going to play for the Dodgers someday. My childhood dream was to be a major-league player. That dream started when I was eight years old because a Washington Senators player came to our playground to conduct a clinic. By the time he left, I had a direction. I knew I wanted to be a major-league player.

"When I was 14 and people were talking about Jackie Robinson, I knew I wanted to be a Dodger. I realized both those childhood dreams. So that's what kept me going all those years in the minors, because I just wanted to be a Dodger. Wherever Jackie Robinson was, that's where I wanted to go. And there were some tough times. There were times I couldn't stay with my teammates. I couldn't eat where they wanted to eat. I couldn't travel the way they traveled. But nothing would deter me from getting to the big leagues."

After spending most of the 1953 regular season at Class B Miami of the Florida International League, where he batted .286 in 93 games, Wills was invited to play on the Jackie Robinson All-Stars after the regular season.

"I got to know Jackie Robinson. I barnstormed with him throughout the South one fall in 1953. He had Luke Easter from the Cleveland Indians, Gil Hodges from the Dodgers, Ralph Branca, a former Dodger then with the Detroit Tigers, and a second baseman named Bobby Young from the St. Louis Browns. Those were the four major leaguers. They filled the rest of the team in with Dodger farmhands. I was one of them and I made $300. Jackie didn't know it, but I would've played for nothing. It was quite a thrill."

Robinson's legacy is remembered by Major League Baseball, which retired his uniform, No. 42, for all teams in 1997 and in 2007 commemorated the 60th anniversary of his historic first game with the Dodgers.

But with the passage of time the ranks of those who personally knew Robinson lessens, leaving today's new generations of players and fans only snapshots and familiar sound bites from his career.

Asked to describe Robinson, Wills said, "He was a very dynamic person. He wasn't someone you'd just walk up to and say, 'Hi, Jackie.' You stood in awe of him. He had that kind of presence. I felt fortunate and blessed just to meet him and shake his hand and be on the same team with him. But he was a straight shooter, no-nonsense guy. He was all business. Whatever he did, it was in a businesslike approach.

"When we went on the barnstorming tour, Jackie drove in a car. Luke Easter and all the other major leaguers were in big cars. And the minor leaguers were traveling with the Indianapolis Clowns on a bus. The Clowns of the old Negro Leagues was the team we played against. We played in places like Birmingham over to Chattanooga, Tennessee; we'd go to Biloxi, Tennessee, and Mobile, Alabama. After every game and before getting in his car to take off for the next destination, he would check the bus to make sure we were all there. One time I was missing because I was in the stands, talking to a cute girl who batted her eyes at me. He said, 'Boy, you get on this bus!' and I said in a high voice, 'OK!' He knew that I was not on the bus, that's how accomplished he was."

Wills' final major-league year was in 1972, when he appeared in 71 games as a reserve shortstop and third baseman. Wills was at Dodger Stadium on June 4, a Sunday afternoon, when the team retired the uniform numbers of Robinson (42), Roy Campanella (39), and Sandy Koufax (32). Koufax was entering the Hall of Fame that summer; Robinson had been elected to Cooperstown in 1962 and Campanella in 1969.

It was the first time the Dodgers had retired a uniform number. The team didn't arrange its first Old Timers' Day in Los Angeles until 1971 when Peter O'Malley was the team president. Before, the Dodgers staged a reunion of the Pacific Coast League's Hollywood Stars and Los Angeles Angels in the early 1960s.

Robinson's appearance was poignant since he passed away that fall of heart failure at age 53. He could barely see those around him at Dodger Stadium as diabetes had rendered him nearly blind at that point.

"The one thing about those historical events, for me, anyway, it doesn't really take on the significance until afterwards," Wills said. "It was years later when I realized how fantastic a day that was at Dodger Stadium when they retired his number and Jackie showed up for that. Jackie, at the time, was not on good terms spiritually with the Dodgers. It might've been because he was traded to the Giants after the 1957 season by Mr. Walter O'Malley at the end. And rather than go to the Giants, he quit. He took on a heavy feeling. I don't want to say resentment, but he wasn't feeling real good about that. He seldom went to Dodger Stadium before that Old Timers' Day ceremony. But Peter O'Malley made amends with him and got him to come out for that occasion. That's another reason why it was so very historical and significant. I don't know if a lot of people know that part of it. And a few months later he passed away. God has a way of putting things back in order in spite of us."

Chapter 6

WES PARKER

NAME:	Maurice Wesley Parker
BORN:	November 13, 1939
BIRTHPLACE:	Evanston, IL
YEARS WITH THE DODGERS:	1964-1972
POSITION:	Outfield, First Base
UNIFORM NUMBER:	28
CAREER HIGHLIGHTS:	Won National League Gold Glove Award six consecutive seasons (1967-72); only player in Los Angeles history to hit for the cycle in one game (May 7, 1970 vs. Mets at Shea Stadium); team MVP 1970; led National League in fielding percentage five times.
THE GAME:	May 24, 1964; Philadelphia Phillies vs. Los Angeles Dodgers at Dodger Stadium

THE CHALLENGE FROM WITHIN

Along with his golden glove at first base and in the outfield, a casual observer might assume Wes Parker's portfolio also contained a silver spoon.

The Southern California native emerged from Harvard Military Academy and Claremont Men's College without much hope for a professional career. Transferring to the University of Southern California for his senior year left him ineligible for the Trojans' baseball team. After spending his 1962 summer in Europe, Parker picked up the phone in early September and called Charlie Dressen, a Dodger coach who was also a friend of Parker's father.

"I want to play for the Dodgers," Parker announced. "What do I have to do?"

Dressen wasn't sure what to tell the 22-year-old college graduate, whom he hadn't seen play since Parker's American Legion days in 1957. Three days later, Parker was assigned to a group of primarily high school players that played every weekend. Parker displayed solid form, both at the plate and on defense.

By December, a frustrated Parker asked Dodger scout Kenny Myers whether the ballclub was going to offer a contract. Myers was startled by the direct question. He took the trademark cigar out of his mouth and stared at Parker.

"That depends, kid," Myers began slowly, "whether you want to play ball, or whether you want money."

Parker needed a challenge, not the money. He had attended games at the Los Angeles Coliseum when the Dodgers first moved to Los Angeles in 1958, daydreaming of playing Gil Hodges' position at first base. Before that, Parker watched the Pacific Coast League's Hollywood Stars at Gilmore Field.

The answer was simple: Parker wanted to play ball.

"I don't think there will be a problem," Myers said.

On December 22, 1962, Parker signed a "no bonus" contract. He was assigned to Single-A Santa Barbara, scheduled to receive $300 per month and $1.50 per day meal money. Parker was the lowest paid player on the squad—the average salary was $450 per month.

Parker batted .305 in 92 games at Santa Barbara and was later promoted to Double-A Albuquerque, where he hit .350 in 26 games. Overall, he compiled 148 hits, 12 doubles, seven triples, 15 home runs, and 22 stolen bases.

When Parker joined the Dodgers as a rookie in 1964, his teammates were the defending world champions, having defeated the New York Yankees in a four-game October sweep. But the Dodgers didn't retain veteran first baseman Bill "Moose" Skowron, who batted .203 during his only season with the Dodgers in 1963.

First baseman Wes Parker won six Gold Glove Awards during his career with the Dodgers.

That opened the door for Parker, who likely wouldn't have made the team had Dodger brass not been afraid of losing him in the minor-league draft. It was commonplace during the era before the amateur draft for teams to "protect" prospects on their major-league roster, knowing the planned payoff in future years wasn't guaranteed.

THE GAME OF MY LIFE

By Wes Parker

It was my rookie year with the Dodgers, May 24, 1964. It was a Sunday afternoon game, and I went through my pregame routine like I was not going to play—lots of ground balls at first base, lots of fly balls in the outfield, running sprints with the pitchers, really working up a sweat. I had my first start in Chicago maybe a week or two before. I started the first game of a doubleheader and went 0-for-5. So I was back on the bench, mainly pinch hitting. I'd never started a game at home. I went into the clubhouse to change shirts. I was soaked from working so hard. I took off my sweatshirt, put on a dry one, and was just sitting there when Pete Reiser emerged from the manager's office and said, "You're in there, you're starting in center field."

I said, "What?" I felt my heart start to race.

I wasn't even close to being confident at the time. I think my batting average was close to .167 from pinch hitting. And I found big-league pitching incredibly difficult—not just kind of difficult—incredibly difficult to hit. It was a huge leap from Double-A, and I never played at Triple-A.

I was surprised to be in the major leagues at the time, although I knew the reason. The bonus and draft rules meant if I was sent to the minors they might lose me to another team in the draft. So they were protecting me, thinking I would be good in the future, not particularly that year. That's pretty much how it worked out, although I was better than they thought I would be.

I had only 20 minutes before game time to get ready. The only good news was the Dodgers were playing a day game against the Philadelphia Phillies. I always saw the ball better and felt better during day games. That's just the way my clock ran, my biorhythm.

But I was definitely nervous. The first thing I said was, "What's wrong with Willie?" because he said I was in center field. Reiser said he had sore muscles and a stiff neck. And I just stared at him. I was trying to think of an excuse not to play. But who else could possibly play there? There was no one who could cover the ground as well as I could. I was not worried defensively, I was worried about what I would do with the bat.

I finally realized as I stared at him that I had to do this. He saw the ashen look on my face and the horror in my eyes. He said, "Look, you can do this. Don't worry, you're a good ballplayer and this is your big chance. Go out there and make the most of it."

Pete Reiser could say that because he was successful in the big leagues. At that point, I made up my mind that I had to do it. I didn't think I was going to be good at it, I really didn't. I thought, "I have to do it because it's my job." I changed my sweatshirt, got dressed, put my shoes on, and got my hat and glove.

I went into the trainer's room to see Bill Buhler because I knew I needed sunglasses. I got a pair of the flip-downs and tried them against the sun. Some are too dark, some too light. You have to pick the model that blocks out the sun to the extent that you like. I did that, checked them, and they were fine. I adjusted the strap so it wasn't too tight, otherwise it gave me a headache. I checked the flip-down mechanism in the sunglasses, and the spring was just fine.

There were 36,000 fans in the ballpark that day. The bleachers were pretty full. I don't remember much about the national anthem while standing in the dugout, but I was probably thinking, "I'll be happy when this day is over." When I ran onto the field, I felt pretty good. My legs felt surprisingly good. Part of it was adrenaline and part of it was because I hadn't played that much, so I was fresh. I don't remember any fly balls or ground balls hit to me early in the game, and if there were, I wouldn't have worried about it. I knew I could catch anything hit my way. I was terrified, though, of hitting.

When I came to the ballpark that morning, I don't think I knew Jim Bunning was pitching. I mainly was interested in starting pitchers to know if I had heard of them before and to have the other players tell me how good they are. Because Wally Moon was also on the bench, Lee Walls was still there for a while. They would talk to me and say, "This guy is really good and throws really hard, you have to watch out for his curveball," or "He'll throw breaking balls when he's behind." I used to love to hear that stuff. That would prepare me for pinch hitting. But in this case, so far they hadn't told me anything. I was going up there without any previous information, but of course, I had heard of Jim Bunning as a fan.

So, first time up, there was nobody on base in the bottom of the second inning. I was hitting seventh in the lineup. There must have been one or two outs. Bunning threw me a high outside fastball and I hit it pretty good to left field. Wes Covington was out there, and he wasn't a very good fielder. He started to run in a circle, and instead of turning and looking at the ball over his shoulder, he backpedaled. The ball sailed over his head and short-hopped the wall. If that happened today, the press would've annihilated him. But back then, it was kind of acceptable to be a really good hitter, which he was, and not a very good fielder, which he also was. So it was a gift double. Even though I hit the ball well, it easily should've been caught. And that really helped me. It made me think, "Oh my God, maybe this is going to work." I stayed on second base, never scored.

The next time up, Bunning blew me away with high inside fastballs. Wham! Wham! Wham! Strike three—it's over. I couldn't believe it. I was thinking, "Oh boy, here we go again." Now, I go back to the bench and Wally Moon is sitting there. Great guy, he helped me the entire year. I sat next to him and he asked, "What did you hit for a double your first time up?"

I said, "High outside fastball."

He said, "What did he just strike you out with?"

I said, "High inside fastballs."

He said, "Forget the high outside fastballs, you are never going to see that again today from Jim Bunning. Look up and in next time you're up—high inside fastball."

The next time I came up, the first pitch was an up-and-in fastball. I doubled down the right-field line. I couldn't believe it. Wally Moon had saved me. Now I'm 2-for-3. We had two runs by then and were ahead 2-0.

Before I hit the next time, I was in the outfield when the Phillies got two runners on base with no outs against starting pitcher Joe Moeller in the top of the seventh inning. Walter Alston came out to the pitcher's mound. I heard a roar from the fans because Alston had pointed to the bullpen. And coming out of the bullpen—and this was very unusual—was Sandy Koufax. The crowd went nuts. I saw him come through the gate and thought, "Well, at least we're going to win the game."

Koufax blew away Ruben Amaro on strikes. Gus Triandos, a pinch hitter, fouled out to Ron Fairly at first base. Then Danny Cater hits a pretty hard line drive to right-center field. Now, if this ball is not caught, the tying runs are going to score with two outs. He hit the ball pretty good, not a blistering line drive, but it was solid. I had been playing straight away in center field, but I probably should've been over toward right field more because nobody pulled Koufax. I had a long way to run. Frank Howard was in right field and he always hugged the line because he wanted no part of a fly ball. He had already told me, "Anything between you and me … you got it, kid. It's all yours."

As I'm taking off toward this ball, I'm thinking, "OK, Frank said to take anything between us, so I'd better keep running as fast as I can." I didn't have time to look to see if he was coming, so then I'm thinking, "If I run into this guy, I'm dead. He's about 6-foot-8 and weighs 300 pounds. He will flatten me—I will not play another inning this year." All those thoughts were swirling in my mind as I'm running for this ball. I was hoping the ball would hang up in the air just a little longer because I was afraid it would lose steam and fall. Right at the end, I looked and saw I had a shot at it. I didn't dive. Instead, I made a full reach while running as fast as I could. I backhanded the ball at about the height of my knees.

The first thing I did was look for Frank, and he cut in behind me, or he would've flattened me. As I ran in, I received a standing ovation, my first one of the day. I went past Sandy. He stayed by the mound before walking toward the dugout, and as I ran by him he said, "Nice catch, kid." My feelings at the time were ones of gratefulness. I hadn't screwed up, at least not yet.

Vin Scully once said to me in an interview, "Wes, the great players welcome and embrace the difficult moments, the moments when the game is on the line. Are you like that?"

I said, "Quite honestly Vinny … no."

Throughout my career, except in 1970, I dreaded most of those moments. Early in my career I dreaded them because I didn't think I could succeed at any time, much less under pressure. Only later did it get to the point where I was comfortable.

In the bottom of the eighth inning, I hit for the fourth time. Bunning was gone and we were still ahead 2-0. There was a runner on first and one or two outs. Fairly was on first. Jack Baldschun, the reliever for the Phillies, primarily threw screwballs. I didn't know what to expect. I didn't talk to Wally Moon. I just went up there. He threw me a hanging screwball—which is unusual, you don't hear that term very often—right down the middle of the plate, letter high. I had a good swing and timed it well. The ball was hit perfectly.

If you took out a measuring stick to find the exact distance between the center and right fielders … this was exactly between Danny Cater in center field and Johnny Callison in right. I'm running and the ball lands on the warning track and bounces off the fence, just like the hit over Covington's head. I just kept running and wound up on third base. Ron

Fairly scored and it was my first big-league RBI. I'm standing on third and Leo Durocher, the coach, barks, "Way to go, kid! Way to go, kid! Damn, that's the way to play the game!" And I got my second standing ovation. So I've got two doubles and a triple and I'm 3-for-4, I've increased our lead with an RBI and made a game-saving catch.

I went to right field in the ninth inning because Walter Alston had talked Willie Davis into playing. Suddenly, those muscles weren't so sore and his neck felt better. So Willie runs to center field and I take Frank Howard's place in right field. As I reached my position, I got the biggest ovation of the day. It was the third one of the day and the longest and most sustained. I remember, even though I had my dark glasses on, I took off my hat—pulling it from under the sunglasses strap—and waved it to the crowd.

It was a feeling of happiness, beyond joy. It was a sense of ecstasy because I knew what it meant, what I had just done. Not only had I succeeded, not only was the team going to win, but I had proven myself in the big leagues. I understood that proving only takes place over a longer period of time. But I had proven to myself that I could play in the big leagues and that I could hit these guys. That was the first time I had the confidence that I could play this game at this level. And to feel that kind of acceptance and love pour out of those stands all over me was exhilarating.

I remember one time hearing John Robinson, the coach of the USC football team, say that one crowd at the Los Angeles Coliseum was so loud he could feel the cheers against his skin. In this game, there was some kind of energy, some kind of pressure from that ovation from the fans. It struck my skin and gave me goose bumps. It was almost like I just wanted to kneel down and pray and thank somebody for what had happened. It kind of snuck up on me. All of a sudden, I was a hero for the Dodgers, a team I had grown up loving and watching with my father's season tickets. I had gone to so many games with him. And suddenly, I'm on the field doing what my heroes had done. It was so overwhelming that it was almost like I never wanted to play another game. I knew I could never top what I had just done. And it happened in my first start at home, one of the most amazing and incredible experiences in my life.

THE RESULTS

The Dodgers defeated the Phillies 3-0 in front of 36,900 at Dodger Stadium. Joe Moeller (2-3) scattered three hits in six-plus innings and Sandy Koufax pitched the final three innings for his only save of the 1964 season. Wes Parker went 3-for-4 with a double and triple. Tommy Davis hit a solo home run off Jim Bunning (5-2) in the third inning.

FITS LIKE A GLOVE

"When Wes is hitting, he looks like one of the best," Dodger manager Walter Alston said in 1968. "When he's not, he looks like one of the worst. Wes would be a lot better ball player if he'd get mad now and then. Sure wish he could get as mad on the ball field as I've seen him in a game of bridge."

While Parker was winning six consecutive Gold Glove Awards at first base from 1967-1972, his offense became a challenge to both Parker and his instructors. Parker was a lifetime .267 hitter. His one breakout season was 1970, when he hit .319 with 10 home runs and 111 RBIs. A *Sports Illustrated* cover story proclaimed him "Baseball's Newest Star," but Parker averaged only 60 RBIs in his last two seasons.

Ask Parker today about his defense and the response isn't something found in any instructional textbook. In fact, the subject taps into his emotions.

"Playing first base suited my personality," he said. "This is something you'll never hear people talk about. I was not an aggressive person. I was really kind of a defensive guy in my personality. I was shy. I always played it safe. I had a hard time asking girls out on dates. So it fit everything that I was all about. If you backed me into a corner, I would fight. I'd fight like crazy. This is the way I was raised because I had parents who were often unfair. And when they were unfair, I would fight like a wild kid. I'd have temper tantrums, trash my room. But I was only like that when I thought I was being treated unfairly.

"And so, as a ballplayer, defensively, if someone hit a ground ball it was almost like I took it as an attack. They were attacking me. And I would fight with everything I had to defend myself. And defending myself, in terms of fielding, was catching the ball, almost as though I was saying, 'Don't you dare hit another ball to me because this is what's going to happen—I'm going to gobble it up, you're going to be out, and your batting average is going to go down.' That was kind of the attitude that I had. And so, as a hitter, it took a long time for me to overcome that because there I had to initiate the action. And if I fought too hard, had great cuts, and fell down while swinging the bat, the opposing pitchers were going to do what my parents did to me—and that was beat on me.

"So fielding, I was safe. I could do all these amazing things and let my athletic ability show and let my personality out and it would be OK as a fielder, whereas as a hitter, I would be punished for it. That's basically what it was."

After the 1972 season, Parker chose to call it quits at age 32. For the player who signed a no-bonus contract, this was not a surprising decision. He spent one season in Japan, both to play baseball and learn about another country's lifestyle and customs.

Parker returned to the United States and launched a successful career as a radio and television commentator. His current hobbies include golf and collecting both baseball memorabilia and antique movie posters. He teaches a weekly class at the Braille Institute in Los Angeles, talking baseball and discussing other current events in the sports world. Parker even treated his students to a game at Dodger Stadium, giving the fans a chance to experience the sounds and atmosphere of the major leagues. Although satisfied with his own career, he does not miss baseball.

Chapter 7

LOU JOHNSON

NAME:	Louis Brown Johnson
BORN:	September 22, 1932
BIRTHPLACE:	Lexington, Kentucky
YEARS WITH THE DODGERS:	1965-1967
POSITION:	Outfielder
UNIFORM NUMBER:	41
CAREER HIGHLIGHTS:	Broke into majors with the Chicago Cubs in 1960; member of the original 1961 Los Angeles Angels; was the only base runner (single and walk) in Sandy Koufax's 1-0 perfect-game victory over Cubs on 9/9/65; hit the deciding home run in Game 7 of 1965 World Series at Minnesota; hit a career-high 17 home runs in 1966 to lead the Dodgers to the National League pennant.
THE GAME:	May 5, 1965; Los Angeles Dodgers vs. Cincinnati Reds at Crosley Field

TRADING UP

When he first walked through the Dodger clubhouse in 1965, Lou Johnson heard the greeting he so longed to hear after a decade of hard knocks in professional baseball.

"We need you," said pitcher Sandy Koufax, who walked across the room to shake Johnson's hand.

Those three words helped change the direction of the 1965 Dodgers, seemingly in trouble after two-time National League batting champion Tommy Davis dislocated his ankle on May 1 while running toward second base at Dodger Stadium. Davis' split-second indecision whether to slide sidelined him for most of the season and jeopardized his career.

The Dodgers called upon 32-year-old Lou Johnson from Triple-A Spokane, who batted .259 in 131 games with 12 home runs and 58 RBIs. Johnson's dream season ended in Game 7 of the World Series when his home run off Jim Kaat at Minnesota gave Koufax the only offense he needed in a 2-0 victory.

"Lou came right in and fit in the clubhouse," said former outfielder Willie Davis. "It was almost as if his destiny was to be there anyway. When he got there, he came in and was so comfortable. The team didn't get excited or panic. We were going to miss Tommy, but we already had talked among the players about winning the pennant. When Lou joined the Dodgers, we had no clue whatsoever as to who he was or whether he could play because we didn't see him in spring training."

Prior to the 1964 season, the Detroit Tigers dealt Johnson and $10,000 to Los Angeles in exchange for pitcher Larry Sherry, the 1959 World Series MVP. Johnson spent the entire 1964 season at Triple-A Spokane, even though the parent club was struggling for a sixth-place finish. Johnson couldn't crack the Dodgers' 1964 outfield of Tommy Davis, Willie Davis, Frank Howard, Wes Parker, Wally Moon, Lee Walls, and Willie Crawford.

Johnson always seemed the odd man out wherever he went. He played in the first game in Los Angeles Angels history on April 11, 1961. He was traded two days later to Toronto of the International League in exchange for outfielder Leon Wagner. From his professional debut in 1953 until he joined the Dodgers, Johnson's contract was assigned 17 times.

"In the earlier years when I played and got released three years in a row, it didn't phase me that much because my mind was still on basketball, even though I couldn't play as well as I played baseball," Johnson said.

After an injury to Tommy Davis early in 1965, journeyman outfielder Lou Johnson became a catalyst to a championship.

"For three years in a row, it finally dawned on me: 'You're getting released, but you keep coming back.' So maybe I had some qualities that I didn't know about—why not stick around and find out? I had nothing else to do either, in terms of employment."

THE GAME OF MY LIFE

By Lou Johnson

I'm a giving person. I got that from my mom. I'm the oldest in my family. But I've always done work to subsidize things that my dad didn't do—not that he couldn't do it, but he didn't do it because of a problem he had. I always worked extra. I'd play football and then go shine shoes, clean up, a whole bunch of things. I've always been the man of the house, so through that process I was able to maintain my little bit. And I thought, "The further I go, the more I'll make" in terms of salary. I never looked at myself statistically, what people idolized. My statistics were winning. From the time I played basketball growing up, I wasn't a great shooter, but I was the glue and kept the team together through leadership. That was a carryover. I worked hard. I worked hard years later in spring training when the regular hours were over.

When I was a kid, I never dreamed of playing in the majors. I played a lot of softball with a ball and a bat, but I never thought I would play baseball—it never dawned on my mind. We all have our dreams sometimes. If you dream of one thing that you know you can make it in, you try to spin off that if you get another shot. The fourth year when I got released, the Kansas City Monarchs of the old Negro Leagues were in town, and I got a chance. That was the spinoff. That was the first time that I had an opportunity to be with some comfortable men and women. Put it into the context of African-American men, solo, where I didn't have to face questions like, "Could I go in here to eat?" or "Could I sleep over here?" or other demoralizing situations that happened. We were all there together, and we all suffered through that. So I was part of that.

And then one of the most surprising things out of that was getting a contract in 1956. Buck O'Neil had put together a deal through the Negro Leagues and the Kansas City Monarchs, and because I learned so much, I thought, "Maybe I have a shot." Then I went to Ponca City, Oklahoma, of the Class-D Sooner State League and stayed a whole year. And I said, "Damn, this is it." Then the next year I stayed the year. And I kept going.

There have been two great incidents in my life. One, I was forced out of the South because I had learned to just enjoy myself, laugh, and just play. It's kind of demoralizing to certain people when you're stealing bases and hitting home runs and sliding in the South. I got through that.

In 1959, I got my first major-league contract. It was really kind of odd, because I didn't expect it. I didn't know what to do, but I knew I was going to get a shot in spring training. Then an injury came along. I had suffered so many injuries, and it got to the point where I was afraid to walk on cotton. I went up and down from the majors to the minors. I stayed in Triple-A for a while, and it turned out well for me. I think after all is said and done, when you don't expect something in life and it comes to you, it's not mind-boggling, but it doesn't come the way you had prepared it to come. And there were two teams that I would've loved to play for—the Cincinnati Reds, because of my mom, and the Dodgers, whether they were in Brooklyn or Los Angeles. The second choice came true.

Before I was called up to the Dodgers in 1965, I didn't think I'd get back to the majors, but I wasn't prepared to quit or make up my mind to do something else. One of the reasons for that was the year I had in 1964, when I hit .328 at Spokane and lost the batting championship on the final day of the season. Then I went to Puerto Rico and won the batting championship. That was an invitation for me to keep going. Where else can I go? I can't do any better than that. So I went back to Spokane and tried to make an adjustment. But 1965 definitely was going to be my last year. I was planning on possibly getting a chance to maybe stay in Spokane. I had met some good people. It just turned around for me after preparing to quit at the time.

I was having a pretty good year at Spokane when Tommy Davis hurt his ankle. If I look at it and am truthful, the promotion was done out of the sense that they tried to make up for what they didn't do, which was not invite me to spring training. I made them pay for it—I did well. I thought to myself, "Now I'm with the Dodgers. I'm going to do well." It didn't matter about the batting average. It didn't matter about the home runs or whether I was driving in a lot of runs. But the runs I drove in were big and the kind of baseball I was playing was needed here at that particular time. They had lost their star—they had lost the man who could carry the baggage for them. When I came in, I was prepared. I went from Spokane to Cincinnati.

Let me back up and tell you about a telephone call. I was preparing to quit anyway, so my thoughts at the time the phone rang were that the Dodgers were going to try to get me out of the organization because I had raised so much hell when they didn't invite me to the big-league camp in spring training. When the telephone call came, I said, "I'm not going to Cincinnati. Of all the teams you could've sent me to, I know I'm not going to play in front of the home folks as long as the Reds have Frank Robinson, Vada Pinson, and Gus Bell. How am I going to break into their lineup if I can't even break into the lineup with the Dodgers?" I thought I was being traded to the Reds. Peter O'Malley, who was running the Spokane club at the time, called back and said, "You're going to Cincinnati, and you're going to meet the Dodgers."

In the span of five minutes, I had packed my bags and run to the airport. I was at the airport five hours before the flight. I was ready to get to Cincinnati before they changed their minds. It was exciting because my mom could go to the ballpark. And at the time I had a sick brother who was in the hospital. All my family and friends were there for my first game at Crosley Field.

When I walked into the clubhouse, there was Tommy Davis, Maury Wills—the whole group of Dodger players. Across the room out of the goodness of his heart, Sandy shook my hand and said, "Welcome. We need you." That was it. Can you imagine me coming through all those channels? The man. Kou-foo. Sandy. That night I was put into the game to pinch run. The next night, the same thing happened, and I scored a run. I had a chance to be part of all three games.

How did it feel to be in a major-league ballpark again? I was with a team I wanted to be with and playing against my other favorite team right there in Cincinnati. I didn't know how long I was going to be there because in my mind, they were just trying to make up for something to please me. That was my attitude and I took it a little farther. You know, some things in your mind you don't get a chance to express. But you try to make up for them through participation and activity and doing the job. Of all the years I had spent playing the game and learning to be capable of what I could do, it was all put together.

We had superstars like John Roseboro, Wills, Sandy, Don Drysdale, Jim Lefevebre, Wes Parker, and Willie Davis. But somehow I fit right in there with them. And I turned out to be the glue. I've said a lot about the home run that I hit in the World Series. But it goes back to when I walked into that room in Cincinnati and Sandy shook my hand. From then on, it was history.

THE RESULTS

The Dodgers defeated the Reds 4-2 in front of 9,753 at Crosley Field. Sandy Koufax (3-1) struck out eight en route to a nine-hit complete game. Jim O'Toole (0-4) took the loss for Cincinnati, allowing three runs on five hits in 4⅓ innings. Third baseman Dick Tracewski and right fielder Ron Fairly hit home runs for the Dodgers. Lou Johnson made his Los Angeles debut in the bottom of the ninth inning as a defensive replacement for left fielder Al Ferrara.

THE UNLIKELY CATALYST

Five days after he arrived, Johnson hit a 10th-inning home run to beat Houston. Three days later, he was beaned and hospitalized. Soon after his return, Johnson crashed into Al Ferrara in left-center field. On June 12, Johnson fractured his thumb after being hit by a pitch thrown by the Mets' Al Jackson.

"I didn't have to worry about staying," said Johnson, who didn't go on the disabled list. "They didn't have anybody else at the time and I began to do the job. I didn't have to give up myself any more in terms of hating. I got a chance to be me. I didn't give a damn who knew it. I clapped my hands. My hands weren't clapping to show up anybody after hitting a home run. I was just proud of myself for hitting a home run. I didn't need anyone to clap for me. I was tired of people not clapping for me. I was going to do it myself."

And Los Angeles was the entertainment capital of the world, with such celebrities as Chuck Connors, Jack Benny, and movie producer Mervyn Leroy making regular visits to the ballpark. Comedian Milton Berle was a big Dodger fan, along with Jerry Lewis, who employed Dodgers Don Sutton, Roy Gleason, and Willie Davis in his war movie, *Which Way to the Front?* Dodger director of souvenirs Danny Goodman was a longtime member of the Friar's Club in Beverly Hills, and his contacts helped fill the early Hollywood Star exhibition games at Dodger Stadium.

"I was in Hollywood," Johnson said. "Where else could you do that and put on that flair? I had flair and it worked. But it was just me being comfortable. I wasn't one of those guys who thought about what I was going to do. I just went out and did it. But what people didn't understand was how jolly I could be and how I could go up and produce without the meditation thing. My stuff was already done. I knew what I had to do—go up and hit the pitch I thought was going to win the ballgame. It didn't matter if I struck out. I kept the fans in the ballpark. And then I always considered myself some kind of a leader. But I couldn't be a leader here in Los Angeles. We had Wills, Koufax, and Drysdale. So I was an unofficial leader. Wills and those guys were great. But I put the glue to it because Tommy Davis would put the glue to it. He was a finisher. I was a finisher. From that day on, I haven't changed. I had a chance to be me."

Johnson helped the Dodgers finished in first place in 1965 and 1966, but no Sandy Koufax in 1967 contributed to eighth place. Johnson appeared in only 104 games in 1967 in part because of a broken leg. The Dodgers traded Johnson to the Chicago Cubs after the 1967 season in exchange for infielder Paul Popovich and outfielder Jim Williams.

After his 30th birthday, which many consider "too old" for a rookie prospect, Johnson appeared in 387 games between 1965-1967. He averaged 65 in each of the next three seasons with the Cubs, Indians, and Angels.

"And so, from the few years that I had left, I was able to put together five good years in the major leagues," Johnson said. "But I don't understand when powers that be tell someone they are too old. ... I think most of us are capable of saying when we are no longer able to do the job. We don't get that chance. I was still a young man. Hell, I hadn't been beat up that bad. I came in and I surprised L.A."

The 1970s were a tough transition for Johnson, suddenly out of the game and battling drug and alcohol abuse. He gave his 1965 World Series ring to drug dealers in Seattle as collateral in 1971, and when he returned an hour later, both the ring and the men were gone. Three decades later, the ring surfaced as unclaimed property from an old safety deposit box in the state of Washington. Days before a scheduled online auction, the Dodgers purchased the ring for $3,457 and returned it to Johnson.

"There are a lot of things I've done that society might frown on, or I might frown on, but whatever I did at the time, it was necessary for what I had to do," said Johnson, a member of the Dodgers' community relations department as a drug and alcohol counselor since 1982. "And very rarely did I have too many sad moments, like striking out with the bases loaded. I can always come back tomorrow. But I had my own thing in Los Angeles and then I got the tag 'Sweet Lou.'

"I lived up to that name because it came from my swing. Clapping my hands, high-fiving, I had my own identity—that was good for me. It enabled me to finally arrive. What better place? The two best places to do that are New York and Los Angeles, and I was received here quite well. I stayed in the African-American community, talking and going down to the people. There were no private clubs for us. I bar hopped and did a lot of things. They didn't catch up with me. I caught up with me. ... I caught up with me."

Visitors to Lexington have no trouble discovering details about Johnson's career, beginning with the hero's welcome following the 1965 World Series when he received the official "red carpet" proclamation at the local airport. Lou Johnson Park is located at 190 Prall Street. The local Roots and Heritage Festival cited Johnson as the first black athlete from Lexington to play in the majors. And in 2004, Johnson was honored with a street sign on the University of Kentucky campus.

"On a campus where I wasn't even allowed to go and watch a basketball game, even after winning a World Series," Johnson said. "That hurt, deep down, because I always wanted to play for the University of Kentucky. I used to come back to Lexington to see certain people and most others didn't even know I was in town. The biggest parade they ever had in Lexington was the one they had for me after the World Series down the main street. It was pouring down rain and when the parade started, there was no more rain. I thought, 'Damn, I can part the waters!' That's the truth. It was raining and I thought, 'I'm the head man.'

"That was big time, but (I still had) that little burning desire to always be a UK person. When the people in my community named two or three parks after me, it was great. But when they named that street sign after me on the campus of the University of Kentucky, that was it. Hall of Fame couldn't be any better than that for me. My mom was wonderful. She cried. The first thing she said was, 'Honey, it happened.' She was 100 years old at the time, and I'm so thankful she saw that moment before she passed away."

Today, Johnson's life is based in Southern California. When necessary, he reaches out to minor-league players or others who might need advice. Just like in the real world, the world of baseball can become a roller coaster of extreme highs and lows. There are still scars from the past, like old statistics on a baseball card, but Johnson the optimist chooses to live for the moment. He shares his smiles, laughter, and spirit in the Dodger offices in Los Angeles. Knowing his presence is valued and appreciated by others at the ballpark feels better than finding his lost World Series ring.

"I've never had a big desire of going back to Lexington to live," Johnson said. "Because there, they know of me. Here in Los Angeles, they know me. There's a big difference. I look at my time with the Dodgers, and respect is all I can get. Sometimes you do things you don't want to do in order to get respect. That's all I ask for—respect. It's not about making money. There are a whole lot of people in the world who have money but have no respect. … Sometimes, it still feels like a fight. … But these days, I feel I've gained the respect of the previous Dodger owners, Peter O'Malley and Bob Daly, and now Frank McCourt.

"Frank's different. Let me tell you how different he is. We're both high-energy people. And when you're a high-energy person, you respect respect. It's not about the money part. When I come in, it's 'Hi Lou' and 'Hi Frank, good to see you.' And that's it. That's enough. I've had everything else. I've had all the clothes, the cars, the money, and everything that comes with it. There's nothing wrong with that, but it's a cover. I don't have to cover up anything now.

"When I walk through the Dodger offices, I hear, 'Hi Lou, good to see you.' But 26 years ago, I didn't have that. I was with an organization that wasn't happy with me coming back, at least for a while. So I took another process, the same one I used to get to the top as a player in baseball, and did it this way. Some didn't like it, but who cares? I like it. And as I say all the time, I consider this Dodger Stadium to be my home. I helped put some seats in here, I helped build some fences around here, and I still take care of the legacy and the tradition of what the Dodgers are all about. You can't beat that. And my heart is straightened out."

Johnson laughed. "I'll have a smile that the morticians won't have to put on my face."

Chapter 8

STEVE YEAGER

NAME:	Stephen Wayne Yeager
BORN:	November 24, 1948
BIRTHPLACE:	Huntington, WV
YEARS WITH THE DODGERS:	1972-1985
POSITION:	Catcher
UNIFORM NUMBER:	7
CAREER HIGHLIGHTS:	Nicknamed "Boomer"; spent 14 of his 15 major-league seasons with the Dodgers; named 1981 World Series tri-MVP along with Pedro Guerrero and Ron Cey; appeared in four World Series and six National League Championship Series; hit career-high 16 home runs in 1977; ranks third on all-time Los Angeles list for most games caught (1,181) behind Mike Scioscia (1,395) and John Roseboro (1,199).
THE GAME:	August 5, 1974; Cincinnati Reds vs. Los Angeles Dodgers at Dodger Stadium

QUITE A CATCH

During the decade of the 1970s, the Dodgers and Cincinnati Reds dominated the National League West standings, finishing either first or second place in the division race on eight occasions.

"In my opinion, the two best catchers in the National League in the 1970s were on the Reds and the Dodgers—Johnny Bench and Steve Yeager," said Al Downing, who pitched for Los Angeles from 1971-1977. "Bench got more publicity because he was a home-run hitter. If you look at the records of both teams, there isn't much difference. A lot of the Reds' success was based on their bullpen, while the Dodgers were always built around their starting rotation. In both cases, the teams needed a strong catching presence."

Bench, who hit 389 home runs during his Hall of Fame career from 1968-1983, was chosen by Cincinnati in the second round of the 1965 amateur draft. Bench spent 2½ seasons in the minors and was the National League's Rookie of the Year in 1968.

The Dodgers tabbed Yeager with their fourth-round pick in 1967. Scout Cliff Alexander, the brother-in-law of Dodger manager Walter Alston, signed the athlete. Alexander monitored Yeager's prep career at Meadowdale High in Dayton, Ohio, where he became the school's first three-sport letterman, playing football, basketball, and baseball, once hitting two grand slams in one game.

"I was a second baseman in Little League in Ohio," Yeager said. "I didn't become a catcher until I got into high school and we tried out for the team as freshmen. There were about 40 players trying to play infield and one tall guy standing in the corner. I asked, 'What does he do?' They said, 'He's a catcher.' Well, now there's only one guy to compete with. He was a senior and I was a freshman and he broke his ankle the first week of practice, so I learned how to catch the hard way. That's when I started catching."

Yeager struggled during his first three years in the minor leagues with batting averages of just .171, .153, and .154. But his defensive skills merited a chance to stay in the organization and blossom.

During a spring training game in Vero Beach, Florida, Dodger minor-league executive Bill Schweppe watched Yeager block a pitch in the dirt and, from his knees, throw out a potential base stealer at second. During that time period, any Dodger executive could "protect" a player from being released if he felt strongly about the individual's major-league

Steve Yeager and Cincinnati's Johnny Bench were the National League's top defensive catchers during the Dodgers-Reds rivalry.

potential. Whether or not Schweppe "saved" Yeager will never be known, but his career turned around in 1971 at Triple-A Albuquerque while playing under manager Monty Basgall. He also listened to the advice from such baseball veterans as Guy Wellman, Goldie Holt, and Hall of Fame catcher Roy Campanella.

"The biggest thing wasn't going into professional baseball, it was leaving home for the first time," Yeager said. "I went to Ogden, Utah, the rookie league, for about 10 days, and then they shipped me to Dubuque, Iowa, where I broke a wrist. The next year I was in Daytona Beach and I didn't play very much. The third year I was signed I went to Bakersfield. I broke an ankle there and then went to Albuquerque. The next year I played every day for Monty Basgall for Albuquerque of the old Texas League. Monty was the first guy who really played me every day. I made the big-league club the following spring. There was a players' strike at the end of spring training and when it was settled, the Dodgers acquired Dick Dietz off waivers from the Giants, so I went back to the minor leagues. After a couple months, I came back to the Dodgers late in 1972 and I stayed with them ever since."

Yeager's offense steadily improved, and consecutive solid seasons at Albuquerque in 1971 and 1972 finally led to a chance to join a Dodger youth movement. Several veterans on the 1972 roster would not return the following season—infielders Wes Parker, Maury Wills, Jim Lefebvre, and catcher Duke Sims. The Dodgers were floundering in third place with a 49-47 record on August 2 when Yeager made his major-league debut against the San Francisco Giants at Dodger Stadium.

Alston penciled Yeager into the starting lineup batting eighth against Giants starter Steve Stone. Yeager went 1-for-3 that night, singling in his third plate appearance against reliever Randy Moffitt.

Dodger starter Don Sutton appeared to be cruising with a 7-3 lead after five innings, but the Giants knocked him out with a six-run sixth. Pete Mikkelsen pitched the final 3 1/3 innings and the Dodgers eventually won the game 12-11 on Bill Russell's solo home run off Jim Barr in the bottom of the ninth.

In three of his next four games as catcher, Yeager was on the receiving end of Dodger shutouts by Tommy John, Claude Osteen, and Sutton. In his sixth game, Yeager set a National League record for most total chances (24) during a 2-1 loss in 19 innings at Cincinnati. Dodger pitchers struck out 22 batters and Yeager added two assists.

The young Dodgers of 1973 included a new infield with first baseman Bill Buckner, second baseman Davey Lopes, shortstop Bill Russell, and third baseman Ron Cey. Buckner switched to left field in late June when Alston decided to give Steve Garvey, a scatter-armed third baseman who had been effective as a pinch hitter, a chance at first base. Other young players such as Von Joshua or Tom Paciorek also contributed to the 1973 Dodgers, who started the campaign with a 61-34 record and held an 8½-game lead on July 17. But the Reds mounted a comeback and won the division 3½ games ahead of the Dodgers (95-66).

When the Dodgers won the National League pennant in 1974, the team started the season 24-0 with Yeager catching, one of the team's most overlooked statistics.

"Yeah, but who was pitching?" Downing jokes about a starting rotation that included Sutton (19-9 in 1974), Andy Messersmith (20-6), Tommy John (13-3 before his season-ending injury in mid-July), and Cy Young Award reliever Mike Marshall (15-12, 21 saves).

Yeager's defense prompted the Dodgers to move their other catcher, Joe Ferguson, to the outfield. Ferguson set Los Angeles records in 1973 for most home runs (25) and RBIs (88) by a catcher, but the Dodgers wanted Yeager's presence behind the plate.

"Joe moved back and forth from catching to the outfield," Downing said. "Steve was basically a catcher. When you catch every day, even on the sidelines or in the bullpen, you pick up on little things about a pitcher. Joe, being bigger, didn't get as far down in the stroke zone, so his target tended to be from mid-thigh to waist. With Steve, the difference was he tended to give you a lower target, from mid-thigh to knee."

THE GAME OF MY LIFE

By Steve Yeager

In 1973, we got so close to winning the National League West and, looking back at the battles that we had between the Reds and Dodgers, it was really a good rivalry at that point in time. When you sit down and remember things that turned a game around or turned a season around, you have some things as an individual player that you did, but you also remember some of the things that your teammates did that did nothing but spark the team. It's all about how to win and how to play with each other. Sooner or later, we were going to figure out a way to beat the Reds.

Joe Ferguson and I are good friends now, and we were good friends back then. Fergie originally was an outfielder, but in 1972 he was learning how to catch. In 1973, he had a great offensive year, hitting 25 home runs as a catcher, and I was backing him up.

In 1974, it started out the same way. I was catching Andy Messersmith and somebody else and I was 24-0 at the start of the season before I got beat. Walt later told me to take Sutton, who had a 9-9 record at the time. I told him, "Why don't I just take them all?" And that's when Walt made the decision to put Fergie back in right field and put me behind the plate. Sutton wound up the season 19-9. As the season went on, we ended up going to the World Series.

Before the 1974 season, we acquired a power hitter from the Houston Astros. They called Jim Wynn "The Toy Cannon," and for a guy who was only 5-foot-9, he hit the ball a long way. Jimmy played a fantastic center field and did a terrific job. When Jimmy Wynn came over and they put Fergie in the outfield, of course we have the infield of Garvey, Lopes, Russell, and Cey playing their first full season together. Those guys got better and better as the season went on. I think we knew what to do, we knew how to play the game, we were young. We were cocky and confident and just went out and played the game the way we were taught.

The game I won't forget occurred on August 5. It was a Monday night game at Dodger Stadium and we played host to the Reds. Jimmy Wynn hit a two-run home run against the Reds' Don Gullett in the first inning to give Doug Rau an early lead. It stayed that way until George Foster hit a two-run home run in the top of the seventh inning.

Gullett was still pitching in the bottom of the seventh when we loaded the bases. Ron Cey hit an infield single and was replaced by a pinch runner, Rick Auerbach. After Ferguson walked, Tom Paciorek reached on a bunt single. Gullett was one of the best pitchers in the league, but I had pretty good success against some of those hard-throwing lefties. Gullett threw the pitch and I hit a line drive into the bullpen for a grand slam. The place went nuts and that just gave us another spark. It was exciting. I've got the radio tape somewhere in the house of Jerry Doggett doing the announcing. The crowd went on and on and on and kept on screaming. It was probably only a couple minutes, but it seemed like it went on forever. It was a nice feeling and a nice thing for me to be a part of, but even better for the team to be a part of. We ended up winning the game 6-3. The Dodgers won the division by four games in 1974.

During my career, I wasn't known for my offense. For me, that hit against the Reds was a big plus. You don't normally see grand slams, and when they do happen, sometimes it doesn't mean anything. But in this case, we were trailing in the game. It put us ahead and over the hump from there. For me personally, it was a thrill. I hit four or five grand slams in my career, and some of them came against the Reds, but when you do something like that on national television, the Monday Night Game of the Week, it's exciting to be able to contribute offensively when you're basically known for your defense and handling the pitchers.

I think when you get kind words from Al Downing or anyone else it's a pat on the back to even be mentioned with Bench, who was a Hall of Famer and a great player. I always felt I wanted to be better than the guy who was playing my position on the other team. So when you play against guys who are great like John, you want to play better and better. Yeah, he got all the accolades because he was a great offensive player. I felt maybe I could catch with him and throw with him. John was such a great leader and a great catcher in those times; it's hard for anybody to go against that. As far as John and I were concerned, we were friends on the field. We even went to lunch a couple times in Los Angeles and in Cincinnati. We talked to each other. He's a terrific guy. I think as a player, you just want to be better and try to be better than the guy across the way.

Whether you succeed or not, it just gives you a little more drive when you know you're going to play against the very best in Bench. You can't sit there and be weak about it. When Sparky Anderson was manager of the Reds, I'd yell at Sparky to send his runners and he always waved his finger and said no, because he knew maybe I had the ability to take away some of his running game, which helped our ballclub, too. You play harder, but that's not to say I didn't play as hard as I could play every day. But it just seems when you go at it with a team like the Reds ... you're in it from the very first pitch until the last pitch and go as hard as you can go.

I think the one thing the catcher has to do is learn the personality of the pitcher, his strengths and weakness, whether or not he likes to work ahead in the count, behind in the count, what pitch he can call for when he needs a ground ball, what pitch can he throw to get a double play and get you out of the inning. I think you have to realize ... with their personalities, some guys you can get on, some guys you can't. Sometimes you go to the mound just to break their concentration, because thinking about getting the ball and just letting it go, sometimes they're working too fast, too slow, so it's knowing the personalities of the pitchers and knowing what you can do. If you can go out and know who to kick in the seat of the pants and who to give a pat on the back, it's something that every catcher should know about.

And learn the relievers, too, not just the starting pitchers. It's just all part of the job. The better you know the pitcher and how he likes to do things, the easier his job becomes and you have the ability to do more thinking behind the plate. The more confidence he has in you, the better performance he's likely to give. He's not just out there thinking about what pitch to throw and where to throw it. And I learned that very well from guys like Don Sutton and Jim Brewer, Ron Perranoski, and Pete Mikkelsen. All the old guys who, when I was a kid, didn't want me to fail. They gave me all the information I needed. There were some catchers who shared a lot of information, but didn't give me all the tricks of the trade. It was something I had to learn through trial and error, along with the leadership from the veteran players I was lucky enough to come play with, they helped me.

One thing I also wanted to make sure was to have fun playing baseball. I think that's my personality. I've always said if you dread getting up in the morning and going to work, then you're in the wrong occupation. How can you not enjoy, I mean thoroughly enjoy, something every young man dreams about doing? Playing professional baseball at its highest level and being successful, how can you not enjoy that? How can you not have a good time playing baseball? If you're not having fun, something's wrong with you, because you should have fun. Realize you'll have ups and downs, but it's still the only profession I know where you can fail 75 percent of the time playing it long enough at this level and they'll put you in the Hall of Fame.

THE RESULTS

Steve Yeager's first career grand slam sparked the Dodgers to a 6-3 victory over the Cincinnati Reds in front of 45,577 on August 5, 1974. It was Yeager's only hit of the game in four at-bats as the Dodgers scored six runs on just five hits against Reds pitchers Don Gullett and Clay Carroll. Doug Rau (11-6) scattered two runs on five hits in seven innings and reliever Mike Marshall closed out the final two innings. The victory improved the Dodgers' lead to 7½ games over Cincinnati in the National League West.

THE CROWNING ACHIEVEMENT

Originally assembled on a whim by manager Walter Alston, the Los Angeles "record-setting infield" of Garvey, Lopes, Russell, and Cey is the Dodgers' version of Notre Dame football's famous Four Horsemen, forever linked as a quartet and always brought together for reunions, autograph signings, and other public appearances. The unit lasted eight and a half seasons from 1973-1981, surpassing the previous mark of longevity set from 1906-1910 by the Chicago Cubs' quartet of first baseman Frank Chance, second baseman Johnny Evers, shortstop Joseph Tinker, and third baseman Harry Steinfeldt. Johnny Kling was a Cubs catcher from 1900-1911.

"I was there before they got together and I was there after they broke up," Yeager says of the Dodgers' infield. "Isn't the catcher part of the infield?"

After the Dodgers lost the 1974 World Series in five games against the Oakland Athletics, the young team looked forward to another trip to the playoffs. But Cincinnati's "Big Red Machine" won consecutive World Series titles in 1975 and 1976 while Alston's tenure as Dodger manager was ending.

Yeager's workload peaked in 1975 when he played a career-high 135 games and caught 736 of the Dodgers' final 759 innings. His career was filled with injuries, including a jarring home-plate collision with Pittsburgh's Dave Parker that left him with a concussion, but none scarier than a freak accident on September 6, 1976, at San Diego.

While kneeling in the on-deck circle, Yeager was struck in the throat by a large piece of wood from Bill Russell's broken bat. Nine splinters were removed from the wound, which barely missed his windpipe, a major artery, and an area that controls muscles in the arm. After Yeager's injury, trainer Bill Buhler invented a special throat guard, a small piece of plastic that hinged on the bottom of the catcher's mask.

New manager Tommy Lasorda led the Dodgers to consecutive pennants in 1977 and 1978, but each fall Los Angeles lost the World Series in six games against the New York Yankees. Yeager posted career highs with 16 home runs and 55 RBIs in 1977. He hit .316 with two home runs and five RBIs in the 1977 World Series.

"I think collectively we felt we should have won a couple more of those World Series," Yeager said. "The 1977 and 1978 playoffs were disappointing, because we felt like we had a pretty good team, maybe even a better team than the Yankees. Weird things happen in short series."

Rookie catcher Mike Scioscia burst upon the scene in 1980, leaving Yeager with part-time duties and occasional starts against left-handed pitchers. He batted .211 in 96 games.

Yeager didn't fare much better in 1981 during a strike-shortened season. He batted just .209 in 42 games and was limited to only 86 at-bats due to injuries. But just as the Dodgers made improbable comebacks against the Astros in the Division Series and against the Expos in the League Championship Series, Yeager became the Dodgers' improbable Mr. October against the Yankees in the World Series.

The Dodgers lost the first two games of the Series at New York, but roared back with victories in Games 3 and 4. Game 5 pitted the Dodgers' Jerry Reuss against Ron Guidry. The pitchers' duel lasted six innings on a Sunday afternoon at Dodger Stadium. Guidry took a 1-0 lead into the seventh, but Pedro Guerrero and Yeager blasted consecutive solo home runs into the Left Field Pavilion. Reuss pitched a complete game and won 2-1. The Dodgers flew back to New York for Game 6 and wrapped up the title with a 9-2 victory behind pitchers Burt Hooton and Steve Howe. Yeager, Cey, and Guerrero were named tri-MVPs of the World Series.

"In 1981, we heard some rumblings about players coming up from the minor leagues, so if there was an opportunity for us to win one together, then it had to be 1981 to do that," Yeager said. "We just came together. It was exciting to hit that ball off Guidry. I think it was the ninth time in history that teammates hit back-to-back home runs in World Series competition. It was thrilling. After the season, some of the players left and that sort of broke up that ballclub."

Yeager played with Los Angeles through the 1985 season, compiling a .228 batting average in 1,219 lifetime games with the Dodgers. He was traded to the Seattle Mariners in exchange for relief pitcher Ed Vander Berg. In his only American League campaign, Yeager batted .208 in 50 games with the 1986 Mariners.

Two decades later, Yeager is a minor-league instructor with the Dodgers. Although such travel and time commitment are too challenging for some former athletes, Yeager doesn't mind life as a teacher. During his post-playing career, he has coached at various Dodger affiliates, including Las Vegas, Jacksonville, and San Bernardino. He even managed two seasons with the independent Long Beach Breakers of the Western League.

"A lot of guys can't do it," Yeager said. "But it's not about me. I've had my day in the sun. It's about being able to give these kids the things that the veteran players and managers passed along to me. When I was a young player, those veterans taught us how to act off the field and taught us how to be better men."

Yeager also remains a popular figure among fans of all ages. He often serves as an instructor at the Dodger Adult Camp in Vero Beach, helping those 30 and older to live out their dreams of wearing a big-league uniform during a one-week camp experience. And throughout spring training, whether he's breaking down the fundamentals of catching to a raw rookie or sharing a good story with an opponent or umpire, Yeager blends into any scene.

One morning in 2006, Yeager woke up early and began to walk across the Dodgertown complex to catch an 8 a.m. bus. At 7:15, the foggy 300-acre facility resembled a ghost town. Yeager's attire included a crisply pressed Hawaiian shirt, khaki shorts, and dark leather loafers. A maintenance worker spotted Yeager quietly walking along the narrow concrete path between housing bungalows and offered him a ride on the back of his truck. Yeager tossed his equipment bag and plopped himself on the flatbed portion of the vehicle, his back to the driver. After 40 years in professional baseball, Yeager looked like a second-hand appliance earmarked for the thrift store as the truck slowly lugged its silent passenger.

By 8:15, the bus was on its way to another game. Players slept or listened to music through headphones while coaches leafed through their stack of newspapers. Batting practice banter was just hours away, followed by another nine innings.

"Baseball is probably one of my first true loves ever, other than my mother and family," Yeager said. "I enjoy the ups and the downs. I enjoy winning. I enjoy the kids when they start off the season and progress and get better. And over the last couple years as a coach in the Dodger minor-league system, the players that we had like Russell Martin and James Loney, Delwyn Young, Jonathan Broxton, Chad Billingsley—I've seen these young guys mature and develop and have a great opportunity to have a marvelous career in the game of baseball and stay up in the major leagues for a long, long time. And that's the joy I get. I enjoy seeing the kids with smiles on their faces. There are ups and downs in this game, even at the minor-league level. You tell them the good thing about tomorrow is we have a chance to do something better than we did today. Tomorrow we have a chance to continue something that we did well today. That's the beauty of the game. Every day is different.

"It's fun to be around the kids, they help keep me young. And I think sometimes they enjoy hearing the stories because I guess I'm an old throwback to the old days where you go from the first to last pitch, get your uniform dirty and play to win, learn how to play the game, know what to do in certain situations. It's nice to see the kids develop both physically and mentally about baseball. When they get to the major leagues and get a manager like Grady Little, he'll know, 'I don't have to worry about this guy. He knows how to play, because we had a few old guys in the minor leagues who taught them well.'"

Chapter 9

JIMMY WYNN

NAME:	James Sherman Wynn
BORN:	March 12, 1942
BIRTHPLACE:	Hamilton, OH
YEARS WITH THE DODGERS:	1974-1975
POSITION:	Outfielder
UNIFORM NUMBER:	23
CAREER HIGHLIGHTS:	Established the Houston Colt .45s/Astros franchise record with 223 home runs (later broken by Jeff Bagwell) from 1963-1973; set career highs with 43 stolen bases in 1965 and 37 home runs in 1967; named the National League Comeback Player of the Year by *The Sporting News* in 1974; uniform No. 24 retired by the Houston Astros in 2005.
THE GAME:	September 15, 1974; Los Angeles Dodgers vs. Cincinnati Reds at Dodger Stadium

THE TOY CANNON

Spanning more than 60 years, only one incoming Dodger has ever graced the cover of a Brooklyn or Los Angeles team yearbook. Looking back, the decision to honor Jimmy Wynn during the spring of 1974 was a bit of a gamble. He was asked to replace Dodger team captain Willie Davis, a 14-year veteran in Los Angeles, in center field.

Wynn was coming off a disappointing .220 batting average in 1973 with the Houston Astros. The Astros decided to trade Wynn to the Dodgers for pitcher Claude Osteen, but they needed Wynn's permission as a "10-and-5 player," a veteran of at least 10 years who has spent the last five with the same team. In case the Dodger destination was not to his liking, the Astros also proposed a deal to the Chicago Cubs.

"I had a choice of going to Chicago or Los Angeles," Wynn said. "I could say no to any trade at that moment. I thought over it real well. If I went to Chicago, I could hit home runs, try to get to 300 career home runs, and hopefully get into the Hall of Fame. Or I could join the Dodger organization, which I loved and respected a great deal, and try to win a championship. Of course I chose the Dodgers to become one of the players to wear Dodger Blue and win a World Series."

Today, the red-bordered 1974 yearbook cover featuring Wynn in the batting cage reminds everyone of that fairy tale season when the veteran slugger and a group of young Dodger farmhands brought Los Angeles its first pennant since 1966. And the Left Field Pavilion became "Cannon Country" after the 5-foot-9, 165-pounder nicknamed "The Toy Cannon" contributed 32 home runs and 108 RBIs.

Coming to Los Angeles meant a new beginning for Wynn, who grew up in Cincinnati and was signed out of high school by the Reds. The Astros drafted Wynn from the Reds' minor-league system after a good season at Tampa in 1962.

Wynn broke into the majors with Houston in 1963. The early games of the franchise were played at Colts Stadium, known for its heat, humidity, and giant mosquitoes. Before a doubleheader, Ernie Banks once told Wynn, "It's a great day to play two, Cannon." Banks passed out of heat exhaustion early in the first game and never returned for the nightcap.

The Astros moved into the cavernous Astrodome in 1964. Wynn hit 37 home runs in 1967, losing the home run title to Atlanta's Hank Aaron, who hit 39. Aaron later said Wynn should have been considered the home run leader that season because he played in the Astrodome. Wynn stole 43 bases in 47 attempts in 1965, but Astros general manager Spec Richardson asked Wynn to concentrate on his power. Wynn's stolen bases were reduced to 13 in 23 attempts in 1966.

Outfielder Jimmy Wynn, nicknamed "The Toy Cannon," is welcomed to Los Angeles by General Manager Al Campanis in December 1973.

The Astros lost at least 90 games between 1962-1968, but gained a measure of respectability beginning in 1969 with the arrival of the expansion San Diego Padres and Montreal Expos. Between 1969-1973, the Astros were generally a .500 ballclub, and an 84-69 record during the strike-shortened 1972 season was good enough for second place in the National League West, 10½ games behind the Cincinnati Reds.

In 1973, the Dodgers won 95 games, but still lost the division to Cincinnati (99-63). Houston's fourth-place finish (82-80) left Wynn looking for the door. It was the perfect opportunity to match the frustrated Wynn with the patient Dodger manager Walter Alston. And in 1974, Alston's batting coach was Dixie Walker, the brother of Harry Walker, Wynn's manager at Houston from 1968-1972. In addition to gaining Wynn, the Dodgers bolstered their bullpen, trading Davis to the Expos for relief pitcher Mike Marshall.

"Going into the 1974 season, we were a team to contend with," Alston wrote in his 1976 autobiography. "We had none of the so-called superstars, although some of our guys like Steve Garvey and Mike Marshall sure came on. We did things a little differently in the spring, and to read about it you'd have thought it was a revolution. I decided to have a formal session with each man at Vero Beach early on, a private session where we could go over our objectives, our training program, what we felt were our strengths and our weaknesses, and similar things as they pertained to each man.

"I was concerned because we were young and didn't have a lot of experience. In fact, there was more than a lot of inexperience at the jobs we were asking guys to handle. So I knew if we were going to win, it would have to be a total effort as a team by the 25 who made the roster."

At age 62, Alston was beginning his 21st season with the Dodgers. The Ohio native inherited the job in 1954 when Brooklyn manager Charlie Dressen requested a three-year contract from team president Walter O'Malley following pennants in 1952 and 1953. O'Malley declined Dressen's proposal, and Alston subsequently worked on a series of one-year contracts from 1954-1976. Alston's veteran teams won championships in 1955, 1959, 1963, and 1965, but the 1974 squad was by far his most inexperienced. The only players with previous World Series experience were veterans Jim Brewer, Al Downing, and Willie Crawford.

The Dodgers jumped out of the gate with a 17-3 record, but the most memorable game during that streak was actually a loss on April 8 in Atlanta, when Aaron surpassed Babe Ruth's all-time home record. Aaron hit No. 715 against veteran left-hander Al Downing, who took his pregame nap and approached the national spotlight with Aaron as he would any other game. Downing handled his place in history with his typical grace, congratulating Aaron on his accomplishment while focusing on his own duties with the Dodgers.

By May, Wynn graced the cover of *Sports Illustrated* alongside the headline "Those Rampaging Dodgers." The Reds fell behind by as many as 10½ games on July 10.

"I know Garvey got a lot of accolades, and deservedly so that season," said pitcher Tommy John, who went 13-3 in 1974 before a mid-season injury led to the historic surgery which today bears his name. "But we made a trade over the winter and got a guy that really made the team go—and that was Jimmy Wynn. He scored 100 runs, drove in 100, walked 100 times, and hit 32 home runs. We didn't have anyone in the heart of the lineup do that in the previous two seasons I was there. Garv had a great year and Wynn was responsible for a lot of the offense we had. I don't think he got credit for what he did. A high on-base percentage is what he brought to the table, then you add in Garv, throw in Ron Cey's power, and Davey Lopes stealing bases. It was a great mix."

THE GAME OF MY LIFE

By Jimmy Wynn

Prior to joining the Dodgers, it was very frustrating having played 10 seasons in Houston without a playoff appearance. When you're drafted by an expansion ballclub like I was by the Houston Colt .45s in 1963, you're hoping to be surrounded by good ballplayers who will help the owner, the manager, and the coaching staff. You hope everything goes well and you win a lot of ballgames. We didn't win that many games during the years I spent in Houston, but it was a lot of fun and there were great managers.

I was always a power hitter in knothole ball and up through high school, thanks to my father, who taught me all the basics about hitting. The nickname "Toy Cannon" came from one of the sportswriters in Houston, a man named John Wilson. The only thing I felt about hitting in the Astrodome was the major-league uniform that I so proudly wore, because it's what I wanted to do when I was growing up. Hitting home runs was just natural, even when I was a kid. Suddenly, I'm hitting home runs in the Astrodome, "the Eighth Wonder of the World." And nobody could hit home runs like me, so I guess it was natural.

I had two favorite home runs when I was with the Astros. The first was at Crosley Field in Cincinnati, which left the ballpark and bounced onto the freeway. The other was in April 1970 when I became the first Astros player to hit a home run into the upper deck in left field during a regular-season game at the Astrodome.

I didn't have any problems fitting in with the Dodgers. When I came to spring training in 1974, I was met by the owners, Peter and Walter O'Malley, and a couple of ballplayers, Davey Lopes and Bill Russell. One of the greatest things that anybody could say to me at the time was, "We need a leader. We know exactly what you can do, but we also need someone to lead this ballclub. And this is the reason why we got you." Quote, unquote, from Peter and Walter O'Malley.

And 1974 was one of the better years I ever had hitting wise, home run wise, playing with the initiative that we could win any time we put on the uniform. Going up against the Reds, I can remember we had a three-game series and we were 3½ games ahead. It was a do-or-die situation, and the Reds won the first two ballgames.

On a Sunday morning, September 15, they were 1½ games behind the Dodgers going into the series finale in Los Angeles. Alston called a pregame meeting and said he thought we were the best team. He told us losing two games to the Reds wasn't the end of the world and that, if we lost again, we'd still be in first place."

Don Sutton started the game for us against Fred Norman, Cincinnati's left-hander. The Reds scored first in the fifth inning on a base hit by Norman. They loaded the bases later that inning and had a chance to blow open the game, but Sutton struck out Johnny Bench on a called strike three to end the threat.

We took the lead in the sixth inning. Bill Buckner was hit by a pitch and I was walked. Steve Garvey hit a ground-rule double to put us ahead 2-1.

In the seventh, Steve Yeager and Davey Lopes each singled, and when Lopes took second on the throw, it set up an intentional walk to Buckner, loading the bases. At that point, I think I had something like four hits in my last 30 at-bats. I hadn't played most of the week due to a sore throat and the flu, and I wasn't feeling that great when I woke up Sunday morning. But all that changed when I hit a grand slam against reliever Pedro Borbon. When I saw Pete Rose turn his back to home plate from left field, I knew the ball was gone. I think Bill Buckner set a new world record for the high jump. He leaped about nine feet in the air ahead of me on the basepaths and then he picked me up at home plate. I think he was more excited than I was.

From that point, we rolled over everybody. I think the ballclub was beautiful. We worked together as a team. Everybody respected everyone else's ability to play baseball. At age 32, I was the senior citizen of that team. That's why the O'Malleys got me from Houston. They needed someone to show the young players the way ... to win. At that time, I didn't know how to win because of the Astros organization, but they knew how to win in the Dodger organization. It was one of those things where everything blended in the Dodger organization. I think that's what makes a good ballclub, when everyone knows their place in the lineup and their place on the bench. They knew exactly what to do and how to do it in 1974. I loved everyone on that club.

As far as our manager that season, I wouldn't trade Walter Alston for anyone in the world. He was a great man who knew the game of baseball and someone a lot of players from around the league would've wanted as a manager.

The Dodger fans were absolutely unbelievable. I loved and respected them. One lady in the Left Field Pavilion, France Friedman, came out to every game and hollered "C'mon Jimmy" and "The Toy Cannon!" I made it a point to say hello to Miss Francis and everyone else who was sitting in the center-field bleachers. One day I saw a big sign that said "CANNON COUNTRY." And I felt like, if people like that give a name like that to an individual, you should be proud. And I was very proud.

Even though we lost to Oakland in five games, the 1974 World Series meant a great deal to me. I think every player wants to reach a World Series and get that ring. We were young and didn't exactly know what was going on in the World Series. But we went up against a club that had dominated baseball for two years, and then they won their third consecutive World Series against us. It was a beautiful experience. I wish we could've won the World Series for the fans of Los Angeles and had a parade for the O'Malleys. But the thing that we were proud of in 1974 was that nobody predicted we would even get that far. Just to win the National League pennant for the fans and the O'Malleys, that was a pat on the back for everybody.

THE RESULTS

Wynn's grand slam on September 15 helped the Dodgers defeat the Reds 7-1 in front of 52,116. Don Sutton (16-9) scattered six hits en route to the complete game, and Steve Garvey went 2-for-3 with a home run as the Dodgers extended their lead to 2½ games over Cincinnati in the National League West. It was the final meeting between the clubs with two weeks remaining in the regular season. The Dodgers won the division by four games.

HOUSTON HOMECOMING

Wynn finished fifth in the National League MVP balloting. Teammate Steve Garvey won the award, as the first baseman hit .312 with 21 home runs and 111 RBIs while earning All-Star Game honors as a write-in candidate. Marshall became the first relief pitcher to win the Cy Young Award, going 15-12 while appearing in 106 games.

Wynn was also involved in one of the most famous plays in postseason history during Game 1 of the 1974 Series at Dodger Stadium. With Sal Bando at third base and one out, Reggie Jackson lofted a fly ball toward Wynn in center field. Joe Ferguson drifted from his right-field position and called Wynn off the ball. Ferguson, whose strong arm prompted the Dodgers to make him a part-time catcher, uncorked a perfect no-hop throw toward home plate. Steve Yeager made the catch and held onto the ball as Bando crashed into him, attempting to score.

"We didn't talk about anything before the game," Wynn said. "Everyone knew that I had a bad elbow. If I had thrown that ball, I would've been no good to anyone because of the elbow. I was fortunate and very happy that Joe Ferguson was out there in right field. He called me off. There's no way in the world I could've thrown out Sal Bando. . . . It was on a fly, it was straight. Steve Yeager did not have to bend over. That ball looked like a jet taking off, that's how quick it got to home plate. I'm just amazed. My mouth was wide open. I was dumbfounded and I stayed out there a few seconds. All of a sudden, I went into the dugout and everyone was hollering and screaming."

Ferguson's throw was an exciting play, but the Dodgers lost the game 3-2. Los Angeles won the second game of the Series 3-2 behind Sutton's pitching and Ferguson's two-run homer off Vida Blue, but the Athletics captured the next three games at Oakland by scores of 3-2, 5-2, and 3-2.

It would be the last hurrah for many of the Dodger veterans. Wynn spent one more season with Los Angeles and Marshall was gone by 1976. Alston stepped down as the Dodgers' manager in September 1976, replaced by Lasorda. By 1977, veterans Rick Monday and Dusty Baker joined the young nucleus, and "The Big Blue Wrecking Crew" won consecutive pennants in 1977 and 1978 and a World Series title in 1981.

But for most of those Dodgers, the first October memories were in 1974.

"Having played in five World Series, I have some perspective," Garvey said. "But when you're playing in your first World Series, you don't know if you're going to make it back again. That's what you'd been waiting for—been dreaming of—and we lost."

"It was the first time for all of us, we were young and very excited," Yeager said. "For the most part, we felt we could have played better, maybe even beat Oakland. But Oakland had a fantastic ballclub. They were in the World Series for the third straight year. The veterans they had on the team, they weren't going to give it to us. But I think deep down we could've played a little better in the 1974 Series."

Wynn batted .248 with 18 home runs and 58 RBIs in his last season with the Dodgers. Although his power numbers were down, he still managed to draw 110 walks in 130 games. Wynn also hit the 100th home run in All-Star Game history during the 1975 Mid-Summer Classic at Milwaukee's County Stadium.

At the 1975 winter meetings, the Dodgers packaged Wynn along with prospects Tom Paciorek, Lee Lacy, and Jerry Royster to the Atlanta Braves in exchange for outfielder Dusty Baker and infielder Ed Goodson.

Wynn spent the 1976 season with Atlanta and part of 1977 with the New York Yankees and Milwaukee Brewers. In 1,920 career games, Wynn hit .250 with 291 home runs and 964 RBIs.

"I was happy with my career. Fifteen years is a long time to play baseball," Wynn said. "One thing I was really disappointed in was a hot start in 1966. I ran into a wall in Philadelphia and dislocated my elbow, broke my shoulder and my wrist, and that killed the whole season for me. I wanted to hit 300 home runs and get to that magic number, but I got a chance to be with some great ballplayers, some super managers, and super owners. I'm proud that I played for the Astros, Dodgers, Yankees, and Braves. But I have no regrets whatsoever."

Wynn wore No. 23 with the Dodgers because Alston wore No. 24, which Los Angeles retired in 1977. The Astros retired Wynn's uniform No. 24 in pregame ceremonies in 2005. The entire Astros team walked with him to the pitcher's mound with the exception of modern-day slugger Jeff Bagwell, who stood at home plate to catch Wynn's ceremonial first pitch.

"His playing career was so important, but he also has been such a big part of this community in Houston," Astros owner Drayton McLane said. "He has conducted himself in such a credible way that we wanted to recognize him. We are very proud to retire Jimmy Wynn's No. 24."

Special guests at the ceremonies included former teammates Ivan Murrell, Enos Cabell, Tommy Davis, Bob Watson, J.C. Hartman, and Mike Cuellar. Hall of Famer Joe Morgan, Wynn's roommate on road trips in the 1960s, also attended.

"It felt like I was going to the Hall of Fame, that's what it meant to me," Wynn said. "Any time an organization retires your number and it's going to be on a wall somewhere and nobody will be able to wear that, it's a beautiful thing when an organization says, 'We love you. We knew what type of ballplayer you were. You were an outstanding athlete, you played with your heart and your guts.' I really didn't think about the emotions involved in the weeks leading up to the ceremony. But once the car wheeled me out and I saw all the fans hollering and saying, 'Jimmy, congratulations, you deserve this,' then a few tears came to my eyes. I went to the podium to say a few words, but then all of the emotions came out and I started shedding more tears up in the Astros suite."

Back problems have limited Wynn's mobility during the past decade, but he still gets around as a community representative with the Astros. He works with kids, telling students to get an education and stay away from drugs. Wynn is also collecting material for an autobiography.

"I have a great life living in Houston and working with the Astros," he said. "I'd love to have a chance to return to Los Angeles for a visit. It's been something like 12 years since their last Old Timers' Day, and I wish they would have a day for the 1974 National League champions. I'd love to see my teammates again. We did some wonderful things. I met a lot of great people, great actors like Telly Savalas. I went to see one of his TV programs. I met Kevin Dobson, who was his cousin, I met Mayor Tom Bradley and his wife. There were also music groups like Fifth Dimension. It was a wonderful two years, I will always have fond and beautiful memories of California."

Chapter 10

FRANK
JOBE

NAME:	Frank Wilson Jobe, M.D.
BORN:	July 16, 1925
BIRTHPLACE:	Greensboro, NC
YEARS WITH THE DODGERS:	1964-Present
POSITION:	Team Physician
CAREER HIGHLIGHTS:	Studied medicine at Loma Linda University and completed internship and residency at Los Angeles County Hospital; partnered with the Los Angeles Rams and Lakers team physician Robert Kerlan to form the Kerlan-Jobe Orthopaedic Clinic, which became the leading sports medicine operation in the western United States; has been the Dodgers' orthopaedic doctor since 1968; performed ligament-transfer surgery on Dodger pitcher Tommy John in 1974 (the procedure became known as "Tommy John Surgery"); developed use of anchors to tighten the shoulder capsule, which he used to preserve Orel Hershiser's career in 1990.
THE GAME:	July 17, 1974; Montreal Expos vs. Los Angeles Dodgers at Dodger Stadium

DOCTOR COOPERSTOWN

The Baseball Hall of Fame held its first election in 1936, and the original class of inductees included the obvious icons of the sport—Babe Ruth, Walter Johnson, Christy Mathewson, Ty Cobb, and Honus Wagner.

And while the museum has opened its doors to executives, writers, and broadcasters, other categories are often lobbied for possible consideration, such as scouts and photographers.

If ever a medical wing becomes part of the Hall of Fame, the obvious first choice would be an unassuming physician whose most famous contribution to baseball occurred after his patient implored him to "make something up." Dodger team physician Dr. Frank Jobe saved the career of Tommy John, thanks to the pitcher's insistence for desperate measures following a career-threatening injury to the medial collateral ligament in his left elbow.

When referring to the circumstances of John's surgery and his arrival a decade earlier on the Los Angeles sports scene, Jobe says he was in the "right place at the right time." A fateful meeting with Dr. Robert Kerlan not only changed his career, but also revolutionized how professional athletes are treated after suffering injuries.

Kerlan, who died in 1996 at age 74, was a former UCLA basketball player who left sports to concentrate on becoming a doctor. He transferred to USC for the rest of his college and medical school studies. He worked with a local minor-league baseball team and was employed by the Dodgers in 1958 when they moved to the West Coast.

Rejected for service in World War II when an exam revealed a form of rheumatoid arthritis in his spine, shoulder, and hips, Kerlan eventually had to give up surgery because his hip could no longer support him long enough to perform an entire operation. He started to use crutches occasionally in the late 1960s and permanently from 1977 on. Athletes knew Kerlan's own pain and physical ailments made him sensitive to their own injuries.

Jobe was a medical supply sergeant in the Army's 101st Airborne Division and originally never intended to become a doctor. Jobe was influenced, though, by watching the doctors who worked to save lives even as they were risking their own. Jobe was one of the soldiers encircled at Bastogne, Belguim, during the Battle of the Bulge. He attended Loma

Pitcher Tommy John and Dodger team physician Dr. Frank Jobe combined in 1974 to make medical history.

Linda University in California, then spent three years in family practice to pay off medical school.

The 1960s Dodger pitching staff featured Hall of Fame workhorses Sandy Koufax and Don Drysdale, whose careers were both finished before their 33rd birthdays. It was a different era in baseball, long before free agency and long before exploratory surgery was considered a positive option.

"Everybody sort of had the same idea that surgery was not something people should encourage, or sometimes people didn't perform surgery they were capable of doing," Jobe said. "The idea was that if you had surgery, you were probably through. Johnny Podres had something very simple—he had been hit in the elbow with a ball. He had bone chips that needed to be removed. So that was not too controversial. But I thought it was interesting the first case I ever had was Johnny Podres."

The physicians formed the Kerlan-Jobe Orthopaedic Clinic, which became the leading sports medicine operation in the western United

States. They were the perfect team, in part, Jobe says, because they didn't have competing egos.

"I guess we were both pretty naïve and innocent in those days," Jobe said. "When we shook hands, we knew it was going to happen and I never even thought about it. We started working together. It worked out pretty well because he was starting to have some arthritis. It was easier for me to go do the surgery and it was easier for him to make the diagnosis and think about the case.

"At that point in my career, I wasn't really a sports fan. My career was medicine, although I know Dr. Kerlan had a great interest in … baseball, football, and basketball. It was all very interesting to me, but back then, I didn't even consider myself an educated fan, although I had played some baseball in high school. When I got to his office, the Angels had come into being, so they were also playing at Dodger Stadium. So he took care of both the Dodgers and the Angels those last two years, which was an every night assignment for him, holding them until I got to the office. Then he took the Dodgers and I took the Angels. What really happened, of course, was I'd go with him to the Dodgers and he'd go with me to the Angels. That way, we'd be on the same page in terms of what we did."

More than once, Jobe has been asked what a typical baseball trainer's room looked like in the 1960s. Some of the theories seem so ancient by today's standards, although not as extreme as the famous quote from Hippocrates (460-370 BC): "What cannot be cured with medicaments is cured by the knife, what the knife cannot cure is cured with the searing iron, and whatever this cannot cure must be considered incurable."

"Dealing with sports injuries it seemed there was only one approach, because no one was doing it any different way," Jobe said. "If you walked into a trainer's room in baseball, you'd probably notice a large bottle of salt tablets. Everyone took salt tablets for some reason. They thought the athletes sweated too much salt, so they wanted to replace that. But what it did was to draw all the fluids in your body to your stomach. Now you need to get some electrolyte balance, and that's where Gatorade came along, to give you a more physiological solution. In addition to the salt tablets, there was aspirin and a lot of hot stuff to put on your muscles. You had one trainer and he did a little rubbing and he did the whole show. Then they hired another person to help, but there was no weight room and no exercise room, because it was felt back then that if you got bulky with muscles, it would slow you down and you couldn't hit the ball. If you had bulky muscles, you couldn't pitch."

One of Kerlan's innovations was the practice of packing a pitcher's arm in ice after a game. Clinically, it seemed to shorten the recovery time between pitchers' outings by 24 hours.

In 1974, the Dodgers were on their way to the National League pennant. One of the pitching stalwarts was left-hander Tommy John, originally acquired from the Chicago White Sox in exchange for slugger Dick Allen prior to the 1972 season. John went 27-12 in his first two years in Los Angeles and carried a 13-3 record into a game against the Montreal Expos on July 17, 1974. With a 4-0 lead in the third inning, John faced Expos first baseman Hal Breeden with no outs and runners on first and second. The only thing on his mind was getting a potential double-play grounder.

At that point, John had thrown 2,164 career innings in 355 games since 1963 with the Indians, White Sox, and Dodgers.

"My first pitch to Breeden was strange," John said. "As I came forward and released the ball, I felt a kind of nothingness. Then I heard a pop from inside my arm and the ball just blooped up to the plate. I didn't feel pain at this point, but just the strange sensation that my arm wasn't there. It was the oddest thing I'd ever felt while pitching.

"I was more baffled than concerned, so I shook my arm and prepared for the next pitch. I released the ball and this time I heard a slamming sound, like a collision coming from inside my elbow. It felt as if my arm had come off. The pitch had barely made it to the catcher. I knew I was done. I immediately called time and started walking off the mound."

THE GAME OF MY LIFE

By Dr. Frank Jobe

When Tommy ruptured that ligament, we really didn't know what to do. But Tommy, being the kind of person that he is, insisted that I do something because he wasn't ready to quit pitching yet. In those days, there were not many surgeries being done on athletes. It occurred to us that maybe we could do something to repair Tommy's elbow, and the idea came from hand surgery that was done on polio victims. What the surgery entailed was using the tendon from the palmaris longus muscle in the forearm to replace a damaged ligament. In Tommy's case, the tendon from his right arm would be used to replace the ligament in his left elbow.

We felt the surgery made sense; we just didn't know if it was going to work. We were confident that we would be able to reconstruct the ligament, but we didn't know if the repair would hold up under the strains of pitching in the major leagues. Tommy continued his period of rehabilitation, but after a few months, he lost feeling in his left hand, which clawed up. The ulnar nerve was bruised and twisted, and another operation was required. We rerouted the nerve on the inside of the elbow. The primary thing we learned from Tommy's experience is that an athlete with a torn MCL should not throw until after having surgery. We let Tommy throw in his rehabilitation program and discovered that this placed a great deal of stretch and strain on the ulnar nerve. We had to perform follow-up surgery, and obviously you want to avoid a second surgery whenever possible.

For the first couple of years, I watched every pitch he made with apprehension, fearing that his elbow was going to blow out again. But it didn't.

The Tommy John Surgery isn't a great surgery, it's a rather simple one. It worked nicely in Tommy's case, and because it worked back then, for 30-plus years it has been a very important aspect in baseball. And two years after we did it on Tommy, we started doing it on other pitchers. Now there have probably been thousands done since. Back then, it was a four-hour procedure. Now it takes under an hour, because we know exactly what we have to do. When we did that first one on Tommy, we did a lot of talking, scratching our heads, and finally came up with it. It was all so new. We didn't know how long to rehab him. We took it very easy, and if he complained of any discomfort at all, we backed off. So we took 18 months with Tommy. Now it's about one year.

Tommy John Surgery has pretty much made my career. His success and those that have followed him are responsible for my reputation."

GAME RESULTS

John walked off the pitcher's mound on July 17, 1974, in the third inning at Dodger Stadium with his team leading 4-0. Left-hander Geoff Zahn replaced John and allowed two inherited runners to score, and later allowed three runs of his own as the Dodgers lost 5-4. In his first game back from surgery after a 21-month layoff, John started against the Atlanta Braves on April 16, 1976. In five innings, he allowed three earned runs on five hits, including four walks and one strikeout. Manager Walter

Alston gave John one more start in the rotation before the Dodgers would make a decision on the pitcher's future. On April 21 at Houston, John pitched seven scoreless innings and regained his place as one of the aces of the Dodger staff, along with veterans Don Sutton and Burt Hooton.

THE SCIENCE OF BASEBALL

John went 10-10 with a 3.09 ERA in 31 starts in 1976 and earned National League Comeback Player of the Year honors. He won 20 games for the first time in 1977 and helped the Dodgers reach the World Series by winning Game 4 of the National League Championship Series at Philadelphia. Pitching in a steady rainstorm, John crafted a 4-1 complete game to beat Steve Carlton and clinch the pennant for Los Angeles. He left the Dodgers following the 1978 season and signed as a free agent with the Yankees.

John won 21 games in 1979 and a career-high 22 in 1980 when he pitched in the All-Star Game at Dodger Stadium. John's career stretched 26 seasons. He posted 164 victories in the 14 seasons following the surgery. His 288 career wins are the most by any pitcher not in the Hall of Fame.

"I should probably have a counseling service for guys who are going to have Tommy John Surgery," John said. "You have to learn to pitch again; that takes a while. You have to go through the experience of making good pitches and winning without your best stuff. Before the surgery, you take it for granted. After the surgery, you learn you just don't bounce back from day one. It's an ongoing process and you've got to hang in there. When I came back in 1976, it was halfway through the season that I finally figured out I could win even if I didn't have my good stuff. It wasn't anything that anyone taught me. I just had to experience it.

"Pitching as long as I did, making 700 starts, I'm proud of that. But after coming back in 1976 until I quit in 1989, I never missed a start because of my arm. That's what I'm most proud of."

John's work ethic became folklore, even if modern-day players aren't familiar with his career. For example, former Dodger pitcher Darren Dreifort was born in 1972, John's first season in Los Angeles.

"I was talking to Burt Hooton when I had my second Tommy John Surgery and he was telling me about a roommate he had earlier in his career," said Dreifort, who gamely battled injuries through his career with Los Angeles from 1994-2004. "He told me about this guy who was the hardest worker he ever saw and people said he didn't have a chance to pitch anymore, but he kept working and it was unbelievable to see what he went through. At the end of the story, he told me the guy was Tommy John. And we all know what Tommy John went on to do after the surgery."

Looking at John's success, one can thumb through the record books and wonder what would've happened had some of the game's early pitching stars had access to modern medical technology.

"If we knew then what we know now, we probably could've saved the careers of such athletes as Joe Wood, Dizzy Dean, and Karl Spooner," Jobe said. "In the case of Spooner, he probably had a rotator cuff tear or a torn labrum. At the end of the 1954 season, he struck out 15 batters in his major-league debut with the Brooklyn Dodgers, and the next game he struck out 12. So they expected him to be the next Babe Ruth of baseball. But the following spring, he didn't warm up before posing for a photographer. He threw the ball too hard and felt pain in his shoulder. Back in those days, the thought was if you were being bothered by a sore joint, it was being seeded by an infection from some other part of the body. And the most common place was abscessed teeth. So the doctors thought Spooner had abscessed teeth because his shoulder wouldn't get well. So he was sent to a dentist and had all of his teeth pulled. So now you have a pitcher with no teeth and still a sore shoulder. So he never was a pitcher again."

Don Drysdale retired just one year after his 58⅔ scoreless innings streak in 1968. It looked like the same fate would befall Orel Hershiser, who broke Drysdale's mark 20 years later with 59 consecutive scoreless innings in 1988. In April 1990, Hershiser walked off the mound after feeling pain during a start against the St. Louis Cardinals. An MRI exam revealed extensive damage in Hershiser's shoulder capsule. Jobe proposed a surgery more radical than Tommy John's. He had performed the procedure on NFL quarterback Jim McMahon and golfer Jerry Pate, but never a major-league pitcher.

"His reputation preceded his advice on the surgery," Hershiser said. "He probably prescribed the most radical thing that could've happened to me and I didn't second-guess it at all. I didn't want a second opinion. I didn't need anybody else telling me what was wrong with me and how to fix it."

After a long and grueling rehabilitation period, Hershiser returned in June 1991 and continued to pitch with the Dodgers, Indians, Giants, and

Mets until 2000. "The Bulldog" won 105 games after the shoulder procedure and posted a 204-150 record overall.

Before the 1990 surgery, Jobe showed Hershiser the tools he would use for the operation. Hershiser joked that if the surgery was a success, he'd have the instruments bronzed. Hershiser went one step further with the plans after making his comeback.

The pitcher ordered a set of the instruments from the manufacturer and had them gold plated. He then hired a trophy maker to arrange them on a granite base in the shape of a baseball holder, which he placed the game ball from his 100th career victory—his first after the surgery.

The inscription on the trophy reads:

Victory #100
June 9, 1991
Made Possible By The Skilled Hands Of
DR. FRANK JOBE
With Gratitude
Orel Hershiser, Los Angeles Dodgers

Hershiser gave Jobe the trophy at a dinner he hosted for the doctors and trainers who aided in his comeback. Jobe has the trophy displayed in his office.

"Every time he won a game," Jobe says, "I felt like crying."

Chapter 11

STEVE GARVEY

NAME:	Steven Patrick Garvey
BORN:	December 22, 1948
BIRTHPLACE:	Tampa, FL
YEARS WITH THE DODGERS:	1969-1982
POSITION:	Infielder
UNIFORM NUMBER:	6
CAREER HIGHLIGHTS:	10-time All-Star with the Dodgers and Padres; played a National League-record 1,207 consecutive games from 1975-1983; won four Gold Glove Awards; had 200 or more hits in six seasons; 1974 National League MVP; All-Star Game MVP in 1974 and 1978; National League Championship Series MVP 1984; uniform No. 6 retired by the Padres in 1989.
THE GAME:	August 28, 1977; Dodgers vs. Cincinnati Reds at Dodger Stadium

THE IRON MAN

It took a famous headache by New York Yankees first baseman Wally Pipp in 1925 for a 22-year-old rookie named Lou Gehrig to get his chance in the first of 2,130 consecutive games played.

Fifty years later, another first baseman embarked on what would turn into the National League record for longevity and durability.

But Steve Garvey's glowing success with the Dodgers, including eight All-Star selections and four Gold Glove awards, occurred only after an amazing omen, followed by an agonizing stretch of uncertainty.

Garvey began his association with the Dodgers as a spring training batboy for the Brooklyn "Boys of Summer" squad in 1956. His father, Joe Garvey, was a Greyhound bus driver in Florida. Given the special assignment of driving the Dodgers team bus, Joe brought along seven-year-old Steve, letting his son miss school to ride along with such legends as Pee Wee Reese, Jackie Robinson, Duke Snider, and Roy Campanella.

First baseman Gil Hodges invited Steve to play catch during batting practice that afternoon, making a lifelong fan in the process. The script seemed out of Hollywood, even if the Dodgers weren't scheduled to move to the West Coast for a couple more years. Hodges was actually tossing the ball around with the future first baseman of the Los Angeles Dodgers.

"The biggest thing any little boy or little girl has is imagination," Garvey said. "And if you happen to be that little boy and you've never seen a ballplayer before, the first time is awe-inspiring. You expect them to be so big because you've always put them up on a little pedestal, and all of a sudden you meet a Gil Hodges and he's just like your dad. I remember him as a very warm human being, inside and out. When he asked me to play catch, I said, 'Gee, Gil Hodges.' It was tremendous. This is where you say to yourself, 'I'd like to be a ballplayer someday when I grow up, I'd like to be like Gil Hodges.'"

When Garvey arrived at Chamberlain High in Tampa, his baseball team needed a third baseman. If he were going to play that position, it would be patterned after Ken Boyer, the St. Louis Cardinals third baseman and National League MVP in 1964. Of course, Garvey didn't know he would win the same award just 10 years later at Hodges' position across the diamond.

"I had a strong arm and had good, quick reflexes and a good bat," Garvey said. "They needed a third baseman in high school and I played there, and I went to Michigan State as a third baseman. But

Steve Garvey receives a curtain-call ovation during his 5-for-5 performance on August 28, 1977, at Dodger Stadium.

unfortunately, at the end of my freshman year, I received a shoulder separation playing spring football and I never quite regained the same accuracy that I had previously."

In Garvey's senior season at Chamberlain, the Minnesota Twins selected him in the second round of the 1966 amateur draft. There were two reasons he didn't sign. After a family huddle, the Garveys decided at least a couple years of college would be good for Steve, an only child. And the Twins did not conjure the same baseball memories as a certain National League team.

"At that time, I had wondered, 'Will the Dodgers draft me?'" Garvey said. "And I think if the Minnesota Twins hadn't drafted me, the Dodgers told me they would probably draft me in the same round. I thought, 'Well, would college be of a little more benefit to me than just signing out of high school?' I talked it over with my parents and we decided it would be beneficial, and a baseball and football scholarship would be the best route to take. It turned out to be the best road. After two years at Michigan State as a defensive halfback in football and a third baseman in baseball, I was drafted in the first round by the Dodgers."

Garvey didn't find out the news until the following day. The baseball amateur draft started in 1965 and was definitely not an event considered worthy of great media attention.

"The football draft is a little different compared to baseball, because in football, you know right away when you're drafted," Garvey said. "But in baseball, unfortunately I had to wait until the next day's newspaper. I built up some anxiety and wondered who drafted me. And then a call came a couple days later from Mr. Guy Wellman, a Midwest supervising scout who came to see me. I wondered why the team didn't call the first day, but still, seeing 'Steve Garvey Drafted by Dodgers' in the paper was very exciting. You really pride yourself being able to play two sports at a major college level. And I did have a decision to make. But what overpowered and swayed the decision was that it was the Dodgers. And people say, 'I thought you could've gotten a bigger bonus for signing.' Well, little do they know that I really would've taken much, much less just to be part of the organization. There was no decision in my mind to be made. Football, I could always coach. I enjoyed coaching high school kids and at the college level. But baseball was my one true love and I thought I could play it for several years and would be able to make a good living—and playing in Los Angeles, with the millions of fans and the large crowds that came to the park."

Garvey made his major-league debut on September 1, 1969, at Dodger Stadium against the New York Mets. And who was the opposing manager? None other than Hodges, on his way to the championship that fall with the "Miracle Mets." Garvey struck out as a pinch hitter against reliever Jack DiLauro, but the Dodgers managed a 10-6 victory as journeyman Jim Bunning beat Jerry Koosman.

In 1970, Garvey edged out four other third-base candidates for the starting job. But the Dodgers lost their first five games in 1970, three by shutouts, and manager Walter Alston was forced to juggle the lineup. Garvey, who went 2-for-23 at the plate, was dispatched to Triple-A Spokane, where he resumed work on his batting stroke.

"When I signed with the Dodgers in 1968, Tommy Lasorda at Odgen worked with me quite a bit," Garvey said. "I never had trouble fielding a baseball, but I always had what they classified as 'quick hands.' The only trouble I had was throwing a baseball. I came to the Dodgers in 1970 and had a problem then. I solved it by 1971 and then unfortunately regressed so that by 1972, my main problem was accuracy throwing to first base. I think 85 percent of the errors I made were throwing."

In 85 games at third base in 1972, Garvey committed a league-high 28 errors. Yet the Dodgers were still intrigued with his offense—nine home runs and 30 RBIs in just 225 at-bats.

The departures of veteran infielders Maury Wills, Wes Parker, and Jim Lefebvre, along with one-time prospects Bobby Valentine and Billy Grabarkewitz, gave the Dodger brass a chance to install a new infield after the 1972 season. The original blueprint included Bill Buckner at first base, Davey Lopes at second base, Bill Russell at shortstop, and Ron Cey at third.

"We decided to go with the kids in 1973," manager Walter Alston said in a 1976 interview. "I always felt like if you could bring a rookie player into the mix every season, they could blend into the lineup. In 1973, we made a lot of rookie mistakes. We threw to the wrong bases. But gradually they came together as a unit and people forget we won 95 games, which is a lot for a second-place team with a really young team."

Cey's emergence at third base in 1973 relegated Garvey to pinch-hitting duties, along with occasional starts in left field. Finally, Alston decided to try Garvey at first base for the second game of a doubleheader at home against the Cincinnati Reds on June 23. Prior to his pinch-hit single in the first game of the doubleheader, Garvey had not played for seven days, and his batting average was frozen at .228 with no home runs in 36 games. In his next four games as the starting first baseman, Garvey went 7-for-17, including his first home run on June 24 against left-hander Don Gullett.

"Walter Alston probably said to himself, 'Well, he has good hands, if we can put his hands to good use and we can find a place for his strong arm ... so I went to left field for the first part of 1973," said Garvey, who batted .304 in 114 games in 1973. "The team got off to a good start, and unfortunately I sat down for two months. He said one day, 'I've seen you play a couple games at first base, would you like to try it tonight?' I said, 'Anything to get into the lineup.' And the rest, I guess, is history since the middle of 1973."

Buckner moved to left field, and Garvey enjoyed a banner season in 1974, batting fourth in the Dodger lineup behind newcomer Jimmy Wynn. Garvey hit .312 with 21 home runs and 111 RBIs in 156 games. He became only the second National Leaguer to be selected by the fans for the All-Star Game as a write-in candidate, joining Atlanta's Rico Carty in 1970. Garvey earned MVP honors at the Mid-Summer Classic in Pittsburgh.

The Dodgers rolled to a 102-60 record during the regular season. They defeated Pittsburgh in the League Championship Series, but lost the World Series in five games to the two-time defending champion Oakland Athletics.

Garvey became the new image of the Dodgers overnight, at least in terms of commercial endorsements. There would be a junior high school renamed in his honor. For a player who struggled to get into the starting lineup, Garvey embraced his success as his "destiny" to wear a Dodger uniform, telling the story of the bus ride to Florida with his father and the Brooklyn players. And the Dodger infield stayed together from June 1973 until 1981, serving as a bridge between two Hall of Fame managers, Walter Alston and Tommy Lasorda, following Alston's retirement at the end of the 1976 season.

The 1977 Dodgers roared to a 22-4 start and enjoyed a 10½-game lead by May 6. Garvey got off to a hot start in 1977, but by late summer was enduring the worst slump of his career. For three years, Garvey had not gone more than three games without a hit. Suddenly, he was stuck in a 9-for-71 drought, a .123 batting average. He went 20 games without driving in a run.

Like Gehrig and later Baltimore's Cal Ripkin Jr., any prolonged drought conjured speculation as to whether the playing streak was taking its toll. But Garvey's streak was still in its infancy stage on August 28, 1977, consecutive game No. 316. Entering the game, the Dodgers were cruising in the National League West, leading Cincinnati by 8½ games.

THE GAME OF MY LIFE

By Steve Garvey

When the 1977 season started, Tommy Lasorda asked me to go for more power. He said, "I'll take a few less hits and a few points off the batting average if you can give me some more power." So I did. I went up to 33 home runs and 100-plus RBIs. Frank Sinatra promised Tommy that he'd sing the national anthem on Opening Day.

I tell people the 1977 Dodgers was the best team I ever played on. We used to put teams away early with speed and power. The speed came from Davey Lopes and Bill Russell. Of course, our team also had the first quartet in history to each hit at least 30 home runs in the same season. The others were Ron Cey, Reggie Smith, and Dusty Baker, who hit his 30th home run on the last day of the season. I remember us going down on the field for a classic picture with a giant "30" in the background on the scoreboard. We made the playoffs for the first of three appearances against the New York Yankees between 1977 and 1981. From the late 1970s to the early '80s, we expected to win. I always say that 1977 was the year we were upset in the World Series. The Yankees beat us in six games, but we probably should've won the series. We finally won the Series in 1981, but overall I think the 1977 team was better balanced.

The infield was in its prime with Lopes at second base, Russell at shortstop, and Cey at third. We spent 8½ seasons together beginning in June 1973. The infield knew what it was doing as a collective unit, and more importantly, Tommy Lasorda was injecting the proper amount of enthusiasm in his first year. And what better way to start for Tommy and the rest of us?

Walter Alston was the Dodger manager at the start of my career in 1969, and both Alston and Lasorda wound up in the Hall of Fame. Walter had a strong influence on me during the first five years of my career. With Lasorda, we were all "Tommy's boys," because he had been our first minor-league manager when we all signed with the organization. The transition from Alston to Lasorda was smooth. But there was a dichotomy of personalities that I really think was the difference. Walt really didn't say a whole lot, but when he did say something, it was after he had watched something for a long time and it was for your benefit. Tommy was more verbal with a lot more adjectives. He was a great psychiatrist in terms of knowing what each guy needed.

The game I most remember as a Dodger occurred on a Sunday afternoon at Dodger Stadium against the St. Louis Cardinals. We held an 8½-game lead over the Reds on August 28, so things looked good as far as making the playoffs.

But I was mired in a terrible slump. I've always said at that point I couldn't hit a beach ball if you rolled it up to home plate. It was Nuns Day at Dodger Stadium. It was also the day I met Annie Ruth, who was a quadriplegic after a recent gymnastics accident. Not only on this day was Annie an inspiration, but being Catholic, the nuns were an inspiration, too.

THE RESULTS

On August 28, 1977, the Dodgers defeated the Cardinals 11-0 as Garvey went 5-for-5 with two home runs, including a grand slam and three doubles for a whopping 14 total bases, one shy of the team record. Garvey tied the National League record for most long hits in a game and most consecutive extra-base hits.

In the second inning, Garvey doubled to left against Cardinals starter Bob Forsch. He scored moments later when first baseman Keith Hernandez made an error on Rick Monday's bunt single. Garvey led off the fourth inning with a double to right field, and he eventually scored on Davey Lopes' bases-loaded single to give the Dodgers a 2-0 lead.

In the fifth inning, Garvey stepped to the plate and blasted a home run—his first at Dodger Stadium since July 27.

The Dodgers blew open the game in the seventh inning. Forsch was gone after issuing a leadoff walk to Russell. Reliever Clay Carroll, a former nemesis with Cincinnati's pennant-winning "Big Red Machine" teams of 1975 and 1976, allowed a single by Reggie Smith. Ron Cey tried to sacrifice bunt, but Russell beat Carroll's throw to third, loading the bases.

When Garvey stepped to the plate, he had just one career grand slam, hit earlier in the season against Carroll on June 22 in a 12-1 victory over the Cardinals at Dodger Stadium. Garvey homered in the rematch, making the score 7-0. He emerged from the dugout for a curtain call and raised his left index finger in the air.

"A game like I had today has a tendency to make you forget all the hard times," he said in the clubhouse. "Everything just seemed to fall into place. The way I had been struggling, I would have taken just about anything. I think I'm back, but more importantly, I think our team is back. The key is we're staying ahead of Cincinnati. When they come from behind to win, so do we. When they win big, we win big. After a while, the Reds are going to think they're batting their heads against a brick wall."

Reporters asked Garvey about his recent slump. Having been spoiled with success, Garvey admitted he was pressing. (It was during a streak in which Garvey reached the 200-hit plateau six out of seven seasons from 1974-1980. The lone exception was 192 hits in 1977, when he set a Los Angeles single-season record with 33 home runs, also a career high.)

"Something like that happens to every baseball player," he said that August day. "It taught me several important lessons, but most of all it taught me to keep things within myself, learn from your mistakes, and to wipe the memory of your last at-bat and concentrate on your next AB. I'd just like to thank all the people for their support during this bad stretch. People have been wonderful to me. A lot of them have sent in rosaries and prayed for me, and that's meant a lot."

In the top of the eighth inning, home plate umpire Ed Montague ejected Cardinals outfielder Lou Brock. Brock, who went 0-for-11 in the series, entered the weekend hoping to tie Ty Cobb's all-time stolen base record at 892. He didn't, but broke the record days later in San Diego. In 1974, Garvey beat out Brock for the National League MVP award—270 points to 233—the year Brock swiped a record 118 bases.

Most players would've called it a day after going 4-for-4 with two home runs and two doubles, enjoying a 10-0 lead. But Garvey usually didn't give way for defensive replacements, and this afternoon was no exception. He opened the ninth inning with a double against reliever Tom Underwood. Standing in the middle of the stadium at second base, Garvey lifted his batting helmet in the air and life resumed to normal at Dodger Stadium. Mr. Consistency was back on track.

NUMBER SIX

Garvey won his only championship during the strike-shortened 1981 season, in which the Dodgers needed to stage comebacks in all three playoff series against the Houston Astros, Montreal Expos, and New York Yankees. The final game of the World Series against the Yankees also marked the final time as a unit for Garvey, second baseman Davey Lopes, shortstop Bill Russell, and third baseman Ron Cey. They spent 8½ seasons together, a record seemingly unbreakable with today's roster shuffles due to free agency.

"We were like brothers on the field," Russell said. "Could you imagine managing every year knowing four guys are going to be there on the infield? And we all played. Garvey played every game and we all averaged 150 games."

Garvey batted .283 during the 1981 regular season, but was hot in the Division Series (.368) and World Series (.417). With Los Angeles two innings away from elimination, Garvey's late home run against Montreal's Bill Gullickson helped the Dodgers tie the League Championship Series at two games apiece. They won the pennant on a cold Monday afternoon with Rick Monday's ninth-inning home run off Steve Rogers at Olympic Stadium.

"That was our year, it was like destiny," Garvey said. "The team was a culmination of something that actually started with the 1968 draft. We all took two or three years to find our niche. In 1973 we started coming together, and it seemed each year (general manager) Al Campanis would add those one or two players to fill our needs, whether it be a Rick Monday or a Dusty Baker or a Reggie Smith. That just seemed to solidify our team through the '70s and early '80s.

"I look back on my Dodger career, and the world championship in 1981 really stands out. While I achieved a lot of individual things that I'm very proud of, this was very special because it's something we accomplished as a team—something we worked hard for."

Garvey remained in a Dodger uniform through the 1982 season. When he became a free agent, Los Angeles couldn't agree on terms and decided to give rookie Greg Brock a chance. Brock struggled in Garvey's shadow, batting .233 between 1982 and 1986. Meanwhile, Garvey signed a five-year contract with San Diego, becoming the highest profile free agent to join the Padres. Garvey's playing streak ended on July 29, 1983, when he fractured his thumb sliding into home plate.

The next season, Garvey helped San Diego make its first World Series appearance, blasting an extra-inning home run off the Cubs' Lee Smith in Game 4 of the NLCS and giving the Padres a chance to win the pennant the next afternoon. Garvey's home run was later voted as San Diego's top baseball moment. The Padres retired his uniform, No. 6, in 1989.

Garvey still ranks near or at the top of many hitting categories in Los Angeles history. He ranks first all-time in RBIs (992) and doubles (333), ranks second with 1,968 hits, and has played the most games of any Dodger at first base (1,672).

Garvey is currently a member of the Dodger marketing department. He also makes annual trips to Lindsay, California, to visit the students at Steve Garvey Junior High School, renamed during the height of his popularity in Los Angeles. The school, located a three-hour drive away from Los Angeles in Tulare County, was originally Lincoln Junior High until principal Bob Edwards staged a contest to rename the facility in 1977. Garvey's name topped the list of candidates, which included both Elton John and Elvis Presley.

When Garvey left the Dodgers, no player or coach wore No. 6 again for 21 years until utility infielder Jolbert Cabrerra in 2003. The only other uniform number kept out of circulation for a significant period is Fernando Valenzuela's No. 34, which still hasn't been worn since the left-hander was released by Los Angeles during spring training in 1991. Like his boyhood idol Gil Hodges' No. 14, the Dodgers would retire Garvey's number were he elected to the Baseball Hall of Fame.

But even if Cooperstown never calls, Garvey will always carry the memories of the Dodgers, both Brooklyn and Los Angeles. And Opening Days at Dodger Stadium are now a tradition for Garvey, who wants to keep his name in the starting lineup of the all-time greats who usually assemble behind home plate during pregame ceremonies. "No. 6" still draws a thunderous ovation.

"Heritage and history come predominantly from success," Garvey said. "And success is always a wonderful story. Whether you talk about the Brooklyn Dodgers and the great players they had, like Jackie Robinson, Roy Campanella, Gil Hodges, the Dodgers also have world championships, starting with Brooklyn in 1955. You talk about the wonderful heritage that was perpetuated by the Brooklyn Dodgers and continued by our generation in the 1980s and now this group. I have always thought that the individual who understands history is the individual who really appreciates success and learns more from failure."

Chapter 12

MIKE BRITO

NAME:	Mike Brito
BORN:	August 21, 1934
BIRTHPLACE:	Havana, Cuba
YEARS WITH THE DODGERS:	1975-Present
POSITION:	Scout
TRADEMARK UNIFORM:	White Panama hat and cigar (sunglasses optional)
CAREER HIGHLIGHTS:	Best known as the scout who signed Mexican pitching prospect Fernando Valenzuela in 1979; also spent two decades stationed behind home plate at Dodger Stadium and dugout-level screen with radar gun; 29 of his free agents have reached the major leagues, including Bobby Castillo, Ismael Valdes, Oscar Robles, Karim Garcia, Antonio Osuna, and Juan Castro; inducted into Cuban Baseball Hall of Fame in 2005.
THE GAME:	A Sunday afternoon semi-pro game in East Los Angeles, 1975

THE UNLIKELY SCOUT

When the baseball-themed *Damn Yankees* hit the Broadway stage in the 1950s, its hero, Joe Hardy, played on the Washington Senators, a theatrical metaphor for a lousy team. "First in war, first in peace, and last in the American League" was the old adage for a franchise that once boasted Hall of Fame pitcher Walter Johnson but hadn't played in a World Series since 1933.

The real Senators averaged 90 losses per season during the 1950s, and the franchise finally moved to Minnesota to become the Twins in 1961. The inglorious history of the region meant nobody paid much attention to the team's fortunes, unless the president of the United States was scheduled to throw out the ceremonial first pitch on Opening Day.

But one of the most interesting chapters in baseball lore belongs to the Senators, who in the late 1950s began signing numerous prospects from Cuba and other countries. Owner Clark Griffin hired "Papa" Joe Cambria as the team's first Latin America scout. Cambria, an Italian-born laundry owner in Baltimore, signed some of the most notable players in history, including pitchers Camilo Pascual and Luis Tiant, outfielder Tony Olivo, infielder Zoilo Versalles, and the world-famous baseball scout Mike Brito.

Of course, Cambria didn't realize Brito's true calling in life when he signed the Cuban catcher in 1954.

"I think the only mistake Cambria ever made was signing me," Brito says with a laugh. "I played seven years of minor-league ball before I hurt my arm. I played in the United States for four seasons and in Mexico for three seasons before getting hurt in a home-plate collision."

In Brito's final year, he played for the Juarez Indians of the Mexican League, who were affiliated with the Senators organization. Trying to maintain his health led to a difficult medical decision.

"In those days toward the end of my career when my arm was hurt, I needed a Vitamin B shot in my vein," Brito said. "That made me throw good for three or four days—very strong. But one day when I went to get the shot, the doctor told me, 'I want to be honest with you. If you keep getting a shot in your vein to keep playing, there's going to be a time when you get it in your blood and then you can get cancer. Then you'll be dead. I give you this advice, so it's up to you.' In my heart, I thought, 'This is my last year in baseball.' I sold all my equipment and moved to Los Angeles and started working here as a truck driver for RC Cola."

Dodger scout Mike Brito (left) and former pitcher Bobby Castillo still laugh about their fateful encounter 30 years ago.

One day, Brito was making deliveries in a liquor store when he met an employee who was a former teammate in the Mexican League. The man was playing baseball on Sundays in East Los Angeles, and he invited Brito to play.

"But I don't have any equipment," Brito said. "I sold everything."

The man assured Brito there wasn't a problem. "We'll get you everything, plus a catcher's mitt."

Happy to regain his association with baseball, Brito started playing again in 1963, earning $25 a game. Slowly, seemingly minor events turned into opportunities as Brito parlayed his love of baseball into another career.

"A friend of mine who was playing in that league became manager of the Reynosa ballclub in Mexico," Brito said. "He told me, if I wanted, to send players from East Los Angeles to the Reynosa club. I said, 'What am I going to gain by this?' He said, 'I'll give you $250 per month.' I said,

'C'mon, you can do better than that.' So he made it $350. So I started sending players to Reynosa of the Mexican League. That was in 1964."

The Sunday league in East Los Angeles eventually broke apart, so Brito decided to start his own. It began with eight teams. Brito was a player-manager, collecting money from the teams, paying the rental fee to the city, and giving out trophies at the end of the season. Today, the league boasts 62 teams. The non-profit status remains in place and revenue is earmarked for trophies and the local parks and recreation department.

THE GAME OF MY LIFE

By Mike Brito

In 1975, there was a game I'll never forget ... at Evergreen Park in East Los Angeles. Bobby "Babo" Castillo was playing third base for the opposing team and I was playing first base for the Latin Stars, which was my team's name. In the eighth inning we were losing 2-1 and had the bases loaded with one out. It was my turn to bat. The manager of the other team went to the pitcher's mound and brought Babo in from third base to pitch to me. When I saw that little guy out there, I thought, "This is a piece of cake." So he's warming up and I'm waiting to bat. First pitch, he threw a pitch that was right over the plate—I swung and fouled the ball. He threw another fastball, which was called a ball, and another fastball, which I pulled foul down the left-field line. Then he gave me another ball, which made the count 2-and-2. At that point, he hadn't shown me anything with his fastball, and that's what I was expecting. Suddenly out of nowhere, Castillo threw me a big screwgie. And I mean, I missed it by this much (holding his index fingers two feet apart). His fastball was decent, in the high 80s, but I had a quick bat. But he struck me out on a great screwball.

After the game, I went to him and asked, "What kind of pitch did you throw me? Was it a changeup?"

"No, it was a screwball," he said.

"Where did you learn that pitch?"

"Well, I was a pitcher at Lincoln High School. Then the Kansas City Royals signed me as a third baseman. (Former Dodger infielder) Spider Jorgensen was the scout. But Kansas City released me."

I told him I was a scout for the Reynoso club of the Mexican League, and I invited him to play in the Mexican League. Like every player, he asked how much the pay was going to be. I said I'd let him know the next day. He gave me all his information.

So I called Reynosa and I told the general manager, who was my friend, and said, "I have this kid who is a pitcher, and he just struck me out on a screwball which looked like a major-league pitch." He asked about his fastball and I said it was hissing and had good life. I didn't have a radar gun. I didn't have one in those days. I thought that fastball had to be in the high 80s. He said, "Well, why don't you sign him?"

The GM asked how much the pay was going to be. The Mexican League was like Double-A baseball at the time, so I said he'd have to pay Castillo at least $1,000. According to the GM, that was going to be too much money. I didn't think Bobby was going to go for that anyway, and I was right. He said he could make more than $1,000 working in the United States.

I spoke to his mother, who was his agent. Finally, we decided to pay him $1,500 a month. That was a lot of money over there. I told the GM, "He can play third base, too, and he can hit a little bit. But he's a pitcher."

So Bobby wins 15 games in the Mexican League the next season. He also threw one of the longest games in team history—18 innings—and he lost 1-0. When I went to Mexico, I asked the manager, "How could you leave him in the game for so long?" By that time, we had already signed him for the Dodgers. So I told his manager that Bobby couldn't pitch for at least five outings.

The bottom line is I sent him to Reynosa and he had a good year in the Mexican League. I offered him a contract with Los Angeles through general manager Al Campanis, who had named me a Dodger scout after Castillo made such noise in the Mexican League. Campanis said, "I want to find out who signed Castillo. He's a local product. How come we didn't sign him?"

Campanis managed in Cuba when I was playing there. Campanis asked if I wanted to work for the Dodgers and I said, "Sure." It was a part-time job for $14,000 a year. That was the beginning and I worked part-time until one year I couldn't sign Eric Davis, who was a local high school player in Los Angeles, because someone didn't like him. I told Campanis, "I don't want to work part-time and at the high school level. I want to go somewhere where I can sign players."

Campanis said, "What about Mexico?"

I said, "I love Mexico."

We signed Babo, and then Fernando Valenzuela started making noise in Mexico when I was scouting over there. I went to see a shortstop and I saw Fernando and fell in love with that lefty. And you know the rest of the story. I signed him for $135,000 in 1979. We brought him over here to Lodi, our team in the Single-A California League. Fernando didn't have a good year in Lodi, he was 4-5. Al went to see him.

"Chief, I'm worried about his velocity," I told Campanis. "His fastball is below average."

"How come you didn't tell me that in the beginning?"

"Well, I told you his fastball was below average, but he had a good curveball."

"So what do you think?"

"I think he needs another pitch."

"What kind of pitch?"

I told Campanis that any time a pitcher has a good curveball, chances are he also has a loose wrist. And since Fernando had a good curveball and long fingers, maybe he could learn another pitch, like a split-finger fastball or a screwball. Campanis said the Dodgers didn't have anyone in the system who could throw a split-finger fastball, so I told him about the Dodger pitcher who could throw a screwball.

Campanis said, "Get Castillo to Arizona and tell Fernando I want him to work with him for a week."

In a week, Fernando was throwing the screwball better than Castillo. And not only that, he had two screwballs with different velocities, a slow one and a hard one. And that was the beginning.

THE RESULTS

Although Brito's team lost the Sunday league game in East Los Angeles 2-1, never has a manager savored such defeat when considering the magnitude of such failure. And unlike the "Mighty Casey" character in Ernest Lawrence Thayer's 1888 poem, Brito doesn't mind that the story of his most important at-bat always ends with a strikeout.

"The big thing was if that was a fair ball hit by me off Bobby Castillo, Fernando would've never joined the Dodgers," Brito said. "And if he did sign with someone else, maybe he wouldn't have been the success that he was without that extra pitch taught to him by Bobby Castillo. If I get a base hit, forget about it. I still remember, 'This little guy pitching is a piece of cake. I'm going to kick some ass.' But it went the other way. Even if he walked me, I would've thought he had no guts to pitch to me."

Looking back from his own perspective, Castillo thought Brito was just another hitter in the opposing lineup. Sitting on the Club Level at Dodger Stadium, the former major-league pitcher smirks when comparing Brito to "Mighty Casey" at the plate.

"I could've thrown Mike any screwball that I had and it would've struck Mike out," Castillo said, already imagining Brito's ears burning with that prophecy. "I didn't fear him or anything like that. But I threw him a good screwball and that opened the door for me to go to Mexico. Mike's right, though, when he talks about the 'Mighty Casey' poem. None of this would've happened if Mike didn't strike out."

THE PRODIGY

Castillo made his major-league debut for the Dodgers in September 1977. He appeared in a career-high 61 games in 1980, posting an 8-6 record, a 2.75 ERA, and five saves.

Valenzuela joined Castillo in the Dodger bullpen in September 1980. He went 2-0 with a 0.00 ERA and one save in 17⅔ innings.

When Don Sutton left the Dodgers via free agency, it opened a door for Valenzuela to join the rotation. After a solid spring in 1981, Valenzuela quietly prepared to pitch the third game of the season. Instead, he became a folk hero when his first major-league start was rescheduled for Opening Day against the Houston Astros in front of a sold-out Dodger Stadium.

Valenzuela, who was staying at Brito's house at the beginning of the season, wasn't nervous the night before the big assignment. At least, he didn't act the part of a jittery rookie.

"The night I took him home, he told me, 'You know, I'm going to start tomorrow,'" Brito said. "Fernando was supposed to start the third game of the season, but Lasorda and Campanis changed their minds because of injuries to Jerry Reuss and Burt Hooton. Fernando acted like he was going to pitch a game in the Mexican League. Nothing upset this guy. Fernando was the kind of a player who never showed any emotion. If he has it, only he knows. I was watching him closely when he had the bases loaded and the big guy coming to the plate. The look he gave me … it was like he was reading the hitters' minds. He knew what they were looking for and he never threw their pitch. That's what made Fernando so successful."

In the ninth inning, Castillo and left-hander Steve Howe were warming up in the bullpen just in case Valenzuela ran into trouble nursing a modest 2-0 lead. When he struck out Dave Roberts to finish his five-hitter, Valenzuela walked off the field with a grin on his face as broadcaster Vin Scully exclaimed, "And a little child shall lead them."

The next day's headline in the *Los Angeles Times* read, "Didn't They Tell Him Batting Practice Was Over?"

"I was right behind the plate, but I didn't use the radar gun because I was afraid of making him nervous," Brito said. "I drove him to the ballpark and brought him back to my house after the game. The only thing I told him about Bob Watson and Cesar Cedeno? 'They liked the ball up,' I said. 'You have to watch it. Watson can hit the ball out of the park in any direction and Cedeno, don't give him anything up in the strike zone. If there are men in scoring position, don't give them anything good to hit.' That was the only advice I gave him.

"I'll tell you one thing, when I was a player, I never got nervous. Even when I had two strikes, I wasn't afraid to swing the bat. But that Opening Day, I felt like I was going to have a heart attack. I smoked two or three cigars because he was in trouble all the time. I was so nervous. There were several times Fernando got in trouble and he had to come up with a big pitch to get out of the inning. On the way home he was happy, but we didn't talk about the game. I just told him, 'You pitched a helluva game.' He said, 'I was lucky.' I didn't want to get too deep with him because he knew he did a good job."

It was the birth of "Fernandomania," the most exciting time in Dodger Stadium history as Valenzuela began the season with an 8-0 record, including five shutouts. Newspapers researched to find the 20-year-old's birth certificate. The document was reprinted in a newspaper with the caption, "Proof: Valenzuela isn't 40."

"I have to be careful when I'm on defense, sometimes I get to watching Fernando too much," left fielder Dusty Baker said. "I'm just like a spectator, in awe of what he's doing."

During the seventh inning at Dodger Stadium on April 27, Valenzuela motioned for Tommy Lasorda to come to the mound. It was a strange moment with Valenzuela cruising to an eventual 5-0 complete-game victory. The manager feared injury, but Valenzuela had simply broken the gold chain around his neck. The superstitious Lasorda didn't want the chain, telling Valenzuela to put it in his pocket. Lasorda's playful mood resumed the next inning when he told Reggie Smith to pinch hit for Valenzuela. "I'm not going out there!" Smith exclaimed, and the dugout filled with laughter.

Lasorda later announced his wife, Jo, had requested Valenzuela's autograph. It was the first time she had ever asked for one of his players' signatures.

The Dodgers roared out of the gates with a 14-3 record. On the road, other Dodgers felt as if they were part of Valenzuela's "entourage."

"It was like following a famous musician or artist," outfielder Ken Landreaux said. "Whenever you hear of someone famous coming to town, people flock to the theater. That's how it was. A lot of people would come to the stadium, hoping it was Fernando's turn to pitch. They wanted to find out about what this phenom was all about."

Public relations director Steve Brener, along with executive vice president Fred Claire, set up guidelines for Valenzuela's media requests. They had watched Kansas City's George Brett feel the pressure of the national spotlight during the summer of 1980 when his batting average hovered near the .400 mark. Spanish broadcaster Jaime Jarrin also played a major role in helping Valenzuela, serving as his interpreter.

"On the mound, Fernando was a Tiger," Castillo said. "Off the field, he was sort of afraid of people because there were so many around. We couldn't go anywhere on the road because people recognized him."

In the middle of the circus, Fernando brought fun to the Dodger clubhouse. On days he wasn't pitching, he loved to pull pranks on teammates, turning a small rope into a dugout lasso.

"I think we came to the realization that this was a guy we liked a great deal, and not because he was winning," said former Dodger outfielder Rick Monday. "At a young age, he understood the kind of commitment that it took individually and collectively. He fit in wonderfully with the nucleus that was there.

"Quite frankly, we looked up to him because he was a young guy and had a lot of difficult things for him—culture and the language barrier—and all of a sudden he's thrust into situations. We were staying in hotels that had a larger population than the entire area of Mexico where he came from. To see the wonderment and the daily challenge of trying to absorb things, he was like a sponge."

In 1981, Valenzuela became the only player in history to win both the Rookie of the Year and Cy Young Awards in the same season. He won 141 games during his career with the Dodgers from 1980-1990, including a career-high 21 victories in 1986. Valenzuela pitched his only career no-hitter in 1990 against the St. Louis Cardinals at Dodger Stadium.

"He made a revolution," Brito said. "I remember the people who liked the other sports, like football and soccer. All ages showed up to the ballpark because they wanted to see him pitch. At my house after he won his first four games, people were waiting outside. I had to come out by the swimming pool in the back of my home. He said, 'Let's go around to the back.' He always took it easy and the attention never went to his head. The only thing is, he's never been the kind of guy who liked to talk to the press.

"I remember when he went to the White House during the 1981 season, he wrote a letter to his mother. That's one of the few times I think he was really excited. I remember him telling his mother, 'I'm going to meet the president of the United States, Ronald Reagan. I never thought that was going to happen to me.'"

And more than 25 years after their fateful encounter at the Arizona Instruction League when an established pitcher tried to help a struggling prospect, Castillo and Valenzuela still remain together with the Dodger organization.

"The Dodgers were my first team," said Valenzuela, a member of the Spanish broadcasting team with Jarrin and Pepe Yniguez. "Mike Brito signed me out of Mexico and I was so excited to think I might pitch for the Dodgers."

The Dodgers traded Castillo after the 1981 season and he enjoyed his best years as a starter with the Minnesota Twins, the team Brito never had a chance to play for. Castillo won 13 games in 1982. He returned to Los Angeles in 1985 and finished his playing career with stops in Mexico and Japan.

"This association with the Dodgers has been a blessing in my life," Castillo said. "You can really say it's a dream come true. I dreamed of playing for the Dodgers and only the Dodgers. I never dreamed of playing for the Padres. I snuck into Dodger Stadium as a kid and rooted for Koufax and Drysdale as a kid. Now, I can give speeches on behalf of the Dodgers' Community Relations department and tell kids if they give it their all, anything is possible."

Brito continues his life as a scout, making trips to Mexico with the same desire to find the next prospect on the horizon. He watched the inaugural World Baseball Classic in 2006 and relished the performances of such teams as Cuba and Mexico. Brito also enjoys collecting equipment and donating it to various youth sports leagues in Southern California and Mexico, hoping to spark an interest among youngsters.

"I think that's Mike's persona," Castillo said. "If you took away baseball from him, I don't know what he'd do. When he played ball every Sunday, he was looking for talent, but at the same time he wanted to preserve a place where those in the neighborhood had to play.

"Later on, when Mike was holding the radar gun behind home plate at the stadium, everyone watching on television knew it was Dodger Stadium if there was a man standing there with a cigar and hat. I think he's a great man, a one-of-a-kind personality, and he's done wonders for the game."

And even though "Mighty Casey" struck out, Brito looks back on his career with wonder. Like Tommy Lasorda, the Hall of Fame manager whose prolific Rolodex would clog any grain elevator, Brito has become one of the most recognizable personalities in the sport.

"In not only Southern California, but the whole baseball world," he said. "Castillo gave me a break and Fernando changed my life completely. He put me in the headlines forever. The other night I went to a scouting dinner, and I was signing autographs. You never see a scout signing autographs. People wanted to take pictures with me, and there was Cal Ripken and Willie Mays nearby. But everybody recognizes me and asks, 'Where's your radar gun? You're more popular than the baseball players.'

"But the whole beginning of the story was Bobby Castillo, Fernando Valenzuela, and the Dodgers. So I have to thank God first, followed by Bobby Castillo, Fernando, and the Dodgers for the success I've had in my career."

Chapter 13

JERRY REUSS

NAME:	Jerry Reuss
BORN:	June 19, 1949
BIRTHPLACE:	St. Louis, MO
YEARS WITH THE DODGERS:	1979-1987
POSITION:	Pitcher
UNIFORM NUMBER:	41
CAREER HIGHLIGHTS:	Major-league career spanned four different decades (1969-1990); was 220-191 overall with 3.64 ERA in 628 games; became second left-hander in Los Angeles history to pitch a no-hitter (1980); was winning pitcher for the National League in the 1980 All-Star Game at Dodger Stadium; pitched 18 scoreless innings in two starts in the 1981 National League Division Series vs. the Astros.
THE GAME:	October 25, 1981; World Series Game 5; New York Yankees vs. Los Angeles Dodgers at Dodger Stadium

STARTING OVER

During his tenure as the Dodgers' general manager in the 1970s, Al Campanis usually built his teams with position players from the farm system. His most effective pitchers were imports from other organizations. Through shrewd trades, Campanis acquired veteran arms such as Tommy John (Chicago White Sox), Al Downing (Milwaukee Brewers), Andy Messersmith (California Angels), Mike Marshall (Montreal Expos), and Burt Hooton (Chicago Cubs).

When John left Los Angeles after the 1978 season to sign a free-agent contract with the New York Yankees, the Dodgers needed to find a left-hander who would balance the starting rotation. On Opening Day 1979, the Dodgers sent pitching prospect Rick Rhoden to the Pittsburgh Pirates in exchange for Jerry Reuss, who had won a career-high 18 games in 1975 but slumped to a 3-2 mark in 1978, splitting time in the Pittsburgh bullpen and rotation. At age 29, Reuss joined the Dodgers with 108 lifetime victories.

"I never had any doubts about whether I still had ability, I just needed a place to go," Reuss said. "I did get some starts, but I pitched a lot in relief in 1979. I proved to myself that I could still start and win in the National League, but the Dodgers were in the midst of a real bad season."

Reuss went 7-14 with a 3.54 ERA for a 1979 Dodger team that slumped to third place in the National League West with a 73-89 record, 11½ games behind the division champion Cincinnati Reds.

Little did Reuss realize that a Comeback Player of the Year honor was waiting around the corner for him the following season. He just needed to figure out a way to get into the starting rotation.

"A couple of things happened in 1980," Reuss said. "A big thing for me mentally and physically was my off-season training. I spent the winter in Los Angeles and it was the first time I was introduced to the Nautilus machines, the weight-bearing machines, and the exercises suggested by our team physician, Dr. Frank Jobe. I became convinced this was a way that would build strength. I liked what it did and I liked how I felt. Then I changed my running program. It was our trainer, Bill Buhler, who suggested, 'Instead of doing sprints and anaerobic work, let's mix in aerobic work, and the combination of the two will probably make you stronger during the course of the season.'

"From a baseball standpoint, the Dodgers acquired Dave Goltz, a free agent from the Minnesota Twins, during the off-season and he was going

After a trade from Pittsburgh in 1979, Jerry Reuss became one of the most prolific pitchers in Los Angeles history.

to pitch in the rotation. I was going to be relegated to the bullpen. I can't say I was happy about that, but it was something that had to be done. The other guys deserved to be there: Burt Hooton, Don Sutton, Bobby Welch, and Rick Sutcliffe. I didn't. One thing that Tommy did was to make a promise to me. I said, 'If a starting spot becomes available, will you give me consideration?' I didn't ask him to give it to me, because he may not have been in a position to do it. But I asked him for consideration and Tommy was fair about it."

Sutcliffe, who went 17-10 in 1979 during his Rookie of the Year season, struggled early in his sophomore campaign. By mid-May, Sutcliffe was 0-2 with an 8.33 ERA. After making some adjustments in the bullpen during the first five weeks of the season, Reuss made a start on May 16 when Goltz came down with the flu. Afterward, he remained in the rotation, taking Sutcliffe's place. Reuss finished with an 18-6 record, a 2.52 ERA, 10 complete games, and a league-leading six shutouts. He was second to Philadelphia's Steve Carlton in the Cy Young Award balloting.

"Pitching in relief the way I did meant I could take two pitches out of my repertoire and stay solely with a cut fastball, which I developed, and a curveball," Reuss said. "And I had command of both and suddenly things were working out for me. I was able to locate the ball unlike I've ever done before. Looking back on it, that stint in the bullpen might've been the precursor to the good season that I had in 1980. Because once I got in that starting rotation, I stayed there. I wasn't going to give it up. When Sutcliffe found out that I was going to start the next time out, he went into Tommy's office. Tommy told him, 'What am I going to do? You're going to have to wait, just like Reuss did, and prove to us you can pitch as a starter. Because I have six guys for five spots.'"

On June 27, Reuss became the third pitcher in Los Angeles history to pitch a no-hitter during an 8-0 victory at San Francisco. He retired 27 of 28 batters he faced—the only base runner allowed occurred on a throwing error by shortstop Bill Russell in the first inning. An interesting footnote to that game was the presence of Hall of Famer Sandy Koufax, a Dodger minor-league instructor who was in town for the series. Wearing a Dodger uniform, Koufax was among the players and coaches who mobbed Reuss on the pitcher's mound at Candlestick Park.

"The no-hitter may have brought Reuss a lot of attention, but he already was pitching like an ace," said former Dodger reliever Bobby Castillo, who appeared in 61 games in 1980. "I think once he got his confidence back, he was just like the Jerry Reuss, who was a big winner for the Pirates."

Things started to click for the Dodgers in the second half of 1980. A rookie pitcher named Fernando Valenzuela was promoted from Double-A San Antonio in September. He allowed no earned runs in 18 innings coming out of the bullpen.

During the final weekend of the 1980 regular season, the Dodgers trailed Houston by three games in the National League West and needed to sweep a series at home against the Astros to force a one-game playoff. With Reuss contributing a complete-game effort on Saturday, the Dodgers pulled off a string of emotional one-run victory margins by scores of 3-2, 2-1, and 4-3. But the momentum ended in the one-game playoff Monday afternoon, when Houston's Joe Niekro defeated Dave Goltz 7-1.

It was a bitter pill for Lasorda and the Dodgers, still in search of the organization's first World Series title since 1965. Sure, there were great players on the Los Angeles roster, but was this group going to disband without a championship?

"Tommy believed there was still talent and the guys still had enough left in their bodies to have one pretty good season," Reuss said. "There were three classes of players on the ballclub. The first class were the guys who came through the organization and played in the 1977 and 1978 World Series—even some who had played in the 1974 Series. So they had been there for a time and they were lifetime Dodgers, but they had yet to win a World Series. They realized that, after so many years, they weren't going to be around as a group much longer. So if there was ever a year to do it, this had to be the year.

"Then there was the second tier of ballplayers, and this included myself, Landreaux, and Johnstone, who had come from other organizations and had enjoyed some degree of success. But other than Johnstone, (none had) enjoyed playing on a World Series winner.

"The third group was a young group of players coming through the system that hadn't been in the big leagues for more than a year or two, and that included Steve Sax, Fernando Valenzuela, Mike Scioscia, Mike Marshall, and Tom Niedenfuer. These were the group of new players coming along, and that first group of players could definitely hear the footsteps, because they kept getting louder as the season progressed. So three different kinds of players and a strike-shortened season, you put it all into the mix and we came out on top."

Reuss was the Dodgers' scheduled Opening Day starter in 1981, but he pulled a hamstring muscle the previous afternoon while shagging flies during batting practice. Burt Hooton had an ingrown toenail, so Valenzuela made his first major-league start, pitching a 2-0 complete-game victory against Houston. It set the tone of the season for the Dodgers and Valenzuela, who would win both the National League Cy Young and Rookie of the Year Awards with a 13-7 record. Reuss went 10-4 with a career-low 2.29 ERA.

A 50-day players strike during the 1981 season split the schedule into halves. The Dodgers, clinging to a half-game lead over Cincinnati when the strike began on June 12, were declared champions of the "first half." That meant an automatic playoff berth when play resumed in August, though no one knew of this plan at the time of the work stoppage.

The Dodgers managed consecutive come-from-behind victories in five games over Houston in the Division Series and Montreal in the Championship Series. That meant the Dodgers would have another chance at their Fall Classic rivals, the New York Yankees. In 10 previous meetings between 1941 and 1978, the Dodgers had a 2-8 record.

THE GAME OF MY LIFE

By Jerry Reuss

I felt good physically when I made my first start for the Dodgers in the 1981 World Series against the New York Yankees. I pitched well in Montreal during the Championship Series against the Expos. I had one bad inning in Game 3 and gave up a three-run home run that was the difference in the ballgame as the Dodgers lost 4-1. But just like our comeback against the Astros in the Division Series, we roared back and defeated the Expos in Games 4 and 5 to capture the pennant.

The following night, we were in New York to open the World Series at Yankee Stadium. For whatever reason, I was hurrying my delivery. Maybe it was the adrenaline. It was my first time in a World Series, and looking back on it, I really didn't have time to get my feet wet. I was thrown into the water and got some pitches up. The Yankees were on everything. They got a ground ball here, a double down the first-base line, and before you knew it, a home run by Watson put them ahead 3-0 in the first inning. That was too big of a lead to catch up with as Guidry pitched a pretty good ballgame and the Yankees won 5-3. The Yankees also won Game 2 by a score of 3-0 behind the pitching of Tommy John and Goose Gossage, so we were on the ropes going back to Los Angeles.

In Game 3, Fernando struggled the whole night, but finished the game and beat the Yankees 5-4. It wasn't a masterpiece by any means, but it put us on the board, stopped the Yankees from taking a 3-0 lead, and pretty much led into the way things went on Saturday. The Yankees really played a lousy game with some defensive misplays, and didn't take advantage of certain situations with runners on base. Of course, we fell behind and the game was back and forth—a sloppy game. But the most important thing was that we won the game 8-7, so we were square at two games apiece.

After that ballgame, I knew a couple of things. One, they weren't going to play as sloppy on Sunday again because this was the World Series, and two, they were the Yankees and their personnel had just too much pride. Plus, they had Ron Guidry, their staff ace, pitching. I knew he was going to take control and it was going to be a tough ballgame. But I made some adjustments mentally. I had seen what it was like in the World Series, I knew how to turn things up a notch, and I was able to do it.

I don't even remember if I had a good night's sleep on the Saturday night before my Game 5 start. You know, I don't even know if I slept all winter—it was an adrenaline rush second to none. I had the same kind of routine every day that I pitched, especially at home: eat something, share a ride, and get to the ballpark. It might have been with Rick Monday, Burt Hooton, or Bill Russell. I can't remember, because my memories run together with the Houston playoff series, which was also on a weekend. But one of us drove and the wives drove in later. It was still a routine, but once you got to the ballpark, you could feel the electricity. This time, you could feel it once we got off the freeway and drove up the hill to Dodger Stadium. That electricity was unlike anything else I had ever felt going into Dodger Stadium.

The Yankees got on the scoreboard in the second inning. Reggie Jackson hit a leadoff double, went to third on an error, and scored on Lou Piniella's infield single. The Yanks still had runners on first and second with no outs, but Rick Cerone hit into a double play and Aurelio Rodriguez grounded out.

Guidry was really on his game, but I didn't focus on Ron's performance because it was something I couldn't control. To be quite honest, I thought Guidry out-pitched me in the seven innings he was out there. The exceptions were the two pitches he threw to Pedro Guerrero and Steve Yeager in the seventh, when they hit back-to-back solo home runs—the margin in a 2-1 victory. Ron had struck out nine batters in the first six innings and walked just a couple, so he was in command the whole ballgame. I was fortunate, working in and out of trouble, falling behind batters but making a pitch when I had to get out of it.

Trailing 1-0 at the time, I figured, "If I can hold the score right now, maybe something will happen." Guidry also bunted into a force play at home when he came to the plate in the fourth and the bases were loaded. Playing those National League rules in our ballpark without a designated hitter really helped out in that situation. One big hit by the Yankees really would've made a difference. So I got key outs behind me and key plays when I needed them.

Once that second home run was hit and I saw Steve run around the bases, I thought, "Now it's my game." I've looked at the ballgame on video, and could see after the seventh inning that I was a different pitcher out there. It was no longer a struggle. It was just locating the pitches and getting the outs to finish the game.

I knew Yeager was going to be in the game because Guidry, a left-hander, was pitching. But I worked well with both Dodger catchers, Scioscia and Yeager, that season. Steve and I worked well late in Game 5 because we both liked to work fast. One thing about Steve, he'd put down a finger with the sign and he was set up. Sometimes it was a little more deliberate with Mike. But at that point, with the adrenaline going through both of us, the feeling was, "Let's go! Let's get it going here and not waste any time."

Then things really changed when we got back to New York. We had a rainout and a day off, which was enough time to get Ron Cey back in the lineup after Goose Gossage struck him on the batting helmet in Game 5. Cey went on and had a pretty good ballgame in Game 6 as we wrapped up the World Series with a 9-2 victory. It was an entirely different attitude in Game 6 than it was in the first two games. The magic that the Yankees had for the first two games just wasn't there for the sixth game.

I had often wondered as a kid growing up just exactly what it would feel like to play in and win a World Series. And everybody who's ever picked up a ball or played in a schoolyard or on a field has pretended to be in a World Series. They could be whoever they wanted to be. And it was a dream—really a dream come true—to be out there.

Although Game 5 didn't win the World Series, there was a moment I'll never forget. It happened in the ninth inning with two outs and two strikes against Rodriguez, the last batter of the game. I actually stepped off the pitcher's mound, rubbed the ball up, and scanned the stands from left field all the way to right field at Dodger Stadium. I saw 56,000 people on their feet, standing and screaming. And I thought just for a moment, I wanted to enjoy it. And I did for about a second or two. Then I said, "Now it's time to go to work." I struck him out on a fastball, and that was it. But it was one of the few times I stepped back and tried to really appreciate the moment, drawing a line … from the time I was playing as a kid with my friends, growing up in St. Louis, to that very instant. Because that indeed was a reality—a dream come true. And until you can actually do it, you never really know what it's going to be like.

THE RESULTS

Jerry Reuss struck out six and scattered five hits in a 2-1 victory over the Yankees in Game 5 of the 1981 World Series in front of 56,115 fans at Dodger Stadium. Losing pitcher Ron Guidry scattered two hits in the first six innings and had retired 14 of 15 batters (permitting only a walk to Reuss in the fifth) until Pedro Guerrero and Steve Yeager hit consecutive home runs in the seventh inning. It was the Dodgers' third consecutive victory over the Yankees and gave Los Angeles a 3-2 lead as the World Series returned to New York for Game 6, which the Dodgers eventually won 9-2. Reuss went 1-1 with a 3.86 ERA against the Yankees in the 1981 Fall Classic, the only World Series appearance of his career.

PITCHING AND PICTURES

After his playing career, Reuss became an analyst for ESPN television from 1991-1993. He later coached in the minor leagues for the Montreal Expos and Chicago Cubs.

"Coaching was what I thought it would be and a lot more," he said. "I found out different organizations have different criteria. Some have low budgets and cut corners, others give you a lot of flexibility and freedom. There were some things I tried on a trial and error basis—ideas I believed would work. Plus, I was able to talk on a level with other major-league pitching coaches. Although it was difficult being away from home, it was valuable as far as putting something back into the game and trying to bring kids to the majors so their dreams could be the same as mine."

In 2006, Reuss joined the Dodger radio booth for selected road games. Paired with former teammate Rick Monday, Reuss also had a chance to witness firsthand the Dodgers' 25th anniversary celebration of the 1981 championship. One of the souvenirs was a two-sided 45 rpm record from "The Big Blue Wrecking Crew," the name given to a singing quartet including Reuss, Monday, Jay Johnstone, and Steve Yeager, who cut two commercial songs—"We Are the Champions" and "New York, New York." Though both known for their sense of humor, Monday and Reuss are true professionals on the air, describing the modern-day game while playing off differing perspectives as a former outfielder and pitcher, respectively.

"Broadcasting is still a teaching kind of setting, but you do it with a different format," Reuss said. "You're not addressing a player, you're not addressing a small group of players. What you're doing is educating and informing people, those fans who are listening on the radio, of just what's going on. I use my experience for what I see with pitching and how it reflects on the rest of the ballgame. And what was especially fun this past year was working with Rick."

During his travels on the road, Reuss carries a digital camera in his briefcase. Using the popular Adobe Photoshop computer program, Reuss has become both an artist and historian.

"Well, it started some years ago when fans would bring pictures up to me," he said. "I'd look at them and say, 'I like that' for some reason or 'I wouldn't like that' for another reason. There was something that was good or bad about it. And then when I started taking pictures while I was broadcasting with the Angels or ESPN, I'd try to incorporate scoreboard shots. I tried to put the scoreboard in the middle of the action, which in a lot of ballparks requires some imagination.

"With the scoreboard behind the action, it actually gives you a good point in time as to what was happening that day, not only in baseball, but … in the careers of those players. I look back on them right now and realize there were a lot of different uniforms and different ballparks. So on film, I was able to capture a moment in time and preserve a bit of history the way I saw it, through the lens."

The Dodgers promoted left-hander Eric Stults late in 2006 once the rosters were expanded to 40 players. After making his debut with three innings in relief on September 5 at Milwaukee, Stults was thrilled to meet Reuss in the clubhouse. Imagine Stults' surprise when Reuss told him he had taken a picture of the player's first major-league pitch.

"That was just so thoughtful," Stults said.

Reuss no doubt remembers the emotion he felt during his first pitch as a starter for the St. Louis Cardinals on September 27, 1969, against the Expos at Parc Jarry in Montreal. The Expos' leadoff hitter that afternoon was shortstop Gary Sutherland, who grounded out. Reuss pitched seven scoreless innings and won his debut 2-1.

"When I think of something that needs to be saved while I'm up in the booth, well, I take that picture," he said. "It's a point in time, and those players who are in that picture may never again be together in that situation. Who ever thinks to capture that on film and who ever thinks to ask for that? It's not the first time I've done it, more like the fourth or fifth time I've shot someone's first major league pitch. Now imagine it's after the season. That's a moment to cherish, especially because so few players ever reach that level. If you can preserve it, you have your own personal piece of history. Imagine what it would be like at Christmastime if you could give that to your mom and dad. That's special."

Reuss has two favorite baseball photos. One is displayed in the executive offices at the Dodgers' spring training complex in Vero Beach, Florida. The other photo doesn't exist—it's more of a composition of Reuss' childhood memories.

"As far as a Dodger picture, there was one taken around the batting cage in 1955 that included all the "Boys of Summer" in Brooklyn. It was just one of those moments in time and it captures them in their youth, the way a lot of people would remember them," he said. "I like pictures of old Sportsman's Park in St. Louis. It doesn't exist anymore, but it was the first major-league ballpark that I'd ever seen. Every time I see a depiction of Sportsman's Park, it takes me back to when I was a kid and that first time I went to the ballpark.

"I could hear the vendors selling the scorecards, smell the stale cigar smoke that has been encrusted into the cement along with the stale beer that has spilled over who knows how many people across the turnstiles. [I remember] walking up the ramp, getting to the top, feeling the warmth of the sunshine, seeing the greenest grass I've ever seen in one particular place, and those Cardinals uniforms in red and the whitest white uniforms you could ever imagine with that sea of green in the background. So when I think of Sportsman's Park, I think of the first time I was there."

Chapter 14

STEVE SAX

NAME:	Stephen Louis Sax
BORN:	January 29, 1960
BIRTHPLACE:	Sacramento, CA
YEARS WITH THE DODGERS:	1981-1988
POSITION:	Second Base
CAREER HIGHLIGHTS:	National League Rookie of the Year in 1982; five-time All-Star batted over .300 in three seasons, including career-high .332 in 1986; stole 444 career bases; member of two Dodger championship teams in 1981 and 1988; also played for Yankees, White Sox, and Athletics.
THE GAME:	October 20, 1988; World Series Game 5; Los Angeles Dodgers vs. Oakland Athletics at Oakland-Alameda County Coliseum

THE SPARKPLUG

When the Dodgers celebrated the 25th anniversary of their 1981 championship in 2006, the invited guests donned crisp, white home jerseys for both the press conference and pregame ceremonies on the field. Although some players may have gained a few pounds or lost some of their hair, the jerseys remained familiar sights: Steve Garvey (6), Steve

Yeager (7), Ron Cey (10), Dusty Baker (12), Davey Lopes (15), Bill Russell (18), Fernando Valenzuela (34), and Jerry Reuss (41), among others.

But Steve Sax emerged from the dugout wearing No. 52, a forgotten footnote in his brilliant career with Los Angeles. Sax donned the number for just two months following his surprise recall from Double-A San Antonio to replace an injured Davey Lopes. He wore No. 23 during his Rookie of the Year campaign in 1982 and No. 3 from 1983-1988 as he became a popular fan favorite.

The Dodgers didn't envision Sax as a second baseman when they drafted him in the ninth round of the June 1978 Free Agent Draft. The former Sacramento area prep star originally was a third baseman and shortstop converted to the outfield.

The Dodgers switched Sax to second base and paired him with shortstop Ross Jones, the club's No. 1 draft selection in 1980. Sax and Jones were dubbed the "double-play combination of the future." Jones didn't last long in the Dodger organization, but Sax's stock was on the rise.

"I went up pretty quickly," Sax said. "Part of it was timing, right place at the right time. I never really played second base for a full season until a year and a half before I got to the big leagues. Jack Perconte was at Triple-A, so I thought he was going to be the next Dodger second baseman—at least until I was ready. My short-term goal process was just to play well where I was playing. All the other stuff I really didn't have any control over. But I knew there were 29 other teams out there in case I couldn't play for the Dodgers. It's not just the team you're playing for, you have to think of those other teams that can use you, too."

At Double-A San Antonio in 1981, Sax won the Texas League batting title with a .346 average in 115 games. He stole 34 bases and struck out just 32 times in 536 plate appearances. After his promotion to Los Angeles on August 18, Sax batted .277 with two home runs, nine RBIs, and five stolen bases in 31 games.

"It was a perfect time for me," Sax said. "We were already going to be in the playoffs and the Dodgers felt their downside was not much. It was going to give Davey Lopes a chance to get healthy. Tommy Lasorda brought me into his office and told me, 'I have to play Davey Lopes in the playoffs. You've proven yourself in the month and a half that you've been here.' But he was going to play Lopes in the playoffs because he was a veteran, and I respected his decision."

Steve Sax celebrates scoring a run during Game 7 of the 1988 National League Championship Series against the New York Mets.

Sax barely appeared in the postseason (four games and just one at-bat) as veteran Derrel Thomas served as the backup infielder during the three rounds against the Astros, Expos, and Yankees.

Three months after defeating the Yankees in the World Series, the Dodgers broke up the longest-running infield in major-league history by sending Lopes to the Oakland Athletics in exchange for two minor leaguers. Lopes, first baseman Steve Garvey, shortstop Bill Russell, and third baseman Ron Cey had spent a record 8½ seasons together since June 1973.

"Our infield with Davey, Garv, and Cey had a good run together, but nothing lasts forever in baseball," Russell said. "It was important for us to win a championship as a unit, and thank goodness we finally beat the Yankees. The Dodgers always had good players in the minor-league system, and Saxie was one of the top prospects."

Sax made sure he was prepared for his big chance. He spent the winter working out at the Nautilus Club, skipping rope, hitting a punching bag, and throwing a tennis ball against a wall, followed by afternoon batting practice.

"Pete Rose is my idol," Sax said upon his arrival to Los Angeles in 1981. "I've patterned my style after him. I'm a very aggressive player and try to give 100 percent all the time. I try to force mistakes, make things happen. This game is a year-round profession for me. I try to improve myself as a player in the off-season. I work out eight hours a day, Monday through Friday."

In 1982, Sax batted .282 with four home runs, 47 RBIs, and 49 stolen bases to edge fellow second baseman Johnny Ray of the Pirates for the Rookie of the Year Award. He was the fourth consecutive Dodger so honored, joining pitchers Rick Sutcliffe (1979), Steve Howe (1980), and Fernando Valenzuela (1981).

But the afterglow of Sax's Rookie of the Year campaign disappeared quickly in his sophomore season in 1983. He suffered through the pain of a mysterious throwing affliction, which had ended the careers of such pitchers as the Pirates' Steve Blass, a 1971 World Series hero, and Brooklyn Dodger pitcher Rex Barney, who pitched a no-hitter in 1948 at the age of 23 and was out of the majors by 1950.

Sax's nightmare began early in 1983 when he suddenly couldn't make a routine throw to first base. On April 6, Sax took a relay throw from the outfield and threw the ball past the catcher. By the All-Star break, Sax had committed 24 errors.

And when a player reveals a vulnerable side, opposing fans are ready to pounce. While the Dodgers were on the road, people held up signs with a red bull's-eye. Even some Phillies players pretended to duck in their dugout when Sax made a throw to first base.

During the 25th anniversary reunion at Dodger Stadium in 2006, manager Tom Lasorda told the story about converted outfielder Pedro Guerrero, who felt hesitant about playing third base.

"Pedro said, 'Please Lord, don't let them hit the ball to me.' Then Pedro thought about it and added, 'And please don't let them hit it to Saxie!'"

It was the first of many Lasorda stories that afternoon. Standing with his teammates at the podium, Sax broke into a grin with his teammates. But it wasn't so funny at the time, especially with his career at the crossroads at age 23.

"I was the most insecure person at the ballpark," Sax said. "I would pray, 'Please don't hit me the ball.' I went through all the steps. First, I was in denial. Then, I was ashamed; I hated myself. Then, I admitted I had a problem. Finally, I got mad. I got really angry. I thought, 'I'm just going to bite this thing in the face.'"

Sax conquered his throwing problems. He also enjoyed a brief chance to play on the same team with his older brother, Dave Sax, a reserve catcher who played a combined nine games with the Dodgers in 1982-1983.

The Dodgers returned to the playoffs in 1983 and 1985, but lost each time in the National League Championship Series. The framework of the team began to change as the Dodgers finished with losing records in consecutive seasons in 1986 and 1987. During his first winter as general manager, Fred Claire planned his 1988 overhaul around free agent outfielder Kirk Gibson, the former Michigan State football star who became the fiery leader of the Detroit Tigers. The return of good times in Los Angeles was just around the corner.

THE GAME OF MY LIFE

By Steve Sax

The most memorable game of my career was Game 5 of the 1988 World Series against the Athletics in Oakland. But what stands out the most is what happened about five minutes after the game. When Orel

Hershiser struck out Tony Phillips to end the World Series, I was just so relieved that this was over. In the middle of the celebration, I stepped into a little room off to the side in the clubhouse. When I took my uniform off, I was so exhausted that I really could've gone to sleep there right there, even as people were yelling in the background and celebrating the championship.

You don't really remember the initial moments of something like that. I think everyone else was in shock just like we were. I put my uniform in a plastic bag, because I had been in the World Series before and knew it was going to be soaked with champagne and alcohol and whatever else was in there. So I wanted to keep the uniform for posterity and put it away. I went in the little room and sat there by myself for five minutes and reflected on everything. I just thought, "We're on the top of the world right now."

Looking back, I don't think anyone could've expected what happened in 1988. When the Dodgers signed Gibson as a free agent during the winter, I thought, "Way to go!" We could definitely use a person with a strong personality like that, a no-nonsense type of demeanor, someone who was going to be all business in the clubhouse and an excellent player in his own right. He had a lot of punch in the lineup, a lot of speed, and all those things worked just right for us, because he was the element that was missing on our team.

Kirk Gibson brought another level of intensity. He pretty much galvanized the team with that kind of a no-nonsense mentality. He led by example. He played lots of times when he was hurt. He never complained about anything. And that's what a leader does. He voiced his opinion now and then in the clubhouse, but not as much as people might think. He wasn't a clubhouse lawyer who would give a lot of lip service. He was a guy who went out and played when he was hurt and was a very humbling type of a person. To some, he was also an intimidating type of person who was like, "I'm doing this, so you'd all better get your butts in gear, too." So that's what we needed on that team.

Kirk was the National League's Most Valuable Player that season, and Hershiser won the Cy Young Award. Orel led the staff with 23 victories and ended the regular season with 59 consecutive scoreless innings, which broke the previous record of 58⅔ innings set by Don Drysdale in 1968. The Dodgers were back in first place that summer, and good pitching was the reason we kept winning. If you look at the talent around the league, people didn't pick us to finish higher than fourth place in our division.

But one thing we had was an excellent team and great pitching. We played together well and played great pitching. That's what Orel Hershiser brought that year. He brought command on the mound and he was the leader of all the pitchers. Look at the year he had—he broke Drysdale's record. When you have great pitching, it can supersede any boundaries you might have.

During Orel's streak, it was natural for people to ask about playing defense behind him. My throwing problems were behind me, but fans might ask of any infielder, "Do you suddenly get defensive and not want to make a mistake to ruin a pitcher's no-hitter, or in Orel's case, a scoreless streak?" No.

My thoughts were, "Please hit it to me, you are going to be out!" That's what I was so glad about, and what made me a better person and a better player was that I had the confidence and knew I could overcome anything. That's why, if there were runners on second and third with two outs, I thought, "Please hit me this ball, because the game is going to be over."

We won the National League West title by seven games over the Cincinnati Reds. In the playoffs against the Mets, I thought everything needed to go right for us if we were going to have a chance to win. I thought the Mets were a better team than the A's, they had a lot more firepower. They had a better pitching staff. We beat the A's in five games, and it took us seven games to beat the Mets. The Mets were loaded with talent and they beat us 10 of 11 times during the regular season. But Mike Scioscia hit a key home run in the ninth inning in Game 4 against Dwight Gooden. Gregg Jefferies was killing us during the year, but in the playoffs, we subdued him a bit and he made a big error at third base that helped us win a game.

The final Game 7 at Dodger Stadium was unbelievable. I thought if we could beat the mighty Mets in the playoffs, then we had a really good chance to win the whole thing in the World Series. It was great to be an underdog the whole way. When you're an underdog, the pressure is on the other team. And I felt there was something magical about our team, because we weren't supposed to win yet we came back and beat the Mets in the playoffs. I felt that once we got to the World Series, the streak was not going to stop there because we had great pitching and our team was really playing together.

What happened then is one of the most famous World Series moments in history. It almost doesn't seem real when you talk about it—ninth inning, down by one run with two outs when Lasorda calls on Gibson to be a pinch hitter. Kirk didn't start because of knee and hamstring problems. Then he's supposed to come off the bench and face their best pitcher, reliever Dennis Eckersley, with the game on the line. The count goes full and then Kirk hits a couple foul balls.

I'm on deck when he hit the home run. I was quite perturbed about it when it happened, because he stole my thunder. No, seriously, I wasn't thinking about Gibson too much. I was thinking, "We have Mike Davis on second base, why aren't they walking Gibson?" I thought they might be able to work me because Eckersley is a right-handed pitcher. I know it would be the go-ahead run, but it might be easier to take their chance with me. So I'm not thinking about Kirk hitting a home run. I'm wondering how I'm going to get a hit off Eckersley and tie the game.

But the A's pitched to him instead. When he hit the ball, I thought, "This is unbelievable." I knew the ball was going to be out once he hit it. He was actually fooled on his swing. He hit the ball at the end of his swing and he caught the ball on the sweet spot of the bat. It was amazing to see Kirk limp around the bases. I was also thinking, "Don't let this storybook ending interfere with Gibson coming to home plate." If you look at the tape, you can see me pushing people away. You know, there's a rule that says if you interfere with a player before he gets to home plate, he technically can be called out. So I didn't want anything like that to happen. So I was saying, "Get away, get away, don't touch him, let him score … and then we'll kick his ass!"

Gibson didn't play again that Series because of his injuries. But we didn't suffer a letdown. Nobody is better at motivating than Tommy Lasorda—that's why he's in the Hall of Fame. It's that personal touch he has with the players on his team, even if they are from different parts of the world and from all walks of life. To be together for eight months out of the year and to keep everybody happy, nobody does it better than Tommy. He's a tremendous motivator. If you need to be motivated, he's the guy to do it.

Just because we were ahead 1-0, we never let ourselves become too confident or overconfident. I felt we were going to win it the whole way, and during the entire Series, I was cautiously optimistic that we were going to beat those guys, because we had great pitching. We really didn't have any pressure on us and we had nothing to lose. We were the small guy in the fight. We were just going to go out and play. Things were going right, we were taking the extra bases. Mickey Hatcher hit a home run when Mike Marshall couldn't play. We were stealing on 3-2 counts and preventing double plays, making good, solid defensive plays. We were getting strikeouts and double plays on defense when we needed them. John Shelby made those great plays in the playoffs against the Mets before the World Series. So everything kept going for us, we had the momentum, and the A's caught us at a bad time.

THE RESULTS

The underdog Dodgers defeated the Athletics in five games to win the 1988 World Series. Kirk Gibson's pinch-hit home run in the bottom of the ninth inning in Game 1 gave Los Angeles a 5-4 victory and set the tone for the Series. Orel Hershiser blanked Oakland 6-0 in the second game. Oakland notched a 2-1 victory in Game 3 when Mark McGwire hit a walk-off home run against reliever Jay Howell in the bottom of the ninth. But the Dodgers wrapped up the sixth championship in franchise history with a 4-3 victory in Game 4 and a 5-2 decision in Game 5. Hershiser was voted the Series MVP. Sax batted .300 in the World Series (6-for-20).

THROWING CAUTION
TO THE WIND

Sax's decision to preserve his Dodger uniform in a plastic bag carried additional meaning when he left Los Angeles, switching coasts after signing with the New York Yankees as a free agent. Those who predicted the California native would melt under the Big Apple spotlight didn't consider Sax's mental toughness. Replacing the popular Willie Randolph at second base for the Bronx Bombers, Sax batted .315 with the Yankees in 1989 and led the American League in fielding percentage.

"I loved playing for the Yankees," Sax said. "I had a great time. I think moving on to New York was the best thing I did in my career. Although I never wanted to leave the Dodgers, it was the right move for me. My career did come full circle, and I think people there had regard for my glove as well as my bat. I led the league in fielding percentage two of the three years, and the other year I was second. I should've won the Gold Glove. Some of the insiders later told me I lost the Gold Glove balloting by one vote. But nonetheless, the numbers don't lie. People can always see the numbers and see that I was a complete player. So I was glad to go for those reasons and maybe I had to be in New York to get that acclaim. It was worth it for me there and I made a lot of money in New York, which is great, I still have a lot of good friendships in New York, and I still have an apartment in Manhattan. If things went right, I would've stayed with the Dodgers. But for some reason, it wasn't supposed to go right. So I left for New York."

Sax retired from baseball after the 1994 season. Instead of pursuing a coaching job, he ventured into other arenas. In 1995, he considered running for public office as a California assemblyman representing a six-county area northeast of Sacramento. Later, he was a network analyst for FOX television.

"I wouldn't have traded anything for my baseball career," Sax said. "It's opened up every door in my whole life. I have a lot of great friendships from the Dodgers. When people ask if I want to be remembered as a Yankee or a Dodger, I'll always be part of the Dodgers because they were the team that I came up with—I had the most success with the Dodgers.

"But now that I'm retired … I've been into martial arts since I've been in my 20s, so I've always liked to do that, and I had a studio for a while with a friend. It was just something fun to do on the side. Then I thought about running for State Assembly and going into politics. So I set up an exploratory committee, but I discovered it wasn't something I was really yearning to do and decided not to run. I still have people ask me, 'Did you run for Congress or Assembly?' No, I never did run, I was just strongly thinking about it, but I wouldn't do it. As far as the commentating, I had to opportunity to join Fox to pick up for Steve Lyons, who wound up being an anchor. It was only suppose to be a week, but I ended up staying for three years. I really enjoyed it. But when they changed their programming from baseball to NASCAR racing, I thought, 'I really don't want to do that because I don't know anything about racing cars.'"

Sax is currently vice president/Private Client Group at RBC Dain Rauscher in Roseville, California. RBC Dain Rauscher is a wholly owned subsidiary of Royal Bank of Canada, one of the nation's largest full-service security firms with more than 1,650 financial consultants and 5,000 employees. The Private Client Group provides financial advice on stocks, bonds, mutual funds, and other financial products.

"When I was playing baseball, I knew that someday I wanted to be in the field that I am in now, which is business," he said. "I love the way the stock market works. I've been involved in the market since I was 21 years old. I've loved it ever since, and I knew when I was out of the game and the time was right that I was going to go back to my studies, get my licenses, and join a firm. And I'm as passionate about my work, being a stockbroker and financial advisor, as I was about playing baseball. I feel like I've never had a job. I think the baseball career was really the ultimate amount of fun and I really enjoyed the broadcasting. I'll be doing what I'm doing 20 years from now."

Sax, whose parents influenced his attitude toward money during his youth, now feels a paternal need to advise today's modern-day athlete in an era of ever-increasing sports salaries. The biggest heartbreak is to see big names end their careers without a solid financial base.

"Four percent of all athletes that were millionaires as players are millionaires when they retire," he said. "Only four percent. I really believe if I could sit down with 100 athletes, I could get 80 of them as clients and change every one of their lives. It's just a matter of getting past the bad influences in their lives, the loyalty that they'll have to some people for whatever reason. A lot of times they get together with these guys who have no licenses, they aren't bonded. They don't have any idea of what they're doing, that's why their clients lose all their money. That's just horrible.

"I'm lucky to say I'm one of the four percent, because I've had the same ethics, the same basic plan as I had when I was a minor-league baseball player. I've been on a budget my whole life and I don't go past my means. My dad was a guy who never had a lot of money, but for the amount of money he had, he made it work. My brother, my sisters, and I all worked. Before baseball, I've had jobs since I was 10 years old. I was buying my own clothes in the sixth grade. My parents made me understand what a buck was worth."

Chapter 15

JAIME JARRIN

NAME:	Jaime Jarrin
BORN:	December 10, 1935
BIRTHPLACE:	Cayambe, Ecuador
YEARS WITH THE DODGERS:	1959-Present
POSITION:	Broadcaster
CAREER HIGHLIGHTS:	Inducted into the Baseball Hall of Fame in 1998; named baseball's all-time best Spanish-language broadcaster in 2005 book *Voices of Summer* by broadcasting historian Curt Smith; selected as one of the top 100 Influential Hispanics in the United States by *Hispanic Business Magazine*; was in charge of all Spanish radio coverage and production for the 1984 Olympics in Los Angeles; received the highest medal awarded to a non-military personnel in his native Ecuador in1992.
THE GAME:	July 10, 1990; All-Star Game at Wrigley Field, Chicago

A FATEFUL MOVE

Jaime Jarrin arrived in the United States on June 24, 1955, the same day left-handed pitcher Sandy Koufax made his major-league debut for the Brooklyn Dodgers. Both Jarrin and Koufax were 19-year-old rookies in their respective vocations and nobody could have predicted their paths would someday cross both in Los Angeles and Cooperstown.

Baseball didn't top Jarrin's list of interests when he emigrated from his native Ecuador to Southern California to become the director of news and sports at Spanish language radio station KWKW. He called boxing matches every Thursday night at the Olympic Auditorium. But the other sport piqued his interest as fans crowded around television sets for a World Series between the Brooklyn Dodgers and New York Yankees.

"I didn't know much about baseball," Jarrin said. "I got involved after watching so many people following the 1955 World Series. They were gathered around the television sets and I said, 'That must be a great game.' I visited Wrigley Field and Gilmore Field to watch the Los Angeles Angels and the Hollywood Stars of the Pacific Coast League. I had always been to Triple-A games, but I never thought I'd eventually be working baseball games."

The Dodgers won the 1955 World Series, but it would be a bittersweet moment for Brooklyn. Without a new ballpark to replace an aging Ebbets Field, team president Walter O'Malley finally moved the franchise to the West Coast following the 1957 season. The Dodgers brought along their English language broadcasting team of Vin Scully and Jerry Doggett, but the new landscape in Los Angeles also meant serving the Spanish population.

From 1954-1957, the Dodgers broadcasted select games at Ebbets Field in Spanish with Buck Canel behind the microphone on WHOM in New York. A native of Argentina, Canel began broadcasting the first of 42 World Series for NBC in Spanish in 1937 and eventually became the first Spanish broadcaster named to the Baseball Hall of Fame.

"One day, Mr. William Beaton, the station manager, called all the employees to his office and shared the great news that he had signed a contract to do the Dodger games in Spanish," Jarrin said. "Looking at me, he said, 'Jaime, I want you to be one of our two announcers.' Then he asked everybody, 'Do you know anyone who can broadcast professional baseball?' An employee by the name of Alex Prada, who used to do news at the station, said he knew of someone who could do

Jaime Jarrin and Vin Scully developed into cornerstones of the Dodger franchise during their respective Hall of Fame careers.

baseball—Rene Cardenas. Mr. Beaton asked him to arrange an audition with Cardenas here at the station.

"In a few days, Rene was there in the studio in Pasadena. Mr. Beaton asked if I would be there too, in the control room, to listen to see if he could really do baseball. He did a couple innings of re-creation and he sounded very professional. He hired Rene and asked if I would join him. I was just there on Sundays to watch the games and I told Mr. Beaton that I didn't think I was ready to be in front of the microphone. He liked me very much and I was only 19 years old. He said, 'Jaime, I want you doing baseball, so I'm going to give you one year to prepare yourself. I want you to be there with Rene in 1959 at the Coliseum.' In my first year there, the Dodgers won the World Series against the White Sox."

Cardenas was born in Managua, Nicaragua, and began his radio career calling boxing matches and basketball games throughout Latin America. He moved to Los Angeles in 1951. Cardenas spent the 1958 season at the Coliseum with a disc jockey named Milt Nava, who didn't know anything about baseball. Neither did Cardenas' next partner in 1959— but he had potential.

"I would say it took me the end of the first year to feel a little comfortable," Jarrin said. "I was very nervous in the beginning. Rene kept asking, 'Do you want to come in?' And I'd say, 'Wait, wait.' Then finally it was in September when I started doing one inning. And that was the start of my love with baseball.

"Another thing that helped was that we didn't travel during the first six or eight years. We re-created the games in the studio, listening to Vin Scully and Jerry Doggett. We had a special line installed from the studios to the ballpark while the Dodgers were on the road. We had to translate. That forced me to really go deep into the game and study a lot and read a lot and do my homework. We had to fill so much time. If Vin started to give one of his beautiful anecdotes, it was very tough for us to translate everything he was saying. We had to have enough material to cover that. Otherwise, we were right on time … strike, strike, foul ball … a single, we were right there. But if it was a difficult play, a triple for example, you had to wait until the end of the play. So the fact we re-created, it forced me to study more of the game. That's how I fell in love with baseball."

Jarrin and Cardenas worked together for three seasons until 1961 when Cardenas left for a job in Houston. Jarrin teamed with Jose "Fats" Garcia (1962-1972) and Rudy Hoyos (1973-1981) before reuniting with Cardenas from 1982-1994.

"In the beginning, I thought I'd do it for seven or eight years and go on to something else," Jarrin said. "But I've loved the game since the first day and the Dodgers have been great with me. My favorite player in the beginning was Willie Davis. He took me under his wing. He would take me out to lunch. He knew I was very young and I was just starting. He was very nice to me, and I'll always remember that."

For decades, KWKW played various forms of Spanish-language music. By 2004, the station stopped playing music and began all-sports programming in alliance with ESPN Deportes, a brand of the ESPN sports empire. Today, KWKW broadcasts the Dodgers, Lakers basketball, and Avengers arena football in Spanish.

"The Latinos are very sports-minded people," Jarrin said. "It started at the Coliseum and then the first year at Dodger Stadium. They made some studies, and I understand from six to eight percent of all the attendance were Hispanics. When KWKW started doing the games in Spanish, I think that helped to spread the love of baseball among Latinos. And that's why year after year the percentage of Hispanics attending ballgames goes up bigger and bigger. So now it's up to 42 to 46 percent. We became very well known because also every year the Dodgers would assign me and someone else to take the highlight film for the year and visit clubs and organizations, and we would do 25 to 30 presentations. They showed the highlights of the year and talked about baseball and we asked one or two players to come along. So we expanded the love of the game by the Hispanics and we are seeing the results now."

The Dodgers purchased the contract of left-hander Fernando Valenzuela from the Mexican League on July 6, 1979, just two months before the death of O'Malley, who became Chairman of the Board in 1970 when his son, Peter, became the team president. According to Jarrin, Walter O'Malley had always dreamed of "a Mexican Sandy Koufax"—someone to tap into the hearts of the Spanish population.

Valenzuela enjoyed moderate success in Single-A Lodi, but his career skyrocketed after his time with the Arizona Instructional League in 1979. General manager Al Campanis sent Dodger reliever Bobby Castillo to Arizona to teach Valenzuela a third pitch—the screwball. With long fingers and flexibility in his wrist, Valenzuela immediately mastered it.

At Double-A San Antonio in 1980, Valenzuela started 5-9, but he won eight straight decisions and didn't allow a run in his final 35 innings. He joined the Dodgers on September 10.

"Everybody believes the Fernandomania started in 1981," Jarrin said. "I think it really started in 1980. He came to the Dodgers just like any other pitcher. He was a reliever who had a great season at San Antonio. He wasn't used right away. It wasn't until we got to Atlanta that Fernando got into a game. The first batter he faced was Bruce Benedict, a catcher who hit a fly to center field."

Valenzuela went 2-0 with a 0.00 ERA and one save in 10 games and 18 innings, which included some clutch performances down the stretch as the Dodgers swept Houston in a weekend series at Dodger Stadium to force a one-game playoff for the National League West title. The Dodgers lost the playoff game 7-1 as veteran Dave Goltz took the loss. Years later, fans wonder what the results would have been had Valenzuela started the game.

"Fernandomania started with the last series of the regular season against the Houston Astros when he came into the game in front of 50,000 people," Jarrin said. "Relieve and win, relieve and win. Some people believe Fernando should've started that playoff game on Monday, but I understand (manager Tommy) Lasorda's position, and he did the right thing. It probably would've been too much to ask of a rookie who has never started a game to start the deciding game of the year. He came into relief in the seventh inning, but by then, it was too late. And Joe Niekro was pitching beautifully. But that's when people started to first notice Fernando and love him, during the series. When he came from the bullpen, the people went wild."

In 1981, Jerry Reuss was scheduled to pitch Opening Day at Dodger Stadium, but he pulled a hamstring muscle the previous afternoon while shagging flies in the outfield during batting practice. The Dodgers' next choice, Burt Hooton, couldn't pitch because of an ingrown toenail. That left Valenzuela, who was told to stop pitching batting practice—he was next day's starter.

Valenzuela pitched a 2-0 complete-game shutout against the Astros. In the next few weeks, the 20-year-old became an international sensation. He remains the only pitcher in the last 60 years to open his major-league career with eight victories in his first eight starts.

"At first, we thought he was lucky," said Jack Clark, the San Francisco Giants' cleanup hitter during Valenzuela's rookie season. "Then you found out real quick that not only was he good, he was great and going to be there for a long time. I don't think I've figured out even to this day any kind of pattern or approach of Fernando. He was just difficult. He hid the ball and was sneaky fast with pinpoint control. Fernando was one of those guys who didn't throw that hard. He didn't try to strike everyone out, although he could if he probably wanted to. He was special."

Valenzuela compiled five shutouts by mid-May and was the starting pitcher for the National League at the All-Star Game in Cleveland. Jarrin served as Valenzuela's interpreter everywhere, from the crowded postgame frenzy of the Dodger dressing rooms in April and May to a regal White House reception in Washington, D.C. hosted by President Ronald Reagan.

"I don't know if Fernando really realized what was going on," Jarrin said. "But at the same time, I think he was aware of everything. He was so smart."

A 50-day strike by the Major League Players Association interrupted the season, but it may have been a blessing in disguise for Valenzuela in terms of rest. After pitching 87 of a possible 91 innings in his first 10 starts, Valenzuela failed to get out of the fourth inning in two of his next three starts. His record was 9-4 with a 2.45 ERA when the strike began on June 12. Play resumed in early August and Valenzuela went 13-7 with a 2.48 ERA overall, including a league-leading 11 complete games, eight shutouts, and 180 strikeouts.

By October, the Dodgers were world champions and Valenzuela became the only pitcher to win both the Rookie of the Year and Cy Young Awards in the same season.

"The 1981 season is a very special chapter for me because I was with Fernando all the time," Jarrin said. "(Executive vice president) Fred Claire asked me to be with him because he couldn't speak the language very well. (Infielder) Pepe Frias was also asked to help for the first two games, along with Manny Mota, but Fred thought it was too much to ask players and coaches to help him. And since I was with the team everywhere, I told Fred, 'No problem.' So I would get ready to go down in the eighth inning to help him.

"By then I was very well known in Los Angeles because of my years with the Dodgers and my years with KWKW, especially the events such as news, special events, the funeral for Kennedy, conferences with presidents. I became very well known, but only here. Nobody knew about Jaime Jarrin in Philadelphia or New York. But thanks to Fernando, I was becoming a well-known person everywhere. But we will never see another year like that."

During the Dodgers' 25th anniversary of the 1981 championship in 2006, players and coaches recalled that traveling with Valenzuela made them feel as if they were part of a rock star's entourage. They thought Montreal would be quiet in early May compared to a frenzied reception in New York, but Valenzuela's face was on the cover of the French language newspapers upon the team's arrival to Canada.

"Even if we signed Alex Rodriguez or Manny Ramirez, nobody would bring that charisma and drama that Fernando brought," Jarrin said. "Several elements led to all this. When he came to the Dodgers, he was only 19 years old. He was a little chubby, had long hair, didn't speak any

English, and his features were very unique. He was built a little like Babe Ruth, wide shoulders and skinny legs. Everything played a big part in what happened in 1981. I went through the years of Sandy Koufax pitching no-hitters and a perfect game and the scoreless innings streaks by Don Drysdale and Orel Hershiser. Nothing compares with Fernando.

"Not only was it a sports event, it was a social awakening for the Hispanics in the United States. Everybody tried to learn some Spanish. Everybody tried to master the language. Agencies tried to hire bilingual people. What Fernando did for the Hispanics no diplomat or a president could do. He really played a huge part not only in Southern California, but everywhere we went—Chicago, Montreal, New York. People came to the ballpark and all the entrances to the stadium were crowded like they were going to the Our Lady of Guadalupe Procession. It was a great year, and it put me on a different pedestal. People suddenly knew about Jaime Jarrin, and that was probably the biggest reason why I was chosen to go into the Hall of Fame."

THE GAME OF MY LIFE

By Jaime Jarrin

I was involved in a very bad traffic accident on March 24, 1990. Because of a labor dispute between the owners and players, spring training started very late. Usually by that time we've played 15 to 20 games in Florida. But in 1990, we played the first game on March 24. The game was in Orlando. I did the game and drove back to Dodgertown in Vero Beach. On the night of March 24, I was having dinner with my engineer, Ken Johnson, and a couple writers. The maitre d' came to the table and said I had a phone call. It was an advertising agency asking, "Jaime, do you have recording facilities there? Because we need right away a spot."

I told them, "If it's something simple, I will be able to do it because we have a small recording studio here. But if it requires a big production, I won't be able to do it."

They said, "No, it's only a 15-second tag for some commercial."

So I said fine. They needed it right away and needed to know I could do it that night because they were sending a messenger from Miami, which was two hours away. It was only 8:30 p.m., so if the messenger arrived at 10, I would have the spot ready. I went back to the dinner table and asked Ken if he could help me record the commercial. He said no problem, so we finished our meal. When we went to the studio, we couldn't find a tape. Ken said, "Jaime, please go and buy a tape." It was almost nine o'clock, so I hurried into town. I went to the only mall that was there in those years. I went to the Vero Beach mall, but I couldn't find a tape. But somebody told me about a Radio Shack store a few blocks away.

I left the parking lot and went onto the U.S. 1 Highway. I went into the intersection and was going to make a left-hand turn. The light was green for me. I had to wait a few seconds because 10 to 12 cars were going in the other direction. I waited until the last car went by. I still had the light and I saw no more cars coming by. It was 9:20. I proceeded to make my left turn.

But immediately I heard a commotion and everything went black. There was a tremendous noise and my first thought was that I had been hit by a train. But I thought, "No, there are no tracks here." I had been hit by a young fellow who was driving a pretty heavy pickup truck. He hit me almost head on and the impact drove me about 100 feet away.

It was a very bad accident and I was in the Indian River Hospital for nearly four months. I had all internal injuries. No broken bones, but I lost a spleen, I lost my gallbladder, my left lung collapsed, and the organ that nearly killed me was the liver, which was leaking. The doctors couldn't see that for the first three weeks. At the point where I thought I was going to leave the hospital, I became very, very ill and they had to take me down for a second surgery because of the leaking fluids from the liver.

And I was really in bad shape. I know the doctors called the Dodgers' owner, Peter O'Malley, and said I had probably only an eight percent chance of surviving the second operation. At that moment, it was Easter Sunday and I had the worst day of my life. I thought I was going to die— I was so weak, everything was aching. I couldn't open my eyes. Everything was in pain. My doctor had gone to Chicago for a convention on that Friday. I was left alone that weekend and my doctor's partner came to see me on Saturday. I said, "Doctor, something is wrong because my stomach is expanding a lot. I feel so bad. So bad." The pain was so strong. The doctor didn't pay attention to me.

But then my physician, Dr. Beckham, came back from Chicago and he saw me at five o'clock in the morning on Monday. I don't know why he came that early, but I had a feeling I had to go to the hospital. As soon as he saw me, I could see that he was really scared. Right away, he picked up the phone and called everyone for surgery. He said, "We can't wait, we can't wait!" When I had the accident, I weighed 165 pounds. My weight was now down to 120 pounds, and the way the doctors looked at me, I knew I was in trouble. They took me to the second surgery and the rehab was so painful, so bad. I suffered so much because of the morphine. My mouth was in such bad shape I couldn't touch anything. For several weeks, the only thing I could eat was a spoon of crushed ice with the promise that when it turned to liquid, I would spit it out because I couldn't swallow anything. And I was fully aware of my condition.

During the first few days at the hospital, I had only been concerned about my voice. Suddenly, I was just trying to stay alive. I have always been blessed with a good voice, a deep voice. After my accident and collapsed lung, I was afraid that I might not be able to announce again. There was no problem talking, but the volume was so low and the sound was so bad that I was afraid. Then I tried to watch some baseball games on TV, but I couldn't because I was so tired after 15 seconds. I just couldn't watch. In the beginning of my rehabilitation, I was conscious of the lung and my voice since I live for talking—I was very afraid. That's why I chose my first game back as my most important game, because of the surgeries and all the complications that I had, I didn't know that I was going to live.

By then, the people of the Indian River Hospital were so great. They couldn't move me to Los Angeles or to a larger facility like the Huntington Hospital in Pasadena. The Dodgers' team physician, Dr. Frank Jobe, didn't give me the OK to be moved. That also became a psychological problem. I saw that I was staying at the hospital and I couldn't leave. My friends said, "This is too small, you need to be in a big hospital." But they couldn't move me. All that played a big part in my thinking.

During this time, the O'Malleys were so great. So was my wife, Blanca. I was in intensive care for seven weeks and she couldn't be with me all the time. She was only allowed to be in my room four or five minutes every hour. So she would spend 55 minutes of every hour in the lobby of the hospital. She paid such a huge price. It was really unbelievable. I was in the room with the doctors and nurses and Blanca had to stay alone. Of course, some people saw her and they became friends. The O'Malleys assigned a car with a chauffer for Blanca because she was the only one in the Vero Beach camp. Everyone else went back to Los Angeles. She was so scared at night. Finally she told me (former Dodger catcher and minor-league instructor) Johnny Roseboro came to Dodgertown and they assigned him to the room next to hers. He said, "If you need anything, just knock on the wall and I will help you in any way." But Blanca had a terrible time for three months because she had to stay there.

One time I asked the doctor how much longer I was going to stay there. He said, "Jaime, I'm afraid at least three more weeks." Three more weeks? No way.

That was in the middle of June and I said, "I can't. I can't." I called Blanca and said, "I can't stay here three more weeks. I'm going to die here."

So Blanca called Dr. Jobe. He said, "Stay there. I don't want him traveling because it could be bad for him and a setback could be fatal. So tell him 10 more days."

My doctor originally predicted another three weeks, but after speaking with Dr. Jobe, he said, "Jaime, in 10 days, I want to see you walking out of the hospital." That really brightened my thinking. After that, those 10 days went by fast and I was OK and I came home. The last week of my stay at the hospital, I was feeling much better. It's unbelievable. Back home in Los Angeles, I was very weak. My voice was coming back, but still I didn't know when I was going to be able to work. Everything was getting better.

Before the accident, I had made my commitment to do the All-Star Game for CBS Radio at Wrigley Field in Chicago. The CBS people called and asked if I would be ready. I said, "I know I'm going to be ready!" I told myself, "I have to do it, I have to do it …" I flew to Chicago and I knew Vin Scully was doing the game in English for CBS Radio. I had lots of problems going up to the booth in Chicago because I still had tremendous pain in my chest. My voice was OK, but I couldn't breathe very well, and there were no elevators at the ballpark, just a lot of stairs ascending to the press box.

The first thing that really made me feel great was seeing Vin there. We have been such good friends over the years, and he was so nice to me at Wrigley Field. We took a picture there and that really set the tone for everything. I don't have enough words to describe how great he has been with me over the years. During the baseball season, it's tough to be on the road. When he used to travel for every game, if he had a night off, you always saw us together having dinner. He has advised me on a few things, and I know he doesn't like to give advice to people. But he gave me a couple of pieces of advice that I cherish very much. He is so full of anecdotes and histories. I feel so blessed to have been with him my whole career. And between us, we have over 100 years of broadcasting experience with the Dodgers. It's fantastic.

Seeing him there at Wrigley Field that day brightened my road. And then hearing the national anthem and seeing the stadium packed really shook me. I had lots of pain, but I started the game. I did only three innings, stopped, and went back to the hotel. I went home but couldn't do Dodger games for a while after that because I was so tired. I was suffering a lot from my chest and didn't return to Dodger Stadium until the last two weeks of September. One of the things that upset me was being with Fernando all those years and in 1990, I missed his best day when he pitched the no-hitter on June 29 against the Cardinals.

Someone took a photo of Vin and me in the broadcasting booth at the All-Star Game. That picture tells me I was probably reborn on that day; that picture tells me so much, and I cherish it like no other one. That's when my life in baseball started again.

THE RESULTS

The 1990 All-Star Game at Wrigley Field was scoreless when Jarrin left the ballpark after three innings. Athletics right-hander Bob Welch, who pitched for Los Angeles from 1978-1987, started for the American League and opposed Cincinnati rookie Jack Armstrong. The Dodger All-Star representatives were pitcher Ramon Martinez and catcher Mike Scioscia. The game was delayed for 68 minutes by rain in the top of the seventh inning with no outs and runners on first and third. When play resumed, Cleveland's Julio Franco greeted Cincinnati reliever Rob Dibble with a two-run double, the only offense needed by the American League in a 2-0 victory in front of 39,071.

FULL CIRCLE WITH FERNANDO

In 2003, the Dodgers brought Fernando Valenzuela back to the Spanish radio booth to join Jarrin and his partner, Pepe Yniguez. It was a chance for both the organization and Dodger fans to embrace Valenzuela after 12 years away from Los Angeles, who released him during spring training in 1991.

"To me, Jaime means a lot, because I remember 1981 and he helped me a lot to answer questions from the media," Valenzuela said. "It's amazing. He's been there for so many years and he's still doing so well. It's great for all the fans and all the people who speak Spanish. Everyone recognizes Jaime Jarrin wherever he goes and it's great to be working with him on the broadcasts."

Jaime's son, Jorge, is a member of the Dodgers' front office as Spanish Broadcasting Manager. Also the voice of KABC traffic reports since 1985, he is an established broadcasting personality. Honored by the Associated Press for his coverage of the Los Angeles riots in 1992, Jorge has followed in his father's footsteps, winning the prestigious Golden Mike Award for broadcasting excellence.

"As special as it is to be a part of the Dodgers, the impact of a long baseball career carries a toll on your family life," Jorge Jarrin said. "I just grew up knowing and accepting that my dad got to do something very unique and important to him that required him being away so much. Now that I work on marketing the broadcast, I truly appreciate, as an adult and father myself, the sacrifices that both my mom and dad have endured along the way—to bring the highest level of commitment to the opportunities God has blessed them with. I am very lucky to have them both."

Jaime Jarrin's family remains a cornerstone to his success, and even the hint of retirement is met by frowns by those who know him best. As long as the game remains fun and he can continue to be a positive influence in the community, age is just a number.

"I will say the love of the game keeps me going," he said. "The fact I consider my job is not only broadcasting a baseball game. I always felt being an immigrant here and being a member of a minority, the Hispanics need a form of relaxation. They are hard workers. And I think baseball is a type of entertainment, so I know I'm doing a public service, giving them the emotions of baseball in their own language. And the Dodgers have been so great with me. That's why I have stayed for so long. I love what I do. I could retire right now. But as my wife says, 'Why should you retire? Because you'd be going to the baseball games anyway every day. You might as well get paid for that.'

"I love what I do. I respect everybody and I demand respect in return. It's great being around people I've known for years and also meeting new people, shaking hands with fans, or posing for a picture. It's really unique. I never thought I would become such a figure in the baseball family and among the Hispanics. It's what keeps me going. I've signed a contract that takes me through 2011. I don't know if I will live that long, but I love what I do."

It's safe to assume that while growing up in Ecuador, Jarrin never thought his destination would include a baseball stadium in Los Angeles. With a great venue and, more importantly, his good health, Jarrin doesn't mind keeping a few routines intact.

"Dodger Stadium is my second home," he said. "I have spent time there more than any other place. And it's so beautiful. I am so happy and blessed to have the best spot in the house. When some people come to the booth, whether sponsors or friends, they say, 'Wow, what a place to watch a baseball game!' And the way the McCourts have kept up the place in the last three years, it's amazing. They have spent so much money fixing Dodger Stadium. It looks so beautiful. I think it's the envy of every other baseball owner. You can walk there and you can see your face. It's so unique for the people. I am a very steady person. I have lived in my house for 40 years. I was with KWKW for 51 years, I've been with the Dodgers for 48 years, the same wife for ... I can't say how many years because she'd kill me! It's fantastic. I am 12 minutes from the ballpark and I'm so fortunate not to have traffic problems. It's an ideal situation."

Chapter 16

NANCY BEA HEFLEY

NAME:	Nancy Bea Hefley
BIRTHDAY:	February 24
BIRTHPLACE:	San Pedro, CA
YEARS WITH THE DODGERS:	1988-Present
POSITION:	Stadium Organist
CAREER HIGHLIGHTS:	Began playing piano at the age of four; later added the piano and accordion; after high school, played music in Las Vegas casinos and worked the horse-show circuit; over the years has amassed a repertoire of more than 2,000 songs; maintains a spreadsheet of every anthem performer she has accompanied.
THE GAME:	1988 Playoffs at Dodger Stadium

THE BALLPARK DUET

They sit together at their favorite Los Angeles restaurant—at the least, the one they most frequent—enjoying a meal at the same tiny table in the corner of the room. The plastic silverware and plate assortment serves just as well as the finest china set, as long as they are together. And the interruptions from other patrons every other minute provide a strange ambiance to the meal rather than an unwanted distraction, even when some individuals merely wave to them through a glass window.

The eating establishment is the Vin Scully Press Box dining room at Dodger Stadium. While not exactly moonlight on the waterfront, it's the perfect destination for a couple looking toward their 50th wedding anniversary in 2007.

Nancy Bea Hefley and her husband, Bill, have enjoyed this routine since the 1988 season, Nancy Bea's first as the Dodger Stadium organist. During games, she sits in the back of the press box, adjacent to the DodgerVision control booth and about 10 feet away from a cabinet top in which media members receive that day's assortment of statistical sheets and game notes. Walking from right to left, those who pick up their notes usually make a 180-degree turn and greet Hefley, even if she's in the middle of a song, as the final part of their pregame routine.

Gifted with perfect pitch as a child prodigy, Hefley doesn't need sheet music when she performs, so distractions are welcome. And behind the radiating smile flashed on the scoreboard every seventh-inning stretch during "Take Me Out to the Ballgame" is a rather dry and clever sense of humor, always needed in the six-month marathon of baseball season.

"To me, the social thing is the part I enjoy the most," she said. "They revamped the press box a few years ago and there was talk of putting me in a booth. Mike Jones, the electrician, said, 'Oh, she won't like that.' Because I do enjoy the people coming by and talking to me, catching up on what's going on. I've always played a few games at Angels Stadium as a substitute, and I always felt like I was eating my dinner, saying hi to people, and then 'going to my room.' I think if I needed to concentrate greatly on what I was doing, then I might really like that. But fortunately, I'm a multitask person. I can do many things at one time. My only problem is when I have the headphones on and people come up and whisper to me. If I have the radio and myself going, then it's hard to hear. Other than that, I can carry on a decent conversation and play. I can't tell you a story or get into any detail that I have to think about, but I can do a decent conversation when I play."

Hefley succeeded the late Helen Dell, who served as stadium organist from 1973-1987 and also played at Founder's Church in Los Angeles. Like Dell, Hefley played the accordion as a child. Although Dodger fans may take their ballpark organ music for granted, more than two-thirds of other major-league teams have gone away from the tradition.

Stadium organist Nancy Bea Hefley joined the Dodgers in 1988.

Organ music at Dodger home games began in 1942 with Gladys Goodding, the sport's first full-time organist and the answer to a trivia question among New York sports fans: "Who is the only person to play for the Dodgers, Knicks, and Rangers?" In the early days, Goodding also sang the national anthem while she played.

When the Dodgers staged their final home game at Ebbets Field on September 24, 1957, only 5,000-plus fans were in the grandstands. Although Vin Scully and Jerry Doggett didn't mention the impending move of the franchise to Los Angeles on that night's radio broadcast, Goodding knew it was the bottom of the ninth inning for Flatbush. Her music selections were of the funeral variety, with slow, maudlin dirges cascading upon the Dodgers and visiting Pittsburgh Pirates. Team president Walter O'Malley tried to change the arrangements, but alas, Gladys had locked the door and the memorial service continued.

The layout at the Los Angeles Coliseum in 1958 didn't allow for an organ when the Dodgers moved to the West Coast, and such tranquil music wasn't exactly appropriate for the usual football games and track and field events staged at the 90,000-plus seating venue.

When Dodger Stadium opened in 1962, a carefully planned stadium sound system supported a Wurlitzer organ played by Bob Mitchell. It was installed by the Telefunken Company of West Germany by the same engineers who designed the acoustical system in the La Scala Opera House in Milan, Italy.

The three longest-tenured organists in stadium history—Mitchell, Dell, and Hefley—didn't bring a great level of baseball knowledge when they first ventured into the press box. Instead, they simply performed for the crowd, learning the nuances of the sport as the games rolled on.

"I try to play mostly off what is happening on the field and be a little creative," Hefley said. "I don't like to be mean with my music. I think the meanest I ever got was when a pitcher from Ohio couldn't get an out. I don't remember who it was. When they pulled him, I played, 'Why, oh why, did I ever leave Ohio?' That's the meanest I've ever been. Otherwise, I try to do it subtly, which a lot of people don't know the title to. If we're playing San Francisco, it might be 'Do You Know The Way to San Jose?' My most fun is when they would bring in opposing pitchers. There was a pitcher named Barry Manuel, and of course, you have to do a Barry Manilow song. And Dennis Martinez, the pitcher from Nicaragua. I played 'Managua' and he said, 'I'm not from Managua!' … One time the first baseman lost track of the outs. He threw to second base after they already had gotten the third out. I played, 'We're Four Little Lambs That Have Lost Our Way.' Just little things like that. I don't like to play 'Hit The Road Jack.'"

Hefley had a chance to spend time with Dell during the Old Timers' Day luncheons in the early 1990s. They discovered each had played the accordion as children. And for Dodger Stadium's 40th anniversary in 2002, Hefley shared a "Take Me Out to the Ballgame" duet during the seventh-inning stretch with Mitchell, who was still playing the organ and performing at the local silent movie theater every Sunday at age 89.

THE GAME OF MY LIFE

By Nancy Bea Hefley

The most memorable moment for me at Dodger Stadium was when Placido Domingo sang the national anthem during the 1988 playoffs.

Before the game, he told me he was going to sing the anthem a cappella. That wasn't surprising because, whether it's a famous singer or someone who isn't a professional, sometimes they prefer to sing it without the organ in the background.

Sometimes they'll ask, "What would you do if you were playing?" I say, "Here's what I would do" and show them. Most often, they'll say, "OK, let's do it with you." That's what happened with Placido. Then we establish the key they're going to sing it in. Most of them know their key. Some do not. Then we'll have to pick, "Are you high or low?" and we go from there. Sometimes we try many keys, but usually we can get it on the first try. I can usually tell from their voice what key they would sing in. But some people surprise you. They have a high singing voice, but a very low speaking voice, so it's hard to tell. Then we might chat about other things. Ask them what they're doing and what's on the horizon.

Looking back over the years, one thing I have found is the stars are more nervous than the regular folk when getting ready to sing the anthem at Dodger Stadium. And I really think I've narrowed it down to the fact that so much is expected of them, so they don't want to let the fans down. People say, "Well, everyone knows the words to the national anthem." That's the problem. And I've heard the words how many zillions of times? But don't put me there in front of people to sing that song because I'll flub those words. It's so automatic when everyone around you is singing it. It does terrify a lot of people, but more the stars than the folks off the street.

I remember Placido Domingo the most, because of the caliber of his voice. He was pretty impressive and he allowed me to accompany him when he came here with the original thought of singing it a cappella. Some come with that thought, and you're not going to change their minds no matter what. But he did and was just great, even though it really wasn't that long of a moment.

Unlike a baseball game that lasts nine innings, the average person takes 90 seconds to sing the anthem. We've had some who were three minutes, and those are killers! When that happens everybody in the press box turns and looks at me like it's my fault. Hey, I'm just following; I'm not leading! We have a couple people who sing it in a minute. You fasten your seatbelt and get ready to go, because they're not going to take any breaths.

People ask if I feel nervous playing if I think someone on the field is nervous. I don't get nervous, but I do get concerned about some of them. Sometimes, they surprise me. We'll rehearse it one day in the press box and when they go downstairs and get in front of the crowd, they get real creative. Then I have to really pay attention to figure out when to put my chords in behind their singing. That can be a little nerve-wracking.

My other favorite game from the 1988 playoffs was Game 1 of the World Series, when Kirk Gibson hit a pinch-hit home run to win the game in the bottom of the ninth inning. When Gibby came out of the dugout, I thought, "Oh, noooo! He can't even walk. What if he gets a hit? He can't even run to first base." It took him several swings before he hit that home run and then it was like, "Oh my gosh!"

During the game, I'm always thinking ahead. Gibson is running around the bases and I have to play something. Well, my routine in those days was always to play "Sing Hallelujah" after the first Dodger home run. The second home run it was time for "Happy Days Are Here Again." It was pandemonium. The game ended. I pulled the cover down on the organ because there was no way I could play over the crowd cheering like that. Someone in DodgerVision said, "Play, play!" Then someone else yelled, "We can't hear!" So I was right in the first place. It was absolute pandemonium.

THE RESULTS

The Dodgers defeated the New York Mets in seven games in the 1988 National League Championship Series. Gibson's pinch-hit home run against the Athletics in Game 1 of the World Series lifted the Dodgers to a 5-4 victory. The Dodgers closed out the sixth championship in franchise history with a 5-2 victory in Game 5 at Oakland.

STITCH AND TIME

While growing up in Bellflower, Hefley played at Southern California horse shows and other venues but didn't may much attention to Bill when he kept suggesting she should audition for one of the local professional sports teams.

"I was a musician, just dedicated totally to music," she said. "I wasn't interested in sports of any kind. I have three boys and a girl and a husband who is a huge Dodger fan. My mother was a huge Dodger fan. So that brought that on. For years, my husband was saying, 'See if you can get that job playing for baseball, particularly the Dodgers.' Well, Helen Dell was the organist at the time and I am not the type of person to put anyone out of work, or even to try. So I wouldn't even call. We were also friends with (former Dodger pitcher) Tommy John and his wife, Sally. Even they said to try for the job. I said, 'No, as long as Helen's there, I'm not going to do that.' Plus, I didn't know that I would like playing every day at a baseball game that much. Then when she said she was going to retire after the 1987 season, I thought, 'I'll give it a try.' I didn't think it was going to be so much fun. It really is."

Bill admits he was caught off guard by his wife's reaction to playing for the Dodgers.

"I would've suspected that she'd get tired of it," he said. "But with her liking the people like she does, that is the main thing right there. That's the reason she's around. She doesn't play as much music at the stadium, but she meets everyone who comes into town. And the announcers and all of them see. It's fun for her, and as long as it's fun, she'll be around.

"I'm not really a musical person. I've listened to it long enough all these years that I should be, but I'm not. In the car, I listen to classical music. I don't like the opera singers, but the artists like Mozart. I have that on every car that I drive. I can push a button and there it is. If I'm driving and I'm listening to something else, pretty soon I feel nervous. That classical music just soothes me."

Playing the same type of ballpark music can dull one's senses, so Nancy Bea plays and listens to more classical music at home.

"My favorite artists are Rachmaninoff and Tchaikovsky," she said. "I don't play their works because they are difficult to play and most need an orchestra in the background. I've become very sloppy because I play the type of music that I do. I'm not as good technically as I once was. But show tunes are my thing; to me, they say something. When they're out there working on the mound, I might play, 'Plant a Radish,' from *The Fantasticks*. They just say so much. Even like pregame when they're announcing groups like the 4-H Clubs, I'll play 'The Farmer and the Cowman' from *Oklahoma*. One time, they had Smokey the Bear down on the field and I played, 'I Don't Want to Set the World on Fire.'

"But to sit and talk about the songs is difficult because it's hard to remember. I react to those situations rather than plan those songs. It's kind of what goes on in my mind. I might be walking along and hear something, or hear someone say something and a light bulb goes off. It's not something I'm thinking about."

When she's not weaving her music into an inning, Hefley brings out her knitting bag complete with her latest sweater project. She has an elaborate sweater collection and creates presents for friends and family.

During Hefley's childhood, she learned to sew by watching her mother. Hefley began knitting in high school, but several years ago she was forced to temporarily give up the hobby because of a true major-league injury—a torn rotator cuff. When she underwent surgery in 2001, the thought of a comeback was music to her ears.

"It keeps my hands occupied while the team is playing," she said. "If I don't have to watch what I'm doing with the knitting—if there isn't a particular design or intricate pattern—I can still watch the game but keep the hands busy. I bring all my boring, boring knitting here, like the sleeves. Depending on the size of the yarn and the pattern and how interested I am in the sweater, I can maybe whip one out in a week."

Hefley alternates between pre-designed patterns and her own creations. She will copy a picture onto graph paper and plot the exact locations for the particular squares and colors. One of her designs consists of a blue and metallic color combination with a bar of music on both front and back. Not just any music, however—the sweater portrays the six musical notes leading to the traditional "Charge" rally verse.

Chapter 17

JIM GOTT

NAME:	James William Gott
BORN:	August 3, 1959
BIRTHPLACE:	Hollywood, CA
YEARS WITH THE DODGERS:	1990-1994
POSITION:	Pitcher
UNIFORM NUMBER:	35
CAREER HIGHLIGHTS:	Made major-league debut with the Toronto Blue Jays in 1982; hit two home runs in one game with the Giants against the St. Louis Cardinals at Candlestick Park on May 12, 1985; saved career-high 34 games with the Pittsburgh Pirates in 1989; led the Dodgers with team-high 25 saves in 1992.
THE GAME:	August 11, 1990; Los Angeles Dodgers vs. Atlanta Braves at Fulton County Stadium

MAKING HIS PITCH

The scene is a Saturday morning in San Marino, California, a small community located in the San Gabriel Valley, just a modest drive from

Dodger Stadium. Little League tryouts are underway and watching the festivities is Jim Gott, the only local resident to ever reach the major leagues. The former pitcher spies a clean-cut, square-jawed construction executive clutching his clipboard and methodically writing down every possible detail about a 10-year-old's potential, checking off categories with the sentiment of a building inspector.

"These dads take this so seriously," Gott says with a smile. "You'd think it was a World Series."

Everyone in town knows Gott, whose good-natured disposition sometimes belied the power and fury generated by his 6-foot-4, 215-pound frame. And the joke is everyone else in the world knows Gott, the loquacious personality who, if paid by the spoken word, would empty the Fort Knox reserve by lunchtime.

More than a decade after his retirement as a player, Gott has found peace back at home. He can visit with old friends, make jokes about neighboring rival South Pasadena High School, and simply appreciate what life has to offer.

As a kid, Gott felt pressure to succeed as a top athlete, so much so that his high school championship was more a feeling of relief than joy.

"I was ready to just leave home, just to have a new chapter in my life," he said. "I had made my decision to play baseball and football at Brigham Young University. My brother was on a golf scholarship up there and I was looking for a calmer way of life. Of course, I didn't choose that, because the Cardinals selected me in the fourth round of the amateur draft. At that point, I decided I was going to do things my way, and I'm gone. My parents were very disappointed that I didn't go to college. My dad needed to sign for me because I was 17, so mom and dad didn't speak for a few weeks after that because my mom wanted me to college and that didn't work out."

Three decades later, Gott has a unique perspective on sports at both youth and professional levels. And, as the parent of an autistic child, Gott realizes even the best fastball in the world can't strike out every opponent.

Of course, Gott will admit he never had the world's best fastball. He went 56-74 with a 3.87 ERA and 91 saves in 554 games with the Blue Jays, Giants, Pirates, and Dodgers.

But some of the stories from his 14-year career are unparalleled, mixing tears with cheers.

Like the time he returned to Southern California with the Toronto Blue Jays to face the Angels in Anaheim. With friends and family in the

After overcoming career-threatening injuries, right-hander Jim Gott led the Dodgers with 25 saves in 1992.

grandstands, he excitedly ran off the mound, adding a few fist pumps and shouts, after striking out Rod Carew.

His manager, Bobby Cox, approached him as he entered the dugout.

"That was only the second out of the inning."

He drove Dodger manager Tommy Lasorda crazy by practicing his Hapkido martial arts in the clubhouse along with pitcher Kevin Gross. It was common to see Gott, a first-degree black belt, practicing spin kicks and other moves during batting practice.

Even the end of his career was memorable. Just days after retiring due to arm problems in the summer of 1995 with Pittsburgh, Gott received a phone call from the Baltimore Orioles asking if he still had the game ball from his first major-league victory.

"Of course I do," he replied. "Why do you want to know?"

Turns out May 30, 1982—Toronto's 6-0 victory at Baltimore in which Gott started and allowed just one hit in six innings—was also the first game of Cal Ripken's record consecutive games played streak. Invited to Baltimore on short notice to celebrate Ripken surpassing Lou Gehrig's mark of 2,130 consecutive games, Gott offered his baseball to the shortstop. Ripken graciously declined the offer, but later wrote in his autobiography how touched he was by Gott's gesture.

Gott wasn't sure one day in the majors was possible after rocky times in the Cardinals' minor-league system. Gone were the days of San Marino and dominating the Rio Hondo League with fastballs. He was just a number competing against so many players. And the high draft status meant the Cardinals had to keep him around for a while, even as he led various leagues in wild pitches and other dubious statistical categories.

"My minor-league career was not very fun," Gott said. "I spent four of my first five minor-league seasons in rookie ball or Single-A ball. So after a while, I'm coming home and my high school teammates are graduating from Stanford and Harvard and places like that. I get a job gardening in San Marino just to survive until the next season."

After his fourth minor-league season, Gott approached BYU football coach LaVelle Edwards, hoping to regain his scholarship. But during a dinner on campus with some of the other recruits, the potential defensive lineman was disheartened to hear he'd probably have to add 45 pounds to his 195-pound frame just to compete at that level.

The Cardinals left Gott unprotected in the 1981 minor-league draft, opening the door for the Toronto Blue Jays. He pitched three seasons there and was then dealt to the San Francisco Giants. It was an exciting time for someone who grew up near Dodger Stadium.

"There are two scenarios working here," Gott said. "When the Dodgers came to Candlestick Park, I was so excited because I was playing against the hometown team. There's Tommy Lasorda and all those guys on the 1985 team, and then just seeing the hostile environment that was there at Candlestick … against the Dodgers, I couldn't believe it. It was unbelievable. They had policemen in the outfield, there were policemen at every aisle. There was an effigy of Tommy being dragged around the stadium and thrown about. Wow. I had never understood the rivalry until I was put in that situation. I knew the Giants were hated in L.A., but I had no idea just how hostile it was."

Gott notched his first major-league hit against the Dodgers' Jerry Reuss in Los Angeles on April 14, 1985. Gott promptly misread the signs from third-base coach Rocky Bridges and was thrown out by catcher Mike Scioscia attempting to steal second base. Gott lasted five innings and picked up the victory that day, but it was one of the few bright spots in a turbulent time in which the Giants posted the only 100-loss season in a franchise history dating back to 1883. The Giants also fired their manager, Jim Davenport, in early September and brought in no-nonsense Roger Craig, whose style didn't help Gott's confidence. Gott went 7-10 with a 3.88 ERA in 26 starts in 1985.

Surgery to repair a partially torn rotator cuff limited Gott to just nine appearances in 1986. He was 1-0 with a 4.50 ERA in 30 appearances when the Giants placed him on waivers in 1987. The Pirates claimed him on August 3, his 28th birthday. Gott found a home in Pittsburgh's bullpen thanks to manager Jim Leyland and pitching coach Ray Miller. Gott went 0-2 with a 1.45 ERA and 13 saves in 25 appearances.

"During my first weeks with the Pirates, I learned that Jim Leyland was a great human being," Gott said. "He was always there to encourage you and to kick you in the butt when you needed it. He was always consistent."

The Pirates finished in last place in the National League East in three consecutive seasons from 1984-1986. But Pittsburgh gradually improved, thanks in part to a pair of young outfielders, Barry Bonds and Bobby Bonilla. By 1988, the Pirates finished second in their division with an 85-75 record. Gott saved a team-high 34 games.

"We had a great group of guys in Pittsburgh," Gott said. "One day after batting practice at home, we all came in to rest from the Pittsburgh humidity. Our clubhouse was big with lockers around the perimeter, a big open area with a couch and some tables for card players, surrounding televisions hanging strategically around the room.

"Well … Barry Bonds went directly to the couch and lay down, quickly falling asleep. Some of the veteran players decided to play a joke on Barry. They went immediately to Leyland's office to get his support. He was in.

"We quietly emptied the clubhouse. The clubhouse attendants moved all the clocks to game time, turned off all the TVs. There was a tunnel at the old Three Rivers Stadium leading from the clubhouses to the respective dugouts. All of us lined up against the walls on both sides while Jim Leyland, fully dressed for the game, ran into the locker room and as only Jim could do, with veins popping out of his neck, started to scream at Barry about how selfish he was. Barry was scrambling to his locker, getting dressed faster than any player in the history of baseball. He was probably still waking up as he ran through the clubhouse doors and through the tunnel as his teammates were laughing at him all the way to the dugout. He was mad and humiliated and he stayed in the dugout for the remainder of the opposing team's batting practice, both infields, and the national anthem. To top it off, Barry ended up winning the game with great plays in the field and an incredible at-bat that resulted in a game-winning home run."

But Gott's career was in jeopardy in 1989 after he missed all but one game due to a ruptured elbow ligament. The Pirates released him after the season, and Gott discovered more than his pitching career was at a crossroads.

THE GAME OF MY LIFE

By Jim Gott

Needless to say, 1989 wasn't a good year. At the end of the 1989 season, I was let go by the Pirates and became a free agent. I continued to rehab my arm in Utah, where my family lived. I filed for divorce in November. My wife and I both got attorneys, but we agreed neither would start the process because of the upcoming birth of the twins in March 1990.

December came around and while I was at a Players Association meeting in Arizona, my agent called and said the Dodgers were interested in me. I flew to Los Angeles to have an examination with Dr. Frank Jobe. The nurse laughed when she retrieved my thick file, because I had been going to that Kerlan-Jobe medical clinic since 1972. My exam went well. My daughter, Jenise, and I drove back to Dodger Stadium and were invited to lunch with Peter O'Malley and Tommy Lasorda at the private dining area. After over a year of feeling hopeless, I had a ray of hope. A job would be nice to start the upcoming year.

Thank God for the Dodgers! Being back home to play at this point in my life was nothing short of a miracle. I needed support and it was here. Fred Claire, the general manager, needed help in the bullpen after trading Alejandro Pena to the Mets in a deal for outfielder Hubie Brooks.

While at the Baseball Winter Meetings in Nashville, Fred—an avid jogger—went for a run with Mike Williams, our public relations director. During their run, Fred and Mike discussed the bullpen. Mike and I grew up in San Marino, played Little League against each other, and then were teammates in high school. We won the CIF championship in our senior year and were co-MVPs. I got a serious endorsement from Mike and, even with my arm still a mess, that eventful run landed me a job with my hometown team.

Thank goodness spring training started late in 1990 due to the labor dispute between the players and owners. My arm was nowhere close to being ready, my divorce was on hold, and my twins were born on February 16. So even though it was uncomfortable, I was there for the birth. They were three weeks early and needed two weeks in ICU. I was grateful to be there to help.

At this time, my two-year-old son, Christian James Gott, or "C.J." as we call him, was suffering every day due to his autism. While most two-year-olds are starting to gain a sense of independence and wonder in their world, C.J. always seemed like he was recovering from a head injury. His balance and gait were off. He was still not talking or looking into anyone's eyes. He was also so oblivious to everyone. When he played, it was always with some object. It could be anything from a toy car or truck to a single block. No imaginative plans, just looking at the object, lining it up, and humming. C.J. didn't even try to talk. He just hummed because he liked the vibration. C.J. could hear airplanes coming from miles away—an unbelievable skill. Yet he became frightened at a sudden noise: a slamming door, telephone, television, anything unexpected. I never heard the term "auditorally sensitive," but I was seeing it and experiencing C.J.'s daily suffering.

During the 1990 spring training, my arm felt bad. By the time the games started, I was praying every moment. Ron Perranoski, our pitching coach, gave me an inning in a game at Port St. Lucie. When I was in the bullpen warming up, I couldn't throw hard. I couldn't find the strike zone and I couldn't get over the helpless feeling that I was done—and definitely not safe going into a big-league game.

So I went out and pitched a tied game in the bottom of the ninth. The first batter had a 2-and-1 count, so I challenged him with a fastball. Whack! Home run. Game over. Of all the defeated feelings I had, I was grateful that day was over. On the bus, I went up to Perranoski and asked to pitch "one more" as soon as possible. His response: "One more what? One out? One batter? One pitch? One inning?"

It was a funny line, but sad. Before my next game, I was in the trainer's room with Dr. Jobe and our physical therapist, Pat Screnar. On the X-ray machine, they showed me a bone spur in the middle of my repaired ligament in my right elbow. My options were surgery and miss a year, or simply pitch with the injury. Bob Welch told me he had the same condition and was still pitching years after being diagnosed. So after crying alone on an empty Field 5 at Dodgertown, I decided my only option was to pitch. I had bills to pay.

The Dodgers were my hometown team and I had read a lot about spring training in Vero Beach and the all-time great players in franchise history. Our 1990 team had some great players. Eddie Murray was my favorite teammate. He was a consummate pro, a hard worker who did everything he could to help his team. Kirk Gibson was the toughest and most influential teammate I ever played with. Then there was Tim Wallach, a great guy and a tough player, quiet team leader, and awesome in the clubhouse.

Fernando Valenzuela was funny, along with being an icon of Los Angeles and a great teammate. I went to a Carlos Santana concert with Fernando in Philadelphia and you would have thought I was with the president. We were ushered to Carlos' dressing room, where we stayed until it was show time. Then we were ushered onto the stage and sat alongside the band while they played. All because of Fernando.

When I think of Kirk Gibson, I remember he played one of his first professional games for the Lakeland Tigers against my St. Louis Cardinals around 1981. All of us had heard of Kirk. What I remember was his presence on the field. Kirk was a true blood-and-guts leader. He was also incredibly fast for a big guy. Gibby later became the spiritual leader of the

1984 Tigers, one of the most powerful teams I played against and a team that had a lot of leaders like Alan Trammell, Lance Parrish, Darrell Evans, and Jack Morris. But Kirk was the impact player!

When he signed with the Dodgers before the 1988 season, I knew he would have an impact. My favorite Gibson story was the eye-black incident with Jesse Orosco and the Dodgers. Not only did that practical joke happen on the field—Orosco smearing Gibson's hat liner with shoe polish—but the clubhouse meeting the next day must've been an awesome experience. Very few players can single-handedly influence a team, but Kirk did, and the MVP season and World Series home run were just icing on the cake.

I, like so many other baseball fans, will remember his walking to home plate, actually limping because he was injured, fouling off a bunch of pitches against Dennis Eckersley before hitting the home run to win the game. Gibson told me his version of that World Series home run during our first road trip to Houston in 1990. Hearing it firsthand with all the behind-the-scenes commentary made the hair on the back of my head stand up.

Getting to know Kirk as a teammate and as a friend was a memory that helped me recovering from my elbow operation in 1989. After a tough spring training, starting the year on the disabled list, and my pending divorce, I was pretty low in self-confidence. Gibson, along with pitchers Tim Crews and Jay Howell, helped me a lot during those early days with the Dodgers.

My first outings back with the Dodgers weren't very spectacular. At St. Louis, I gave up three runs in one inning in my debut, prompting a sportswriter to jokingly ask, "How does it feel to have a 27.00 ERA?" referring to my earned run average. He was my favorite writer in the world and is still a great friend, but at the time I wanted to grab him by the throat.

One time, I was shelled in San Diego. After I was taken out of the game, I showered and walked back to the hotel. As soon as I got to the hotel, I called Fred Claire and asked to meet with him. He asked me to come right up to his room. He had me sit down and I told him I was close to giving up. I didn't think I could regain my form from 1988. Fred listened and he told me how he learned a few years back to give injured players extra time to heal and regain their form. He was ready to give up on Alejandro Pena a few years back when he was watching the team play. Alejandro, coming back from an operation, was going through a tough go of it early on. Something made Fred stick with him, and a few months later, Alejandro was back on track.

So, in closing, Fred gave me a big boost in my abilities. I was more determined than ever to get back to my old form. When we got back from that road trip, I went to Dodger Stadium to start my ritual in the training room. I went to the clubhouse and then to my locker. Most of the players were already there. Our equipment manager, Dave Wright, came by to give me some mail and I noticed he was wearing a T-shirt with my baseball head shot with the words, "JIM GOTT FOR MAYOR" on it in bold letters. With a smile on my face, I looked up and saw everyone in the locker room had a "JIM GOTT FOR MAYOR" T-shirt on. I was incredibly touched by this show of acceptance. It was just what I needed to help me through this tough time. Gibby, Tim Crews, and Jay Howell organized this showing of friendship that I will never forget.

Finally, the big day came in Atlanta in August. The game went into extra innings and Kal Daniels hit a two-run home run in the top of the 10th inning. I was brought in from the bullpen to save the game. Ron Gant hit a line drive out to left field. Then David Justice struck out. I knew my stuff was working when I struck out Justice, because I had so much trouble with him throughout my career. When I struck out Jim Presley to end the game, it felt like I was back. Totally back. I had my stuff again. I was able to get guys digging in the dirt for my slider. And my fastball had some pop to it again. That's what I didn't have up to that point. I struggled in spring training: the fastball was straight. Even though I was able to get it into the high 90s on the radar gun, I wasn't throwing it by anyone. The Dodgers had been patient with me enough and I don't think I could have done what I did if I had been rehabilitating with another club. No other club was where the Dodgers were in terms of Dr. Jobe doing surgeries and Pat Screnar serving as physical therapist. And then I had people like Orel Hershiser with incredible work ethics. So, by following their paths, it was awesome.

THE RESULTS

The Dodgers defeated the Braves 6-4 at Fulton County Stadium on August 11, 1990. Stan Javier and Juan Samuel each had two hits for the Dodgers. Kirk Gibson and Kal Daniels each hit home runs. Jay Howell (4-5), who pitched a scoreless ninth, earned the victory and Jim Gott notched his first save since September 27, 1988, with the Pirates at Chicago's Wrigley Field.

A NEW BEGINNING

Jim Gott's 1990 season with the Dodgers breathed new life into his pitching career, but another important milestone occurred during the summer. During a photo session on the field at Dodger Stadium, Gott met Cathy Fischer, who was working for the local Hollenback Youth Center in Los Angeles. Cathy heard Jim speak at the center's preseason luncheon, and was introduced to Jim by the team's community relations director, Michelle Foxx.

Before the longest road trip of the year, Gott invited Cathy to have breakfast at the Pacific Dining Car. They had a good time and when it was time leave, Cathy wanted to show Jim the baseball glove in her car, which she used to play softball.

"It was an Alan Trammell model glove," Gott said. "But I thought it was signed by Alan Trammell, so I said something like, 'Oh, you know Alan Trammell.' She didn't even know who had signed the glove. Kooky me—I was trying to make conversation. But it was pretty much love at first sight when I met Cathy."

Gott later donned a tuxedo and proposed to Cathy on the pitcher's mound at Dodger Stadium. Fortunately for him, she didn't signal to the bullpen.

"Here's where Cathy is a godsend," he says. "We get married on October 25, and all of a sudden, she's with someone who has four kids. She was just 27 years old at the time. During the 1991 season, the kids stayed with us for a few months, and Cathy started seeing and was helping me to see what C.J.'s challenges were. C.J. would throw his head on the ground when he got frustrated. He'd bite his wrist. With autism, the kids don't like change at all. Any change to these kids is bad for them.

"As a parent, here I am crying because I can't comfort my child. And here Cathy is, feeling sorry for this little guy, and wondering what we can do to take care of it. Cathy had really worked hard at Pacific Enterprises with the corporate contributions, so as an administrator, she really knew how to take a problem and try to solve it. That's what she ended up doing with C.J. She started talking to different people, and lucky for us, one of Cathy's friends was an educational advocate. She started giving Cathy the best advice on where to go, so we saw the best pediatrician, the best speech therapist and physical therapist. It was on and on and on. Here I am, I'm happy my career is going again and I'm happy in my career. Meanwhile, Cathy is administrating the welfare of my children."

Jim and Cathy participated in their first Dodger Family Game together in 1991, along with the four kids—Jenise, age six, C.J., age three, and twins Ryan and Tyler, age 16 months. The happy occasion soon turned into a drama when C.J. disappeared from the field. After 15 minutes of searching, Cathy returned to the old Angels clubhouse beyond the regular Dodger clubhouse, which was being used by the Family Game guests. All alone in the room was C.J., sitting in the corner and holding a piece of cake. He had retraced his steps from the field after first spotting a decorated Family Game cake at the clubhouse entrance an hour earlier.

As Gott gradually gained knowledge about autism, his status as a major leaguer also helped other fathers of special needs children because Gott was willing to share his family's story. Jim and Cathy had two children of their own in the subsequent years, Danny (1993) and Nicholas (1995). Danny was also born with autism, but a strong social component allowed him to participate in more activities while growing up, including three years in Little League. C.J., who turned 19 in 2007, lives in a group home in Pennsylvania, learning masonry and textile skills. C.J. will always need assistance in his life, whether at home or in the workplace.

"Each week, I see dads who don't understand or know what to do about their special needs child," Gott said. "For me, the beginning was confusing. After Jenise was born, we just expected another 'perfect' child. Crawling, standing, walking, babbling, and talking just seem to happen without any effort on the parents' part. Just be proud parents. That's all I expected.

"That didn't happen from day one with C.J. He was born when I was in spring training with the Pirates. I was so happy to get out of San Francisco in 1987. I did well and really seemed to fit in with my new team. That off-season, I was gearing up for a great season and the birth of my son—the future big leaguer. I was always so envious of my teammates with their sons during the annual family games at the ballpark. Mine was on the way. When they said 'autistic,' I really had no idea of what it looked like. I didn't know if C.J. was going to be like Rain Man and living in an institution or if he'd be working at the Jet Propulsion Laboratory in a little cubicle."

For Gott, it was the beginning of two extremes. His professional life flourished again, saving a team-high 25 games in 1992, which produced an annual income in the millions. If he struck out a feared home-run hitter such as Fred McGriff to save a game, the euphoric feeling might not last long if there was a crisis brewing at home.

A pro athlete's injuries might change one's outlook on sports, but what about becoming the parent of a special needs child?

"Learning humility and accepting things," Gott said. "It was a huge step, just being able to accept things as they are, and not the expectations that C.J. was going to be okay. I tell that Family Game story about C.J. disappearing and now we can relate when we hear stories from other families. It was just too loud on the field for C.J. Now I've completely changed my mind what's okay for C.J. and what's okay for Danny. And it's also eased my expectations for my other kids.

"The other thing I realize is how it's easy as an athlete to become self-centered, because you have people there who are tooting your horn and telling you how great you are. When things are going good, you're in the paper and people want your autograph. It's really easy to forget about what life is really about. You're riding high, and it's so easy to get out of whack."

Although C.J. never played Little League, Gott had a chance to share the game with his son. They often arrived at the ballpark hours before batting practice when it was quiet.

They ran around the field and went inside the clubhouse. C.J. knew the attendants and always gave them a high-five greeting.

For the past 15 years, Jim and Cathy have worked in many arenas dealing and coping with autism, from schools to charities to fund-raising events. Their most important challenge is making newcomers feel welcome so they don't have to face autism without a support group. And they watch the stages of recognition.

"Most come in with defense in their eyes, some come in with sadness in their eyes, but we all have bewilderment in our eyes," Gott said. "What is the problem with my child? Will they ever grow out of this? Will they have a job? Will they get married? Will they be safe when they're not with us? Whether it's the schoolyard bully or the resident caregiver, will my child survive without me?

"The dads that have the kids with the most severe autism get it quicker than the high-functioning ones. Most are happy to drop off their kid for an hour or two just to get some rest. They all love their kids but feel very overwhelmed. Mom at home is struggling, too. She is the one who is the main caretaker, driving to all the therapies—occupational, sensory, auditory, social skills, neurological—and special pediatricians. Some kids take medication, some have odd eating and sleeping habits, but all on this crazy autism spectrum have a number of issues that the dads try to help out, but because of work, they are outside of the circle. The parents hope for guidance, but are either too proud or embarrassed to ask for help. The best thing is to join the team surrounding your child. The sooner the better, for your sanity, your child's development, and your partnership with your partner."

It's another Saturday morning in San Marino and it's time for Little League. Danny no longer plays, but 11-year-old Nicholas Gott takes his place for tryouts. He takes batting practice and catches baseballs with ease as the row of league managers furiously make notes in the margin of their draft scorecard. Nicholas runs the basepaths and tweaks an old ankle injury, but he bounces up and continues his sprint toward third base.

All the while, Jim sits silently in the grandstands. He might be a little nervous; he might feel a twinge of nostalgia for when he ruled the local school playgrounds during the Nixon Administration. But most importantly, he knows it's a time to be proud.

"I think about how good things are," Gott says. "I'm so grateful Nick is out there running around and having fun, which is the perspective of what Little League should be. These tryouts have nothing to do with me. C.J. never played because of his autism, but Danny played for three years.

"What really happened was the other team always let Danny come to the plate after the third out. They would make anywhere from one to 15 pitches until he made contact. And whether he hit a foul ball that went behind him or just a little dribbler, Danny would be so proud that he made contact. He'd start running the bases and you'd see all the guys in the field make *Bad News Bears* plays.

"Nobody ever tagged Danny out. Danny then ran to the immediate area where the people were, whether it was the opponent's bench, the opposing parents, or our parents. He would get high-fives from everyone and it was just a wonderful moment when the community could come together to give him that experience. They loved Danny and accepted him for who he is."

Chapter 18

TOMMY LASORDA

NAME:	Thomas Charles Lasorda
BORN:	September 22, 1927
BIRTHPLACE:	Norristown, Pennsylvania
YEARS WITH THE DODGERS:	58
CURRENT POSITION:	Special Advisor to the Chairman
UNIFORM NUMBERS:	27 (player), 52 (coach), 2 (manager)
CAREER HIGHLIGHTS:	Hall of Fame manager; spent 20 seasons in Dodger dugout from 1976-1996, led Los Angeles to two championships, four National League pennants, and eight division titles; member of the 1955 world champion Brooklyn Dodgers; only man in history whose teams have won both a World Series and an Olympic Gold Medal; uniform No. 2 retired by Dodgers in 1997.
THE GAME:	October 15, 1988; World Series Game 1; Oakland Athletics vs. Los Angeles Dodgers at Dodger Stadium

FOREVER DODGER BLUE

When Tommy Lasorda broke into organized baseball, he wasn't a high-priced bonus baby earmarked for stardom. Instead, the 5-foot-10, 175-pound left-handed pitching prospect barely received a passing glance during his first spring training at Dodgertown. But those humble beginnings sparked within Lasorda a competitive spirit that still burns 50 years later as a distinguished member of baseball's Hall of Fame.

Lasorda's story is one of survival and persistence, of heartaches and humor. Of the 600-plus minor leaguers who were at Vero Beach competing for jobs in the late 1940s, only Lasorda is still active with the Dodger organization. Although his major-league career consisted of only 26 games with Brooklyn and the Kansas City Athletics, Lasorda's plight as a brash rookie became the backdrop to one of his favorite stories.

In 1955, Dodger general manager Buzzie Bavasi had to make room for a wild left-handed pitcher whose contract stipulated that he remain on the major-league roster for at least two seasons. That prospect was Sandy Koufax, whose greatness wouldn't surface until the next decade.

Bavasi called Lasorda into his office and explained his roster dilemma. He asked Lasorda which pitcher should be sent to the minor leagues. Lasorda wished farewell to Koufax, until overruled by Bavasi. "I can honestly say it took one of the greatest left-handed pitchers in baseball to knock me off that Brooklyn club!" Lasorda would later boast.

Lasorda, who once struck out 25 batters in a 15-inning minor-league game in 1948, holds the all-time career International League record with 125 victories for the Montreal Royals. After his pitching career ended with the Dodgers' Triple-A Spokane team in 1960, scouting director Al Campanis offered Lasorda a chance to become a scout. As Lasorda searched the country for talent, he crafted his powers of persuasion when describing the Dodger tradition to potential free agents. Along with scout Kenny Myers, he was also sent to Japan to conduct baseball clinics.

When Bavasi decided to make Lasorda a manager at rookie-level Pocatello, Idaho, in 1965, he told the new skipper that developing prospects was more important than winning ballgames. Lasorda was excited at the new challenge, but realized he couldn't change his attitude in the dugout.

In his autobiography, *The Artful Dodger*, Lasorda recalled his reaction to Bavasi's winning-is-secondary advice.

Hall of Fame manager Tommy Lasorda piloted the Dodgers to a pair of championships in 1981 and 1988.

"Telling me I didn't have to win was like telling the Wright brothers to take a train," he wrote. "I'd spent my entire life striving to win, fighting to win, I didn't know any other way. I understood that my primary job was to introduce young players to professional baseball in the most positive way, but I believed that creating a winning atmosphere was the most positive way. I intended to teach, just as Buzzie wanted me to do, and what I intended to teach was how to win."

Lasorda gradually worked his way up the ladder in the organization, winning minor-league championships and developing prospects like Steve Garvey, Ron Cey, Bill Buckner, Charlie Hough, Tom Paciorek, Joe Ferguson, and others. His 1970 Spokane team is considered one of the greatest minor-league squads in history. Lasorda also nurtured more than his share of future managers and coaches. At the start of the 2001 season, six major-league managers had played for Lasorda—Bobby Valentine, Dave Lopes, Dusty Baker, Mike Scioscia, Phil Garner, and Johnny Oates.

Lasorda was always up for a challenge, even when pitching batting practice. He once predicted that he could throw batting practice to every Dodger player in camp during spring training. Bavasi stopped Lasorda because he knew he'd deliver on his promise. And even if Lasorda volunteered to throw batting practice, he couldn't resist using the occasion to motivate hitters.

"I remember Tommy Lasorda pitching to a bunch of us minor leaguers during an over-the-line game in spring training during the 1990 lockout in Vero Beach," said Eric Karros, a first baseman who, between 1991-2002, became the all-time Los Angeles franchise home run leader with 270. "One day after batting practice, Tommy challenged us and said he could pitch against us in a game. Well, it went on and on and finally there was a simulated game. We spotted Tommy a 5-0 lead and predicted we'd easily beat this 63-year-old man. We sure were wrong. Tommy taunted us after almost every pitch and really gave us a good lesson in concentration. We ended up with one run and heard about Tommy's victory for the rest of the day."

During Lasorda's 20-year reign as Los Angeles manager, the Dodgers enjoyed a winning tradition, including World Series titles in 1981 and 1988, along with countless highlights and pennant races.

The Hollywood crowd also flocked to see Lasorda's teams, and his office was filled with celebrity photos ranging from Danny Kaye and Jonathan Winters to the Pope and Frank Sinatra. It was Sinatra who performed the national anthem for Lasorda's first Opening Day as manager in 1977. And it was another Hollywood personality, comedian Don Rickles, who joined the fun late in the 1977 season as the Dodgers enjoyed a big lead in the National League West.

"It was Fan Appreciation Day, the final home game of the season," Rickles said. "The outcome of the game was not in doubt and what was about to happen would have no effect on the pennant race. It was very late in the game and Lasorda was going to change pitchers, so I got into a Dodger uniform and he sent me to the mound to make a pitching change. When I arrived, the pitcher, who was of Hispanic descent, obviously knew I wasn't one of the coaches. Although I didn't speak the language, I had a pretty good idea of where he was telling me to go in Spanish. I kept talking to him, trying to get him to leave so I could wave in the new relief pitcher, but he wouldn't exit.

"Finally, the umpire approached the mound, trying to get things moving. When he got close enough, he recognized me and I really became worried that he might lose his cool at the gag. Instead, he simply said, 'You're playing in Vegas next week aren't you? Can I get two tickets?' Needless to say it was a Dodger Stadium moment I won't forget."

When Fred Claire became a Dodger vice president in 1975, one of his marketing ideas was the color "Dodger Blue." Claire later wrote that he provided the paintbrush and Lasorda went to town throughout Southern California, spreading the virtues of the home team. Claire was later promoted to general manager of the Dodgers in 1987. Together with Lasorda, they enjoyed the sixth championship in franchise history in 1988, the year of Kirk Gibson, Orel Hershiser, and a band of bench players and reserves who blended into an October juggernaut.

Lasorda's "bleeding Dodger blue" personality over the years became synonymous with the organization, along with his on-field theatrics with umpires.

"What would baseball be without Tommy?" wrote *Los Angeles Times* columnist Jim Murray in 1995. "You don't want to know. A meal without wine, a day without sunshine, a dance with your sister. Any cliche you want. A life without song.

"Not to see that wonderful character bounding out of the dugout, belly first, fist pumping, bowlegs churning, throat yelling on his way to the umpire to straighten him out and tell it like it should be one more time? Never!"

THE GAME OF MY LIFE

By Tommy Lasorda

There are so many great games to remember. I can think of Orel Hershiser breaking Don Drysdale's record for scoreless innings; I can say four guys became the first quartet to hit 30 or more home runs in the same season. I didn't have any great moments as a player that would equal the great moments as a manager. Scioscia's home run put us in the World Series, Monday's home run put us in the World Series. It's so hard to put it down to one.

The one that had the most drama attached to it was Gibson's home run. What makes it so great is he never showed up for the introductions, because he was seriously hurt during the playoffs at New York when he dove for a ball in left field. It was the only time he came to the plate in five games. He lay on the rubbing table for practically the whole game. Then he came out and told me he could hit. I knew I couldn't put him in the game until there were two outs. I didn't want them to walk him because I was going to give him two strikes to hit the ball out of the ballpark. Then I was going to play for a tie.

When Mike Davis stole second base, I knew Gibson wasn't going to be walked because there were two strikes. That's why I didn't want him to steal the base before that—they would've walked him. With two strikes, a lot of them get burned. They'll hardly walk a guy if they have two strikes. But they would walk him if the count were different, so why should the count make a difference in the first place?

After Gibson's swing, I didn't watch the ball. I watched Canseco in right field. When I saw him go back against the fence, then I knew the ball was out. To watch him run around those bases was quite a sight. And a lot of people don't realize that home run actually paralyzed the Athletics for the rest of the Series. They had tremendous talent on that team.

We played with a bunch of nobodies who played together and wanted to win. They played for the team. Anything positive you can think of, those guys had it. And that's what makes it so interesting. What they lacked in talent they made up for with energy and desire and will. Whenever I watch the Gibson home run on video, I get tears in my eyes because that was something that will be remembered for years and years and years to come.

We got along together very well. He was a great competitor. He was the kind of guy you wanted on your team. Our young players followed him around like young puppies following their mother. That was inspiring to me. Guys like Saxie, Hershiser, Marshall, and Scioscia, those guys were so impressed with him, which helped a lot as far as the team was concerned. When there was that prank in spring training, I didn't worry about fallout the following day in a team meeting. I fined him because he left the ballpark and I told him that I had to fine him. He said, "I know it." So I fined him. He knew I had to do it. It was the question of not doing it that would've hurt.

That's the thing about it. The best relief pitcher in baseball was on the mound and they were leading by one run. I wasn't counting on a home run, but I was playing it that way as far as strategy. I was hoping he'd win the game with a homer, and I gave him two strikes to do it. Then, when they got the two strikes on him, I was just hoping for a tie. I was still rooting for a home run because he couldn't run in the event he hit a grounder somewhere. He couldn't run at all. It was a night of infamy. We'll remember that the rest of our lives. And when the Los Angeles Sports Council tried to come up with the top 100 moments in the history of Los Angeles sports, Gibson's homer was voted number one.

THE RESULTS

Kirk Gibson's two-run home run as a pinch hitter in the bottom of the ninth inning gave the Dodgers a 5-4 victory over the Oakland Athletics in Game 1 of the 1988 World Series. The Dodgers scored in the first inning on Mickey Hatcher's two-run home run off former Los Angeles right-hander Dave Stewart. Oakland took a 4-2 lead on Jose Canseco's grand slam against Tim Belcher in the second inning. Relievers Tim Leary, Brian Holton, and Alejandro Pena combined on seven scoreless innings. The Dodgers added a run in the sixth with one out on consecutive singles by Mike Marshall, John Shelby, and Mike Scioscia.

Dennis Eckersley replaced Stewart after eight innings and quickly retired Scioscia on a popup and Jeff Hamilton on a called third strike. Mike Davis, who batted .199 during the regular season, pinch hit for Alfredo Griffin and drew a walk. With pinch hitter Kirk Gibson at the plate, Davis stole second base on a 2-2 pitch. Gibson then hit his storied home run into the right-field pavilion. It was the first time in history that a home team won a World Series game with a pinch homer in the bottom of the ninth.

THE GOLDEN TOUCH

Lasorda continued to manage the Dodgers until June 1996, when he was sidelined by a mild heart attack. After a month of rehabilitation, Lasorda decided to walk away from the dugout and become a team vice president. He retired with 1,599 career victories, two championships, four National League pennants, and eight division titles. His 16 victories in 30 National League Championship Series games were the most of any manager at the time of his retirement. And his 61 postseason games managed ranked third all-time behind Bobby Cox and Casey Stengel.

In 1997, the Veterans Committee elected Lasorda to the Hall of Fame in his first year of eligibility. He was the 14th manager and the 52nd Dodger inducted into the Hall. Lasorda continued to serve the Dodgers in a variety of capacities, including interim general manager during the 1998 season.

But the biggest surprise of all occurred in 2000 when Lasorda, at age 72, was selected to coach Team USA baseball at the Summer Olympics in Australia. Baseball had been a medal sport since the 1992 Barcelona Olympics, but the 2000 Sydney Games marked the first time professional players were eligible.

"First of all, I want to do something for my country," Lasorda said at a Dodger Stadium press conference, announcing his Team USA coaching assignment. "I'm proud to be an American. I'm proud to be living in the greatest country in the world. And if I can do something for my country, I would be more than honored. This is a privilege. You know, I've been with the Dodgers 51 years (through 2000) and I say this with humility—all the Dodger fans love me. But when you're the coach or the manager of the Olympic team, you represent the United States of America. Everybody's going to be pulling for us, and that's what I want. We're going to go after that gold medal because I want to bring it home to the United States, because I think we have the players and I think we can do it."

Throughout the summer, skeptics figured Lasorda didn't have a chance at winning the Olympic tournament, which included two-time defending champion Cuba, along with entries from Japan and South Korea.

One of Lasorda's supporters was Rod Dedeaux, the longtime University of Southern California baseball coach who played two games for the 1935 Brooklyn Dodgers. Dedeaux, who passed away at age 91 in 2006, coached the USA squad when it was a demonstration sport during the 1984 Olympic competition at Dodger Stadium.

Dedeaux and Lasorda were longtime friends, thanks to their Southern California connection. At Lasorda's press conference, Dedeaux presented him with his cap from the 1984 Olympics. When asked to compare the atmosphere of a major-league game and the Olympics, Dedeaux said the increased level of intensity would surprise Lasorda's players.

"They'll walk out on the field and hear the chant, 'U-S-A, U-S-A' and it makes your blood tingle when you see all the flags waving in the stands," Dedeaux said. "But the same thing goes for the other countries. It will be more than these fellows have ever come close to experiencing. In 1984, we had all the major-league ballplayers to be. And all of them talk about how that was their most exciting moment."

During his playing career, Lasorda often needed a passport as he traveled around the world. He pitched in Panama, Cuba, and Puerto Rico. He managed winter ball in the Dominican Republic and also made visits to Mexico and Italy. After the 1993 season, Lasorda's Dodgers participated in a Friendship Series of exhibition games in Japan and Korea.

"Baseball is truly a world game today more than ever," Lasorda said. "That's what makes the sport so great. Right here in the major leagues, the Dodgers are the melting pot for the world."

Before leaving for Australia, Lasorda motivated himself by walking on a treadmill at home while watching John Wayne movies on a wide-screen television. And before the tournament, Lasorda told his players that they had a chance to shock the world.

So was it really any surprise when Team USA returned with the gold medal after defeating Cuba 4-0 in the championship game? Milwaukee Brewers pitching prospect Ben Sheets hurled the complete-game shutout. And Mr. Dodger returned to the States as baseball's Yankee Doodle Dandy, with a chance to blend patriotism into his cachet of after-dinner speeches, including the trademark claim of "bleeding Dodger blue."

Life is still a whirlwind adventure for Lasorda, ready to fly across the country at a moment's notice. In his current position, he reports directly to the office of the chairman, serving as an advisor on all areas of the

Dodger organization for owner/chairman Frank McCourt and vice chairman/president Jamie McCourt.

"Having dedicated more than half a century to the Dodgers as a player, scout, coach, manager, and executive, Tommy Lasorda represents an incredible resource of information and perspective for this organization," McCourt said upon promoting Lasorda in 2005. "His name is synonymous with Dodger baseball and he is recognized around the world as one of the sport's most notable goodwill ambassadors. We will utilize his incomparable talents and keen mind on many varied projects."

And watching Lasorda's career from nearly the beginning was Vin Scully, the Brooklyn and Los Angeles icon who joined the Dodger broadcasting booth with Red Barber and Connie Desmond in 1950. The Dodgers selected Lasorda from the Philadelphia Phillies organization in the November 1948 minor-league draft. With the exception of a 15-month hiatus beginning in March 1956 when he was sold to the Kansas City Athletics, Lasorda and the Dodgers have remained together.

"There are two things about Tommy I will always remember," Scully said. "The first is his boundless enthusiasm. I mean, Tommy would get up in the morning full of beans and maintain that for as long as he was with anybody else. The other thing was his determination. He was a fellow with limited ability and he pushed himself to be a very, very good Triple-A pitcher. He never quite had that extra something that makes a major leaguer, but it wasn't because he didn't try. Those are some of the things: his competitive spirit, his determination, and above else, this boundless energy and self-belief."

Chapter 19

DON DRYSDALE

NAME:	Donald Scott Drysdale
BORN:	July 23, 1936
BIRTHPLACE:	Van Nuys, CA
DIED:	July 3, 1993
YEARS WITH THE DODGERS:	1956-1969
POSITION:	Pitcher
UNIFORM NUMBER:	53
CAREER HIGHLIGHTS:	Spent entire 14-year playing career with the Brooklyn/Los Angeles Dodgers; elected to Baseball Hall of Fame in 1984; uniform No. 53 retired by Dodgers in 1984; won National League Cy Young Award in 1962; set records in 1968 with six consecutive shutouts and 58⅔ consecutive scoreless innings; broadcaster with the Montreal Expos, California Angels, Chicago White Sox, and Dodgers.
THE GAME:	October 5, 1963; World Series Game No. 3; New York Yankees vs. Los Angeles Dodgers

BIG D

When the Dodgers moved to Los Angeles, most of the players had never before traveled west of the Mississippi. One of the exceptions was a tall, skinny pitching prospect from Van Nuys High School in the San Fernando Valley. The other notable local product was Duke Snider, multisport standout at Compton College.

The power-hitting Snider suffered a change in locations, switching from the cozy Ebbets Field in Brooklyn to the cavernous Los Angeles Memorial Coliseum. But Southern California fans watched Drysdale blossom into a dominant pitcher.

Drysdale is best known for teaming with Sandy Koufax to form the greatest one-two pitching punch in Dodger history. From 1962-1966, Koufax and Drysdale combined to win 210 games en route to three pennants and two World Series titles.

"When I think back to my playing days, I just think about all those years we won," Drysdale said in a 1993 interview just one month before his death at age 56. "Wearing a Dodger uniform meant a lot to those who had grown up in the organization. It was like a family. When you played somebody else, they treated you like an outlaw-type, the quickest gun in the West. I think that attitude made us all better ballplayers."

The Dodgers were defending World Series champions when Drysdale joined the team in 1956. There was an opening in the rotation thanks to Johnny Podres' one-year service in the Navy. Other veterans such as Carl Erskine were starting to slow down or were hampered by arm injuries.

Drysdale made his major-league debut at age 19. When veteran Sal "The Barber" Maglie soon joined the Dodgers as a waiver-wire acquisition early that season, Drysdale watched the former New York Giants star live up to his nickname, pitching inside and giving hitters "a close shave."

"It's not the first knockdown pitch that gets their attention," Maglie said. "If the next pitch is also inside, the batter knows the first pitch wasn't an accident."

Drysdale went 5-5 in 1956 and was the team's best starter in 1957, going 17-9 with a 2.69 ERA. His pitching motion became the most feared sidearm delivery since Ewell "The Whip" Blackwell of Cincinnati Reds fame.

"Drysdale is the toughest guy I've had to face since I've been in the league, and I've looked at some good ones," Giants Hall of Fame

Hall of Fame pitcher Don Drysdale spent his entire playing career with the Dodgers from 1956-1969.

outfielder Willie Mays said in 1957. "You can't guess with him; you might get hurt. Don pitches you in and he pitches you out, but you never know when he's going to do it. I've run into faster pitchers like Don Newcombe and Sandy Koufax, but man, oh man, when Drysdale comes in sidearm …"

Drysdale got off to a rough start during his first month in the Los Angeles rotation. He went 0-4 with an 8.58 ERA in his four starts in April 1958 and finished with a 12-13 mark. But by 1959, Drysdale was again a 17-game winner, and this time on a World Series champion team.

Drysdale's biggest year was overshadowed by a disappointing ending to the 1962 season, when the San Francisco Giants overcame a 4-2 deficit to score four runs in the ninth inning at Dodger Stadium to win the third and final playoff game. Drysdale won a career-high 25 games during the inaugural season at Dodger Stadium and later received the Cy Young Award, but it was the rival Giants who enjoyed a trip to the World Series.

Koufax's 1962 season ended prematurely due to circulatory problems in his finger. But he captured three Cy Young Awards in 1963, 1965, and 1966, which likely prompted baseball officials to give the award to a pitcher in each league beginning in 1967. Koufax retired after the 1966 season and was elected to the Hall of Fame at age 36 in 1972. Drysdale entered the Hall of Fame with former Dodger shortstop Pee Wee Reese in 1984.

"Koufax was God, he was the best I've ever seen, but not until he turned it around in 1961 and used his mind as well as his arm," said Stan Williams, who pitched for Los Angeles from 1958-1962. "Drysdale was an extremely tough competitor. He was mean on the mound. He took charge and intimidated the hitters. He had great stuff. He threw from a low three-quarter or sidearm delivery. That was very tough on right-handed hitters. He'd give you a good effort every four days."

In the beginning of his career, Drysdale was known for his temperamental actions. He was involved in brushback incidents on the field and occasionally popped off in the press, whether reacting to criticism or getting fined by the commissioner's office for allegedly throwing at hitters. He led the league in hit batsmen in 1958 (14) and 1959 (18). By 1966, Drysdale plunked 17 hitters in 273 innings while Koufax had none in 323 innings.

"His animosity was on the field," Williams said of Drysdale. "He was a good person off the field. You'd go out drinking with Don and it was a hard time to pay the bill because he always had his hand in his pocket. He was just a good person overall. But when he got on the mound, he became a Jekyl-Hyde type, where he was tough and mean. But that's the way the game was played in those days. There was an intimidation factor going on. He wouldn't back down from anybody."

THE GAME OF MY LIFE

By Don Drysdale

The game I'll never forget was the third game of the 1963 World Series when I shut out the Yankees 1-0. We swept New York four games that October and Sandy (Koufax) won two games and Johnny Podres won the other. Any time you're in a World Series it's exciting. I didn't have a chance to pitch in the 1956 World Series as a rookie. When we beat the White Sox in 1959, it was a special moment. But I think a lot of people in the Dodger organization felt that 1963 was special for several reasons. First, we should've been in the World Series in 1962 and we just didn't get the job done. If you were there, you'll never forget watching the Giants steal the pennant from us when we had a lead in the ninth. But that's baseball and that's why they play nine innings. You didn't expect the Giants to just roll over. Not in that kind of rivalry.

The other reason 1963 was so special was because we swept the Yankees in four games. There were some great teams in Brooklyn, but they always seemed to have a problem with the Yankees. The Dodgers won in 1955 and could've repeated as the champs, but remember what happened when the 1956 Series was tied at two games apiece? Don Larsen went out and threw a perfect game. Nobody ever remembers we came back and won Game 6 behind Clem Labine, because we lost Game 7 at Ebbets Field, and the Yankees had their crown again. This Yankee team in 1963 had Mickey Mantle and Roger Maris in their lineup. It's hard to pick out the toughest hitter because there were so many of them. I've always said I don't know about my career, but the players in the 1950s and the 1960s were some of the greatest of all time. In the National League, I played against Hank Aaron, Willie Mays, Stan Musial, Roberto Clemente. When we'd face the Yankees in the World Series, we'd see Yogi Berra.

The World Series is the ultimate competition, but I also remember a game in Wichita in 1957. I was with the ballclub in 1956, but had a bad spring in 1957. Don Newcombe, Carl Furillo, Jim Gilliam, and Sal Maglie wouldn't fly. We were somewhere in Oklahoma, going back to New York. We got into Wichita for a game with the Braves and we didn't have a starting pitcher. Our manager, Walter Alston, said, "Who wants to pitch?" Hell, I had nothing to lose, so I said I'd start. I shut out the Braves

4-0 and pitched nine innings. I made the team and had a good year, winning 17 ballgames.

Walter Alston was the best I ever saw at handling a pitching staff. That was his great asset, probably the best-kept secret about Walt. He gave the pitchers to Joe Becker in the spring. Joe was a mule trainer from St. Louis and that's the way he worked us. Once the season started, Joe continued to condition us and talk to us, but Walt took it from there. That's the key of any successful manager, knowing how to handle the pitchers. And a catcher makes a lot of difference. You can't put a dummy back there. You have to have a catcher who can think about the strong suits of the pitcher that night. The ideal situation is to have a catcher and pitcher who have been together for a long time and know each other. You always felt different in spring training when you were working with a kid out of the minor leagues. You go into a different thought process. You have to think about what you've thrown to the hitter the last time he was up there. Is the kid putting down the right sign? That's always been a strong suit with the Dodgers, they've had good receivers. The longer you can keep a staff together, the better. Nowadays, with free agency, you don't know how long you can hold it together. That's one of the big reasons you see changes in the game. We had to stay together, so consequently, we learned to play together.

The most disappointing moment of my career would have to be 1962 when we lost to the Giants in a three-game playoff at the end of the season. That was quite a bitter moment. We had some sweet times, but with the sweet come the bitter. That was bitter right there.

The best advice I ever received in baseball was from Buzzie Bavasi, our general manager with the Dodgers. When he signed me to my first contract in Brooklyn, he said, "Let me tell you something, kid. It's hard to get here, son, but it's even harder to stay up there, because somebody always wants your job." I never forgot that.

People ask me how I would like to be remembered as a ballplayer. I think just the saying, "Give him the ball and he'll try and get the job done."

THE RESULTS

After winning the first two games of the 1963 World Series at Yankee Stadium, the scene shifted to Los Angeles. Los Angeles scored a run off right-hander Jim Bouton in the first inning. With out one, Jim Gilliam walked. After Willie Davis lined to right, Gilliam advanced to second on a wild pitch. Tommy Davis singled to score Gilliam with the game's only run. Drysdale loaded the bases in the second inning but retired Bouton on a strikeout to end the threat. Tony Kubek opened the third inning by reaching first on Maury Wills' error at shortstop, but Drysdale promptly picked Kubek off first base. He then retired 17 of the next 18 hitters. Kubek notched the only two hits for New York over the final seven innings. Drysdale struck out nine batters, walked one, and finished with a three-hitter. It was the only career shutout in six World Series starts. Sandy Koufax beat the Yankees 2-1 in Game 4 to wrap up the 1963 championship, which remains the only one of six overall Dodger titles to be clinched on their home field.

THE MEMORIES

"Do you have any idea where Annie is?"

That was the frantic call to Southern California from the press box at Montreal's Olympic Stadium on July 3, 1993, when members of the Dodgers' traveling party were informed that Don Drysdale had suffered a fatal heart attack in his hotel room. Drysdale's absence from the ballpark that Sunday afternoon prompted team and hotel officials to investigate, which led to the pitcher's room, still double-bolted from the previous night. Just hours earlier, Drysdale was interviewing first baseman Eric Karros on the postgame show.

Broadcaster Vin Scully couldn't announce the news of Drysdale's death to the television audience until Ann Meyers Drysdale had been notified. Don and Ann married in 1986 and had three children: sons Darren and Don Jr. (D.J.), and a daughter, Drew. Drysdale also had another daughter, Kelly, from a previous marriage.

Ann was at a baby shower in Orange County and wondered why Don didn't appear on television in his customary slot, the top of the fourth inning. When Ann was finally notified by telephone, Scully grimly broke the news to his audience in the seventh inning after calmly broadcasting the game.

"Never have I been asked to make an announcement that hurt me as much as this one," Scully said. "And I say it to you as best I can with a broken heart."

The news was a shock to the Dodger organization, still reeling from the death of Hall of Fame catcher Roy Campanella at age 71. Drysdale had attended Campanella's funeral. The former battery mates died seven days apart from one another.

Life went on at Dodger Stadium, and Ann joined Roxie Campanella in representing their husbands' memories at various team and community functions. Roxie Campanella passed away in 2005 and Ann's visits to the ballpark weren't as frequent, thanks to her kids' ever-increasing schedule of activities.

Ann continued her work as a basketball commentator on television. Her Hall of Fame status in basketball, following a prolific career at UCLA and subsequent tryout with the NBA's Indiana Pacers, made her and Don the first married Hall of Famers from two different sports.

In 2007, she started a new career as general manager of the WNBA's Phoenix Mercury. Widowed at age 38, Ann never remarried, raising the kids while juggling her broadcasting assignments. She wishes the two youngest children had more memories of their father and sometimes wonders what might have been. But mixed with the melancholy is a touching sense of humor, especially when remembering her husband's organizational skills.

"I miss him as much today as I did then," she says. "I know if Don were here, my house would be a lot cleaner—the beds would be made, the showers would be squeegeed. Of course, my middle son Darren is very much like Don. All the clothes are in order, the bed is made a certain way, and that's the way Don had to have things. Darren is around to reinforce that memory.

"I'm sure there are times when they're going to miss having a father around when they see other friends who have fathers and they're doing family gatherings. That's why it's so important for me to include them in the things that I do and try to enjoy things as a family. It's hard sometimes when I go with them, whether it's a school picnic or a movie thing. You see a lot of moms and dads together, but there are also a lot of single-parent homes. I'm sure they miss deep down what Don could've taught them as a father and as a man. He led a special life, and we certainly miss that, but we miss him more than anything else. You think about father-daughter situations with someone going on their first date, or even being there to watch them play sports, or how they do academically. They certainly miss him."

Different individuals knew Drysdale at different stages of his life. Former players remember the competitor who won 209 career games and retired at age 33 in 1969 due to a torn rotator cuff. Drysdale also owned a bar and restaurant, was a football broadcaster for the Los Angeles Rams, appeared in several television sitcoms including *The Brady Bunch*, and liked to raise horses on his ranch. He also displayed an artistic side after his career, once sketching a horse portrait in pencil with his initials, "DSD," in the corner. The title of his 1990 autobiography was *Once a Bum, Always a Dodger*.

"I miss the stories when he'd get together with the guys and laugh and talk about things that happened when he played," Ann said. "Even when he was an announcer, he'd tell great stories. I remember I always enjoyed having him come home from Dodger Stadium and I'd always ask, 'Who won?' if I couldn't listen to it on the radio. He'd say, 'We came in second' or 'We came in first,' that kind of thing. I thought it was very cute. We never lost. He was not about losing. For him to say, 'We came in second,' was a great way to be positive."

Drysdale didn't talk about baseball much at home. He preferred to focus on his family, leaving Ann to later ask those who knew Don to share their memories. At the ballpark, he talked about the "good old days," rarely making himself the center of the story.

"I saw that modest side when I was dating him and we came to the Dodger Adult Camp in Vero Beach with the other former players who were instructors," Ann said. "Just to see him around those guys when Campy was alive and Duke was there—Labine, Erskine, Preacher Roe, all those guys he played with and learned from. They didn't talk about how good they played, per se, but they told the stories and how much fun they had. Or they would talk about the other person and how well they would do."

One of Ann's favorite second-hand stories involved Don and infielder Don "Popeye" Zimmer. Supposedly, Drysdale got into a fight outside a bar just about the time Dodger general manager Buzzie Bavasi was driving by. Zimmer and Drysdale returned to camp after curfew and didn't get caught. As the story goes, Zimmer pretended to slam the clubhouse door on Don's hand so he couldn't pitch.

Drysdale participated in many of the Old-Timers' Day ceremonies at Dodger Stadium between 1971-1993, unless they conflicted with a broadcasting assignment for another team. The Dodgers retired his uniform, No. 53, in 1984, the summer both he and Pee Wee Reese entered the Hall of Fame.

"Whenever there was Old-Timers' Day at Dodger Stadium, Pee Wee would be the leadoff hitter," Ann said. "Don would pitch against him and the first pitch always knocked him down. Always. And that's when those guys were in their 50s. Duke also tells a story when he was playing for the Giants and went out drinking and wasn't supposed to play the next game. They sent Duke up to the plate against Drysdale and he drew a walk, which really upset Don. Even at the Old-Timers' games and at Dodgertown, those former players just laughed. They told stories, silly things they did as young men off the field."

Drysdale took his job in the press box very seriously in terms of integrity. Oh sure, he could have fun behind the microphone, but he stated his opinions about the organization both on and off the air. Such candid remarks weren't always appreciated, especially during a dreadful 63-99 campaign in 1992, but nobody questioned his love for the Dodger organization.

"He'd walk into the stadium and people respected him," Ann said. "When I was there with the kids, he'd sit with me for maybe an inning when he wasn't working. But he really enjoyed talking to the beat writers and members of the press. He loved working the game. He loved calling the game, and he had a smooth voice and people trusted him, just like they do with Vin. Of course, he wasn't Scully, but he still was a very special broadcaster in a lot of ways. For him to come back to Dodger Stadium, it was like going full circle."

Drysdale was behind the Dodger radio microphone in 1988 when Kirk Gibson hit his storybook World Series home run at Dodger Stadium. The two most famous calls are Scully's on national television ("In a year of the improbable, the impossible has happened") and Jack Buck's on CBS Radio ("I don't believe what I just saw"). Drysdale was describing the action for the Dodgers' home radio network.

When Gibson slowly walked out of the dugout as a pinch hitter, it was a gamble—knee and hamstring injuries had prevented him from playing. Drysdale brilliantly conjured a "Casey at the Bat" analogy, comparing the situation to the famous baseball poem, and then described Gibson's subsequent battle with Oakland reliever Dennis Eckersley. As Gibson's home run disappears into the Right Field Pavilion, Drysdale's voice hits an unusually high octave: "Way back … it's gone!" The thunderous cheers prompt Drysdale to pause for a few seconds, but he kept his cool and delivered the line of the night: "This crowd will not stop … they can't believe the ending … and this time, Mighty Casey did NOT strike out."

Flash ahead to 1990, when Gibson, struggling with injuries for the second consecutive year and pondering retirement, approached Drysdale one day and told him he often played a tape of Drysdale's home run call for inspiration. Drysdale wasn't even aware that Gibson had a copy of the tape, let alone what it meant to the burly slugger.

"You could've knocked me over with a feather," he said.

That passage of time has also put Drysdale's broadcasting career into context. He has been mentioned as a candidate for the Ford C. Frick Award, the broadcasting wing of the Baseball Hall of Fame. Nobody has been voted into the Hall of Fame as both a player and a broadcaster.

One of his best friends in the industry was Bob Uecker, internationally known for a wry sense of humor and a .200 career batting average. They were "partners in crime" at ABC Sports during the 1970s. When Uecker made his major-league debut with the Milwaukee Braves on April 13, 1962, it was as a pinch hitter in the ninth inning against Drysdale at Dodger Stadium. Drysdale, on his way to a 6-3 victory, retired Uecker on a groundout to second base.

"I look at Don and Uecker, or Don with guys like Sandy, Snider, (broadcasters) Dick Enberg and Dave Niehaus," Ann said. "And it was almost like Don was a brother to them. Not to say that Sandy and Duke weren't close, or Tommy Davis and Willie Davis weren't close, but there was something about Don—he just like, brought them together. To see him with them individually was pretty remarkable. Sandy stayed with us for three or four days in the 1980s and just to see those two talk, they enjoyed and respected each other so much. It was the same thing with Duke. They just laughed. He could spend an hour on the phone with his friends, easily."

Drysdale met Ann while he was covering ABC's *Superstars* competition, a multi-sports event where athletes of different sports tested their all-around abilities against each other. Meyers was three-time champion of the women's *Superstars* and the first woman to compete in the men's competition.

Ann compared Drysdale and Uecker to the *Mutt and Jeff* comic book characters from opposite ends of the spectrum. During an event for ABC Sports, Drysdale and Uecker knew Ann was in the production truck, watching behind the scenes. Before the real taping of an interview, the subject matter was a colorful non-sports topic, and "Mutt and Jeff" launched into a pretend conversation in front of the camera. Uecker proceeded with a German accent, keeping a straight face while he "interviewed" Drysdale. After two minutes, Drysdale couldn't keep his composure and he burst out laughing.

Uecker gave the toast at the couple's wedding. During their first dance, Uecker approached Don and Ann and asked if he could cut in.

"He didn't dance with me, he danced with Donnie!" says Ann with a laugh. "And I'm just standing there, watching those two go around the room."

Years later, Uecker stood on a stage and told a string of jokes about Drysdale. He pointed to various "bruises" on his body, courtesy of his friend's beanballs. The crowd was howling with laughter.

It was an amazing performance. Uecker kept a straight face for this monologue—delivered during Drysdale's memorial service. He checked with Ann to make sure it would be appropriate and she agreed. Don would've wanted laughter any day.

Uecker told everyone what a "neat freak" Drysdale was and how he would intentionally leave a glass on the coffee table or any other flat surface he was behind, knowing Don was just seconds behind with a paper doily or a coaster.

"No exaggeration," says Ann, who always asked Don why he insisted on buying high-maintenance furniture. "Donnie would always clean the glass tables. And he'd have the squeegee to clean the glass shower. Everything was tight. Everything was organized. We seemed to make it work with each other. I came from a family of 11 children and balls are lying around the house. 'Well, it will get picked up later.' Not with Donnie. He told a story about when he was young and his basketball kept bouncing into his mother's rose garden. She finally took the ball and popped it with her garden tool and said, 'That's enough of that.' She didn't mess around with him."

In November 2006, MGM Studios released *Bobby*, a movie about the life of Senator Robert Kennedy, who was assassinated in 1968 after winning the California Democratic primary on June 4. During his acceptance speech at the Ambassador Hotel in Los Angeles, Kennedy paid tribute to Drysdale's streak of six consecutive shutouts, the last occurring only hours earlier against the Pittsburgh Pirates at Dodger Stadium.

In his next start, the Dodger players wore black armbands on their uniform sleeves in memory of Kennedy as Drysdale broke Walter Johnson's record of 56 consecutive scoreless innings. The streak reached 58⅔ innings and remained the major-league record for 20 years until Orel Hershiser's 59 consecutive scoreless innings for the Dodgers in 1988.

Dodger owner Frank McCourt, whose family moved from Boston after he purchased the team in 2004, invited Ann and her children to a special screening of the movie, knowing there were many references to Drysdale's consecutive scoreless innings streak. The McCourt and Kennedy families have been friends for generations, and Drysdale was a friend of Robert Kennedy.

"It was a special night," Ann said. "I had heard about the movie. I didn't have D.J. with me, but I had Darren and Drew. Darren is 17 and Drew is 13, so they were too young to remember things about their father. We have pictures up all over the place in the house, so we see him every day. But certainly my children didn't know anything about the Civil Rights Movement or the war in Vietnam going on in the 1960s and '70s.

"I couldn't believe how prominent Don was in that movie. Even at the end of the movie, Darren said, 'Mom, I thought they were going to show Dad at the end of the movie.' Just to sit there and to feel how it impacted them, even though they didn't see him on the film—just to hear his name and how he was talked about with such passion in the movie—you could really feel that come across. I would certainly like to thank Emilio Estevez for including Don how he did, which was very special. Just to see the effect on my children was pretty neat."